Season of Sorcery

On Becoming a Wisewoman

Poppy Palin

Season of Sorcery
On Becoming a Wisewoman

©1998 Poppy Palin

ISBN 1898307 96 2

ALL RIGHTS RESERVED

Internal and cover illustrations by Poppy Palin
Cover design by Paul Mason

Published by:

Capall Bann Publishing
Freshfields
Chieveley
Berks
RG20 8TF

B

To my parents, for their constant love.
To the memory of my lovely Aunt.
To Claire Louise and Barbara, with my thanks.

And to Julien de St Pierre, always.

"Once a person has an insight as to their true self and starts to 'be' who they are, it is a constant effort to maintain that state. Society speaks through the mouths of the many and their message is repeated over and over again. . . . a person's worth is based on their work and wealth. The advantage of meditation with the Avatars and Beings of the Otherworld is that it brings you into contact with true values based on the worth of 'know thyself'. The self is, after all, immortal whereas work stops at sixty and money ends at death."

M. Austin, 1995.

Contents

Foreword

I am very fortunate in being able to write this book today, a book that has, to my mind, a dual purpose. As a spontaneous psychic I have been party to some bizarre, inexplicable, and often frightening events. As these events appeared to occur, for many years, solely around me, I used to believe that I was somehow responsible for them. Consequently, the natural psychic ability I have, which I now consider a gift to be worked with, I used to view as an affliction to be eliminated.

The events which occurred around me made me feel alienated from my peers, who considered me to be 'weird'. People would often avoid me for fear they might become 'infected' by the strangeness that afflicted me. Later on, certain people felt that I would curse them if I so much as looked at them. My experience of psychism was not a positive one for many years, and for this I partly blame the media who are keen to foster the medieval view of life and the afterlife, even in the late twentieth century. I have the clarity now to see how people are still lead to be xenophobic, but for many years I felt I was at fault for having the ability to make things I could not control or understand occur.

The only books I came into contact with seemed to emphasise my inherent 'difference' and thus perpetuated my feelings of fear and isolation. I recall my confusion as I searched the local library shelves for volumes that could shed some light on my situation. Even in the early nineteen eighties the shelves could only offer me lurid exposes of sex magic, Satanism, spontaneous human combustion and blurred photographs of UFO's. The more I looked, the more I grew to feel I was mad, bad and dangerous to know. The books, revealing the names of demons, imps, familiars and recounting tales of pacts signed in blood, were all that was available to me under the broad heading of the Occult and Paranormal.

For one who had spent their childhood and adolescence desperately trying to be 'normal', it was of no comfort as a young adult to discover that I was not. Not only was I abnormal, but nobody could help me. Those dreadful and prolific volumes scarred my perception of myself for many years, and I lived alone and in fear for a period of time when I could have been enjoying the usual pleasures of youth. None of what I read related directly to me, after all, I was only a girl from an average background in an average town on Merseyside. But then, I could find no reference point anywhere which helped me deal with my own

1

2

'skills' and, I discovered, the more I ignored them, the worse it got. My life, both waking and sleeping, was filled with disembodied voices, strange smells, eerie music, poltergeist activity and prophetic visions. It mattered not if I moved house or changed my situation, I could not escape from myself, but the more I tried to 'deal' with it, the less help I found. A vicious circle, as my psychism, and the things that it attracted, did not seem to want to be ignored.

Although today there are a range of sensitively written and informative works available to the average person in any bookshop, I feel there is still a need to speak out to anyone who was born with, or who has acquired, the gift of psychism. There can still be a lot of wading through irrelevant literature just to get some simple, basic, practical advice. I know I am not unique in the respect of having 'a gift', and that I should use the knowledge I have gained to help anyone else who is trapped in that terrible darkness that fear brings.

In sharing my own life, I hope to bring greater understanding and inner peace. By this, I do not mean that I have all the answers, and that I seek to preach or to convert. This is not a religious work, nor is it a 'new age' piece. The message is a universal one, relevant to anyone, in any age, and the message is not that I alone know the truth. This book is designed to empower the individual, as well as inspiring and giving encouragement to the reader to know themselves. In this book I champion personal growth and understanding, and I do so by questioning everything, re-assessing old established ways of being which are not productive and challenging those who offer a convenient 'answer on a plate'. I am able to share my experiences before I move on, ever onwards, on my own path of the soul. One of the purposes of this book is to share and to pass on, through story and through suggestions.

The second, more basic purpose of this book is for it to reach people through entertainment. Perhaps some of its readers will not come to the work with their own personal experiences of psychism which they wish to compare to the authors own. Perhaps some readers simply like a good tale of the unexplained. For these two purposes I have tried to write in a manner that is neither overly simplistic or wordily complicated.

It is my hope that which ever path you are walking in this life, you will gain from this book, and take what you will from it on your own journey.

Find your stars,
Poppy Palin, Bath 1996.

Introduction

When I began to compile this book, after many years of interaction with the Otherworlds, I was faced with a dilemma. I knew exactly what the book was to be about, and I knew my reasons for writing it. However, I could not decide whether to use the emotive word 'Witch' in the title. It seemed the correct thing to do, seeing as the word aptly describes who and what I am. It would be a word, if used in the title, which would attract a lot of attention, curiosity and intrigue.

No doubt my choosing to use the word 'Witch' on the cover of my book would have brought me a great deal more attention than my present choice. Obviously, I chose not to use it. In explaining why I made this decision, I would have to tell you a story. It is a story that would stretch the bounds of credibility in even the most spiritually open and aware person. Yet it is a story that I must tell for if the reader cannot accept this story then I am afraid that the rest of the book will also be unacceptable.

This is a volume of work which contains much in the way of fantastical but true tales. The story I am about to tell explains why I am the Wisewoman that I was born to be. It is said that Witches are born, not made. In this life my experiences have made me understand that this is a truth. I was also born as a Wisewoman with gifts of the Sight, prophesy and healing in the year 1284.

Back then I was born into service on the manor of a French lord, my mother having been a lacemaker to his family. Although that was my Mother's official position, she was also unofficially present at the births within the big house and was on hand to assist with the family's ailments. She was a fine midwife, herbalist and healer as well as a skilled craftswoman with her lace.

I have no recollection of having a father figure, although I do remember a sister. She was older than I, a female who had no interest in my mother's talents, but who sought to marry a wealthy man. She did indeed marry a man who was a frequent visitor to the estate of the Lord. My mother continued her good relationship with her employer as she trained me in her ways, and we were allowed to stay in a tiny, one roomed cottage which was on the edge of his land, almost in the woods.

I recall a happy life surrounded by the warmth of my mother and of the women who worked in the kitchens of the manor. There was security in our little dwelling and great peace, and I had hardly anything to do with the world as it was in those times. We wanted for little, as our basic needs were provided for in return for the lace and healing. No money came our way but we managed. My mother educated me in what was edible in the woods and I still feel the happiness I felt when sitting outside our home, peeling and chopping roots and plants to store or to eat. Inside the cottage was one plain, rough hewn table, what served for chairs and a large fireplace. I do not recall how we slept, nor do I think there was any other area to sleep in. But we had an undisturbed life with food and shelter, the support of women, and the beautiful trees right outside our door. I had no idea anything bad existed, I honestly believed that life would always be that simple and cosy.

As I was not as comely as my sister and as I lacked her tenacity in acquiring a husband, it seemed natural that I would succeed my mother as lacemaker to the small community. This also included the art of midwifery and a knowledge of herbal lore. As I had grown up observing the ways of nature and the birthing of children, it was a natural progression for me to be responsible for these things. My mother lived a healthy life and we had all we genuinely needed, but my mother grew tired early into her middle age. There was nothing physically amiss with her, but as she was so close to the cycles of life and death herself, she had obviously known somewhere within herself that it was time to move on. I had no fear of death and nor did she. With a little help I would bury her somewhere in the woods, as it should be, and in time I would train someone else's daughter to be the community Wisewoman. My mother's view of spirituality was as simple and basic as her life, and it really was her life.

My knowledge of working by moon phases, my talking with the dead for guidance, my relating to larger beings in the universe, my conversing with stones, trees and animals and my rudimentary divination methods were all passed on to me by my mother. It was all second nature to me and to her, like breathing, it was just something that we did. Nobody questioned us, we were accepted and if not revered, then certainly respected for who and what we were. When my mother died I had no fear for her or the future.

When my mother had passed on, I would spend more and more time alone in the woods, walking for hours in the dappled light under the trees, looking for a particular plant. The woods seemed to stretch on forever, and it pains me now that it is so hard in our modern times to recapture this feeling of being totally enveloped by the realm of the green ones. More than once on my journeys I chanced upon a man who introduced himself as Julien de St Pierre. I was called

Marguerite, I believe my only other identification was being of the house of Mirabeu or possibly Mirabel, but Julien called me Maman. I thought he was wonderful.

The man was a traveller with mousy brown hair which was shot through with grey, moss-on-granite eyes and hands like knotted like tree roots. He used a staff to walk with and preferred to travel alone and keep away from the towns. He was a mixture of a seer, a poacher and a bard and I longed to meet him when he was passing through near my house. Ours was never a physical relationship but I believe we were deeply in love none the less, more with each others souls than the flesh. He was skilled at survival in the wood, but that was not his main reason for distrusting the people of the villages. He told me stories of friends and relations turned in by their neighbours, accused of heresy and witchery. He said it was like a fever, a terrible fear of anyone different in any way. He was only ever drawn into communities to heal the sick or to provide spiritual comfort to the terrified peasants. I could not relate Witchcraft or the like to anything to do with me or my life and I continued to feel safe despite his dire tales. He was disillusioned and filled with pain for the folk he saw in trouble, but he was also worried for himself. His spells of hiding in the trees became more regular, and I was pleased, but never afraid. My mothers curious blend of Pagan, Christian and possibly Eastern traditions, as well as her handed-down knowledge and ways of relating to the cosmos were totally removed from Witches' doings, as far as I was concerned. I was safe.

The end of my peaceful existence came quite unexpectedly in my forty-second year. A new lord had succeeded the old one and his young wife was at last pregnant. She was very small and delicate and was taking to the pregnancy very badly. She was weak and uninspired, despite the lord's obvious love and encouragement, and the birth was proving difficult. Although I had the kitchen staff working alongside me, and all the comforts possible for the young woman, I lost both her and the child. She had bled profusely but I could have saved her had she the will herself.

The lord became incensed, transformed with a blind fury as he realised she had been lost by me. The kitchen women wept and wailed as he set about beating me terribly. He too was young, and had lacked the steadiness of his father, the old lord. As well as my beating, I bore the shame of losing a woman and babe, something my good mother had never done. I accepted the fate of the woman's demise, but had no way to reason this with the man who rained blows upon me. At some point somebody must have carried me back unconscious and left me in my own dwelling.

It had been some days later when I had recovered myself sufficiently to leave my house. I was weak, but I needed to go to the manor to see how I would be received. I also needed to beg some bread. However, I could not have imagined what sight would greet me upon my arrival. I had expected harsh words and the unforgiving attitude of a man still grief-stricken, but I had not expected to see the place deserted. The sight was profoundly shocking, empty stables, barns and kitchens, all my women friends gone. I recall feeling disorientated, and then I felt fear for the first time. They were my protection, my means of trade and support and they were my friends. The silence in that once bustling house was ominous, the haste of their departure evident. The Lord had obviously taken the whole household rapidly away from the scene of his heartache. I could not imagine life without them. I had no thought to steal from what they had left behind, nor did I think to stay in the abandoned house in relative luxury. I simply went back to my home.

I have one memory of an abortive attempt I made to ply my wares in the village nearby. I needed bread but all I had to sell was my lacework. After Julien's warnings I decided to stick to my most innocent of wares. The village was a long walk, almost a day's round trip, and my skirts became muddier and more torn as I tramped onwards. My experience of people was that they were good and friendly as a rule, so I could not believe the hoots of derision and cat-calling that awaited me when I finally arrived, exhausted, clutching my little basket. Immediately I could see that they would have no need of my delicate lace. Tripping over chickens and pigs, I braved their stares and as I turned tail. They had been rude about my wares, but about me myself they were curiously silent, and whispered as I walked away. Once out of their sight I became dejected and afraid. As the season was turning there was an abundance of berries to eat, but I worried what I would do come winter. I was isolated in my little home and for the first time I really did worry as to my fate.

I waited in the woods for Julien many times after that, often hungry and with an ever growing sense of unease. I was not a trapper, or a hunter and as the weather grew colder I feared how I would find sustenance. On one trip to the woods I returned to find my home had been burned to the ground. I wept, not for the material security, or the meagre possessions, but for the carefully stored herbs that my mother had passed on to me and I had collected myself. The memory of her patience, her love and her skills upset me more than anything. Less than that, I wept for I knew I was now the target of hatred for some reason. I still had not really grasped the situation. All I could do was drag my tired and hungry body back to the woods to await Julien.

He eventually arrived, alerted by whispers that he heard here and there, to see if I was safe. An emotional scene ensued and I remember the mists shifting and revealing us as they moved in the trees. It was early October then, and October even now in this life can make me feel the same terrible fear and yearning that I experienced then. There was a mixture of sadness and frustration, anger and pity involved as we talked through the night. I vowed to triumph over their ignorance and cruelty but Julien said that I must flee. That mixture of fear and flight has remained with me, indelibly etched into my soul, as has my feelings against injustices of any kind. I would have to say goodbye to the man who I had never made love to, but who I loved so completely, in order to run from the bullies and bigots in the villages.

Julien said that I should make in the direction of my sister's house as her husband could protect me with wealth and power. It was a long shot. I was no longer young, not well nourished and I had never been outside of my home area before, but I had the spirits to guide me and the trees to protect me, so I agreed reluctantly to head for the border. I could move by the stars and by my senses. I believe that we were somewhere south of Lyon at this time. I begged Julien to come with me, but he would not. He said he would catch me up, he promised me that. But first he must try to put people off my trail and find out what they intended to do. I left alone that morning before the mist thinned.

By the time I fell down and hurt my back I had been travelling steadily for several days. I was weak for lack of sustenance and made clumsy by fatigue. I allowed the thought of seeing Julien again be my inspiration and I focussed on my sister's house. I was a small woman who felt even smaller in the unfamiliar areas of forest. I did not dare to leave the trees shelter but I found that they were growing thinner and more spindly as I went. I slipped down a bank of shallow soil and landed painfully on my back, immobilised in an area of patchy cover. It was there that they eventually found me, painfully hungry and sobbing with pain and frustration. I could not escape.

A man rode up to me and slung me roughly over the back of his horse like a sack of grain, so I dangled stupidly there in great agony. He wore a helmet and did not speak. To scream was pointless. I gritted my teeth and endured the ride which took us many many hours. We eventually came to a walled city where I was taken directly to a barn-like building and thrown unceremoniously inside. I found I was sharing my huge prison with numerous other humans, all in a state of hysteria. This image had haunted me in this life, so much suffering, men climbing the walls to try to get to the arrow-slit windows only to fall again. There was no escape. The terrible, incoherent cries and babblings, pleadings and moans within those walls nearly drove me mad. My pain kept me sharp and alert and I walked the best I could to a corner. Ordinary poor people like me shrank away as I passed by them, their eyes round with fear. I tried not to frighten them more with my stares. What on Earth was I meant to be that was so terrible?I reached an empty corner, wrapped my cloak, such as it was, around me, and curled up in a ball on the stone floor.

Incredibly, I must have slept. I came to my senses as a shaft of light hit my face as the gates of the building were opened. The guards came in and before I could regain my wits, I was grabbed, yanked to my feet and marched out of the barn. The injury in my back made me grind my teeth in pain as I was dragged to another building, this time a place of immense grandeur, or so it seemed to me. It was a curious cross between a castle and a church. I was furious by the silent, rough treatment I was receiving from the guards, none of the men with the helmets that made them so anonymous and ominous would communicate a thing. I was taken up a corridor lined with dangling pennants of red and gold and richly carved dark-wood furnishings.

I have no idea who the three men were that I was finally brought before. Two of them flanked the most important man, who sat on a raised dais in a great hall. I hadn't a clue what position of power they held, but I was forced to kneel before them and my head was pushed roughly down onto the strip of carpet. When I was allowed to raise my head a little, I saw that the main man had a glimmer of the psychic about him, what would be termed now as an aura. I thought I may be able to communicate with him more easily, despite his authority, because he had the strong bright colours around his head that I associated with those of good spirit. However, his two cronies, who I perceived to be clergy, seemed to have more say than him. It was they who accused me of all manner of foul crimes and practices. My head was yanked up for me to view certain objects that they held as evidence against me, some of which were my own innocent items, others which were alien to me.

I was not allowed to speak as I was accused of brewing poisonous potions and harmful lotions, some of which had been used to kill the lady of the manor and her unborn child. I had, apparently, also killed various villagers by my meddling, not to mention their livestock. My denials were silenced. You have to remember that I had only ventured to the village once in my entire life, my interest in those folk was minimal. Some items like bones and iron nails were shown as items I had cursed people with. I had never seen any of them before, yet I was told that I had used them for ill wishing. I was a skilled woman in many ways but a simple and uneducated one and so the combination of my fear, exhaustion, pain and confusion left me totally bemused and at a loss. I knew all was lost when I was not allowed to meet the eyes of the senior dignitary. I had

wanted to appeal to his sense of decency and honesty, but my gaze was regarded as further sorcery. I was dragged away, spitting and kicking feebly down the length of that lavishly decorated, dark, long room. That had been my trial, I gathered. I was found guilty.

Once more outside, with the morning's pale sunlight almost blinding me, I was taken roughly by three men into a smaller empty barn. I was almost unconscious in my poor physical state, which was just as well. As the others watched, I was beaten bloody and raped by one man whilst I was repeatedly insulted for the state of my body, appearance and smell. I have only scanty recall of this devastating experience but I know of its outcome. My arm was broken and I lost an eye, no doubt for the sport of it, but perhaps to stop me cursing them with the evil eye. I remember that this was a gesture by which one covered one's own third-eye, in the centre of the brows, and extended the right arm with the index and little fingers pointing outwards at the 'victim'. It could be used to curse, but I had been shown it was a way of psychic self-defence, to ward off unwanted thoughts or actions by protecting the third-eye.

Whatever the reason, I was further disabled and humiliated, I was broken and bleeding with my clothing shredded. I was as degraded as it was possible to have made me, and I knew that they would claim they had had to protect themselves against my witchery. I was so puny and undernourished that this was ludicrous, but there was a genuine fear of witches and the devil's work which could actually make people believe I was capable of harming three strong men by the power of thought. Indeed, had I been taught the arts of hexing and cursing I would have probably been able to do just that. But my mother's teaching was that of 'harm none', she and I had never had to protect ourselves before to have had to consider the other side of magic. My instinct was only to regain my freedom, which was all I owned and valued. I did not wish to hurt anyone, my only struggle was to escape and be left alone. Still, for fear of my actions I was placed in a single stone cell, stripped naked and manacled to the wall.

There was a solitary stone seat, a tiny window and nothing else. I was glad to be alone again but the constant pain was driving me half mad. As darkness fell I felt things crawling over me in the blackness that I was powerless to stop, but at least no human hands touched me. When the light finally returned I was reminded that I only had partial sight, but I felt stronger and brighter, a little of my old self returning. It was incomprehensible to me that I could have ended up in such a state, it must have been a terrible mistake. I believe that this naive optimism and lifting of the spirits had come because I was near death, although I did not know it then. I still thought I could return to the woods, somehow.

Eventually, people came to the cell, unchained me and threw my ragged, disgusting clothes back at me. I was given a bowl of water although I don't know why they bothered. Why sustain someone you are about to kill? Maybe it was better for them to keep me alive, so that I could endure the ordeal to come with more clarity. Maybe they actually thought it would teach me a lesson and save my soul. I struggled to dress, my body had let me down and betrayed me, its weakness disgusted me. My soul felt like a tiny walnut hiding within the frame of my shrivelled physical self. The lack of connection I felt between my body and soul helped me in what was to come. I was taken outside and thrown into a cart which appeared to have a wooden cage-like structure over it. It was up quite high as I could see people's heads and faces as I lay inside the wooden, moving structure. My empathy with wild creatures who are caught and paraded, far from their natural environment, has been strengthened by that memory. I was an exhibit to be taunted and teased, as if I was not really alive, as if I had no feelings. I was being driven slowly to a square on that overcast late-autumn day, with the leaves blowing in circles on the ground. It was only as I was dragged down from the cart that I saw what had been prepared for me and I howled in fury and sorrow. I can see the stake now, in that hideous square in Avignon. I can see the slate-grey sky above me, filled with birds that I so envied, so free. The stake was so crude, so devastating, that I screamed and screamed, powerless to resist or struggle. It was then that I noticed two further stakes, set apart.

At this point, things become decidedly more hazy as it must have been one of the most traumatic experiences a soul can have. Not only was I to be burned in total innocence before a crowd of hateful strangers, but I was also to witness the burning of Julien de St Pierre, the man I loved and had left reluctantly behind. I did not understand how it was that he too had been captured but it seemed to be the cruelest trick that fate could have played. I was yelling to him but my voice was drowned by the crowd and was lessened by my lack of strength. He did not hear or even appear to see who I was. His head hung low and he was horribly silent.

It was so painful to know he would not see me before we died, together yet terribly separate. The third victim was another woman, someone that I did not know, and she did not hold my attention. My vision was poor from the lack of an eye, but I saw him and it increased the agony. Then as the fire was lit, I have trouble remembering anything, I drifted in and out, always screaming. I think that my memory, even my far-memory, may have erected a screen between me and the all-consuming, excruciating pain of being burned alive. I have snippets of recall, my spitting in the face of a clergyman offering me benediction, of a terrible smell, of feeling the cold sensation of blood coursing down my limbs, the omnipresent noise.

12

What an end to a life of such peace and tranquillity.

Out of my body I did not spend much time hovering above the scene in the square. I did not forgive, but I understood. Everyone was afraid, and their reasoning was that if I was being burned then at least it was not them. I did not want to feel connections to them by revenge or hate. Never once since recalling that life have I ever wanted to meet the souls of those men who brutally treated me, in order to retaliate. All I did want was to meet Julien again, with a passion that was deep and strong. I did not stay close to the human scene in order to wait for his soul. I did not want to view his smouldering human form, or my own. I knew he would come to me. I kept my love for him pure, and I drifted off over the disgusting scene below, over the walls of Avignon in late October 1326. That was my last memory of that incarnation.

That is part of my story, but by no means all of it. A story may be all it is. I have as yet no means of discovering if a lacemaker called Margeuritte lived and died in medieval France, although I hope to try to find out somehow, someday. The only way I have found to prove that this is not just a rather gruesome fantasy tale is to verify the information I have with the separate information of another individual who was present all of those centuries ago. Independently from me, he filled in the gaps that I have in my story and had his own version of the extraordinary tale. My whole life was haunted with this incarnation, by dreams and inexplicable phobias, until I met the man who was Julien de St Pierre again in this life. My love for him had been born into this world with me, and I knew I had to find him. This search and the struggles involved make up the rest of this book. From here on in, things get more extraordinary, not less so.

So, why do I feel I cannot use the word Witch in the title of this book?Should I not be proud of all I am and what I stand for? The root of my reluctance stems from that terrible time, my being abused and insulted and finally killed. Amongst the many ripe descriptions that were hurled at me as I suffered was the word Witch. It was indeed an insult and the memory of its use still hurts. It was their word, the ignorant in all their guises, the church, the poor, the rich and privileged. It was not how I saw myself then. The memory is as vivid as any from my childhood in this life, it is real and it affects me, whatever body I occupy. It is soul-memory and my soul had suffered for being labelled a Witch. Of course, I could reclaim the word as so many others have done, I could be proud to reclaim it and use it to describe who I am. My screamed denials "I am not a Witch!" are as valid now as they were then. The word had no meaning to a woman who lead a simple life in a wood.

I am no longer so insulted by being called a Witch but I prefer to use the title that I was happy with in simpler days. The things that matter, herbal lore, healing, communing with spirits, venerating nature are the things that continue, unaffected by time, in my modern life. My aim is the same' to become wise and wiser, to use all I know and will know for the good of all and the One. I am always becoming a Wisewoman, always becoming more the way my soul has the potential to be in life. My thirteenth century mother's word for us was the Mascarati. She spoke an ancient language which she used to commune with the green folk in the woods. It was a magical name and a magical language. In this life I have remembered the old language. The mother I have now has the same soul as she who I loved then. In this life there are many connections to that one in the burning times.

I believe that this incarnation is an important one for me, and no doubt, for many other souls who seek to follow the path of the Wise, and become wiser.

It is my hope that in writing this book it will become another of my tools in helping others, as once again that is what I am here to do.

Chapter One

Reincarnation has always been, for me, a truth. By truth, I mean a personal rather than a universal truth... in this book I tend only to deal with the former. As a personal belief which fits into my own modus operandi it feels right, although I am open to be questioned and challenged on the matter. As with any personal truth I must accept that one day I may be faced with evidence, or a gut feeling, which will make it impossible for me to no longer accept the concept wholesale. I do not wish to be resistant to growth and to refuse change. I am always looking for new ideas or experiences to assimilate into my current system.

Part of being a working psychic is to constantly give credit to feelings and instincts, no matter how irrational they may seem to the logical mind. I feel that the best possible approach is to combine these feelings with well researched facts. In the case of reincarnation, it is not always possible to research things fully, as evidence given in dreams, meditation and guidance can be obscure and the characters involved will probably have had little historical importance. Although no belief system should be written in stone, my current view, weighted with much personal evidence and feeling as well as that of countless others, is that we have 'more lives than one'.

As soon as I was able to speak, I gave my mother evidence that I had memories from another life. Although I was not informed of this until many years later, as a tiny child I was able to relay information that I should never have known. For instance, I would inform my mother about the location of a house longsince demolished, that had belonged to another woman that she had been close to.

The woman had died before I was born, and I had never met her, yet I was able to give information about her life and to sing the songs she had sung. I had certainly not picked these things up at home, as my mother had found it painful to talk of the dead woman. As the woman and she had been so close, it was possible as a babe in arms that I was telepathing with my mother, picking up strong memories. I could have been acting as a medium to comfort my mother, relaying this information to give her proof that the woman still existed, somewhere. Either of these two ideas could have remained possibilities, had it not been for the fact that at the later age of fourteen I had a series of spontaneous, powerful visions. I had no idea that I had given those childhood revelations when these visions began. My mother had never told me about them.

I simply slipped into trance alone one afternoon whilst listening to music. I have an enormous amount of interest in all things musical, although my own talents are primarily artistic, and certain pieces of music can send me into an altered state of consciousness without any preamble. It was the first time it had ever happened to me and I simply found myself in another time and space. In fact, I was in another bedroom which I perceived as my own, which was obviously of earlier in the century by its design and decoration. I felt a strong connection and familiarity with the room, and could see it in fine detail, down to the wallpaper print.

I did return to the present when the music stopped, but I discovered with repeated plays of the same piece I could simply access this 'parallel' life. I was excited by the discovery, unnerved but not frightened. Unlike so much of the psychic activity that plagued my life, I seemed to be able to control the phenomena. I could spend as much time as I liked accessing the old house, starting in that bedroom and eventually 'walking' around the whole house in my mind's-eye.

I was so intrigued by this experience that I wanted to share it desperately with someone. I thought that it would be ridiculed or dismissed by my peers at school, as I was more often than not a source of great amusement to other, more popular, students. I was odd and weird in their eyes, and my blurting out of my experiences once in a religious education lesson had done little to enhance my appeal to the masses. I knew that my life was far removed from theirs, and besides a couple of close friends who were also misfits in their own way, I was not part of the pack. I was also an only child, and spent a lot of time alone engaged in creative pursuits. My art especially was advanced in skill and highly imaginative. It was an outlet by which to express my experiences with the Otherworlds, my dreams and images.

In that respect my work was praised and I was not ridiculed. My role at school seemed to veer from a verbal punch-bag to a counsellor. I spent many hours listening to and advising the same girls who would later bully me. I see now that they were so insecure that they needed someone to make them feel better about themselves, so they made me feel smaller than they did. As with the terrible men in my French incarnation, I do not wish them to suffer as they made me suffer. Perhaps they had their own problems at home, or with others. I generally took their abuse and continued to help them, accepting that as my function in that mini-society of school. At home, I struggled with my own strange inner world, and I rarely confided in anybody. My ability to be in tune with my own psychism had not ended when my fontanel closed over, as with a lot of children.

Eventually, I let it slip to my mother that I was having visions of another home that I had once had. My mother has extraordinary psychic ability, but also a great deal of Catholic guilt and repression which she is none to happy to deal with. As a younger child, I was brought up with a great acceptance of all things psychic, with Mary and Jesus existing alongside past-lives and predictions. I was not taught of reincarnation as a truth but my mother would often exclaim "oh, I was just in my American life then" and would not be interested in certain countries as she thought she had been murdered in them in other lives. She would mention her own recollections quite naturally, but as the years went by she became less happy to discuss my own experiences. I think sometimes that her powers of prediction and her psychism scared her and challenged her Catholicism too greatly.

When I told my mother about the room and the house that I had once lived in, she was immediate and certain in her response. It had been the room of the dead woman she had known, the one that had died before I had been conceived, and it was correct in every detail. My mother did not seem particularly surprised that I had seen the house, after all, she had heard me reveal the hidden information about the woman when I was tiny. She told me about that occurrence then and I was amazed. My mother believed that I was being guided by the woman, who was my guardian angel, whilst I maintained privately that it had been my house that I had seen, and my bedroom, so I had been that woman in my last life. It would explain in part the extraordinary bond that I share with my mother, as she and that lady had been very close indeed.

As I did not wish to embellish the house with my new knowledge about its owner, I stopped going to see it in my imagination. I felt that I had seen all I needed to see, and that the temptation to begin fantasising about that life would be too great. I hoped that a different piece of music would trigger further memories in the future, but it had to be spontaneous, and not something I engineered. Then, as now, I was aware of how the rational can creep into visions, guidance and meditations, telling you how it should be logically. I was happy with my memories of that house, and unless I got anything else without trying too hard, it was time to leave it. I did get the odd flash for sometime afterwards, and I was able to piece together more of the woman's life. This included a dream about her visiting a lovely old fashioned shoe shop, where I was seeing through her eyes all the prices and products of her day. 'We' then went on a train together. I told my mother a little of these dreams to clarify if the information I had seen was authentic, and indeed it had been, again to the finest detail. Also I recognised that 'feeling' that goes with a real recall of memory, a personal, deep gut feeling.

At the age of fourteen I was no stranger to the idea I had had other lives. At the age of seven I had had a vision in a history lesson about Tutenkhamun and Ancient Egypt. I thought the whole process of drifting off to another time, another 'self' was totally normal. I had no qualms about accepting that I may have been male, not female, in another life. It was the simplicity with which I experienced these things that convinces me of their authenticity. I often 'became' a young Victorian girl who lead a comfortable life in a big house set in beautiful grounds.

This was not fantasy based on television or books but again had the clarity of detail and feeling that were so convincing. It seemed a charmed life for a young girl, I remembered my favourite tree and a building that I now know was a summer house. However, I know that I died before I was ten years old. The images are one thing, details of clothes and furniture that I did not care about as a very young child myself, but which I saw in my mind's-eye, but the feelings of happiness, loss, frustration and bewilderment are the ones that feel right, personal and eternal things.

Undoubtedly as a person grows older, the wealth of images that we come into contact with are there for the taking and can easily be cobbled by the unconscious into a perfectly feasible past-life experience. They may be technically brilliant in terms of authenticity, but they will lack that resonant 'That was me and I was there' feeling that I have experienced on many occasions. However, perhaps the Self has a need to express something about how it feels through a fantasy of images which it can relate to.

Perhaps all past-life memories are just aspects of the Self all clamouring for recognition by wearing various symbolic guises. I will discuss this possibility again later, but for now I will reaffirm my belief that other lives have a relevance for all of us, be they fictitious or no, and they can bring greater understanding by looking at them with an openminded view. The personal memories I mention here were my first contacts with my own lives and I had no reason to believe that I hadn't lived before, perhaps many times. There was no pressure on me to believe this, or indeed, not to believe it. So I just accepted it.

As I grew up, I became increasingly aware that I was sharing my life with an ever expanding variety of spirits. I would go to sleep with voices in my head, voices in my pillow and voices in my room. When I was small I remember talking back to them, but as I became older I became alarmed by the relentless disembodied chatter. The noise that resulted was something like having access to fifty or so busy phone lines all at once. Sometimes I caught a word or phrase that meant something, other times I was spoken to personally but mostly it was a selection of non-sensical conversations. Perhaps I was tuning into the collective of humanity in the area where I lived, the conversations of our neighbours, the noise of their televisions etc. After they made me afraid to go to bed alone, the voices became singular rather than plural and I was always addressed personally.

Not one of the voices ever scared me terribly, although I often became confused and unsettled sharing my space with nameless others, until one morning when I received a message loud and clear. I was lying in bed, having woken on one bright and sunny morning, when a voice said, in a booming voice, right in the middle of my room "you hurt me!". As a little girl who hadn't yet seen her tenth birthday I was terrified at being yelled at by an invisible source who was obviously extremely angry with me personally. I shot under the bed clothes, to emerge slowly to find the room was still empty and sunny.

That was all it had said, but the accusing tone and personal feeling of the message haunted me for years afterwards. I have recently hypothesised a suitable answer for its sudden burst in my room. Strangely it was the voice of a man who I had had a terrible relationship with in my twenties, who is very much incarnate now, but whose yelling at me somehow reached me even as a child, before it had happened. This proves, perhaps, the concept of time as circular rather than linear, maybe events occur simultaneously on many levels. Also, I had known the man in another life in an equally disastrous relationship and he had yelled at me then too. I do not know why the message came through then, but it did and it succeeded in making me afraid to be alone in my own space.

The more scared I grew, the worse the paranormal occurrences around me became. The more I feared being in my room, the worse the activity haunted me, what would commonly be recognised as poltergeist phenomena. Things often moved about in my room without me touching them which I found a terrifying thing. Did a ghostly figure materialise and move them, did they fly through the air or did they vanish and reappear? I never saw how they did it, but they moved none the less.

My mother, worried about my reluctance to sleep in my own room alone, invented a lucky pixie to protect me. She told me it was he who moved my things around. This did little to alleviate my fears, although she meant well. I was still having many different things happen around me, including haunting music which filled my room each morning before I got out of bed. It sounded like nothing I have ever heard since, a kind of faery music, which seemed to be played on tiny bells. I had no other reference point for faeries than the Cottingley faery pictures which were faked. The image of the two sisters gazing beatifically at the hoaxed images of the ethereal little winged figures was one I found disturbing.

Somehow I thought faery folk to be at least knee-high to a human, not minuscule things. I knew that I wouldn't find them living at the bottom of a suburban garden, which was hardly in the countryside, but I did think that the music came from some faery folk, wherever they were. The music was odd and eerie, but I could never have been scared by it. I think it was there to comfort me, as it was often there as I drifted to sleep, and upon my waking.

By this stage, I had devised a chant to ward off the bad creatures that haunted me, which I repeated three times when I went to bed. I believed that daylight would disperse the spirits of whatever haunted me so I did not repeat it all day. However, the odd happenings did not cease, for all my chanting, and neither did the music I heard. The music I recall with fondness, having experienced the green folk myself in later life. I perceive the elemental beings, the faery folk and elves of myth, to be either light forms or embodied in a way which I can visually interpret as a human, i. e. a leaf-being, a flame-being, or a giant made of mist. For me, any place where there are enough trees is the right place to meditate and see the green people.

I am sure that there are more 'magical' places to commune with elemental spirits, such as barrows and stone circles, but I prefer any wild green place, wherever it maybe, with as few humans in its vicinity as possible. The woods which I have been living close to are alive with the flitting forms of nature spirits, and I look with my third, or mind's, eye to see them as they really are. In meditation, contemplation and indeed, in appreciation, I have often sat and waited to speak with the spirits or to just observe their dances. They sometimes feel obliged to appear as a twee green and brown clad elf to be acceptably perceived but I prefer to catch them au natural, glowing life forms which are totally free and at peace. Why they still wish to commune with humans is beyond my comprehension, but they do come and I am always overwhelmed by their forgiveness and understanding for our species, far beyond my own limited tolerance for the way we behave.

The music I heard as a child has seldom been repeated in adulthood, but knowing the essence of their beings as I do now, I feel that my hearing their music was certainly a comforting thing and I feel pleased to 'go to them' now in their own environs, as they once sent their music to me. The music was always separate from the moving items and the voices. I just wish that I hadn't seen that dreadful picture of the faeries of Cottingley as a child, as it was difficult to disassociate the beings I believed made the music, from that twee image which I found disturbing if it were true. So, the activity in my room continued, and I felt powerless to stop it and guilty if I kept fussing about it.

When I was eight years old I experienced my first omen sign. We were about to celebrate Halloween, a festival that I then had little understanding for, as these things are seldom explained to children. I will discuss my understanding of this important time of year in a later chapter. I was visited, shortly after coming home from school, by a raven. The huge black bird, the likes of which I had never seen before, landed outside a window and began to stare at me for several minutes with what seemed like singular intent.

My mother also saw the bird, although she passed no comment on its ominous presence. I did not know what it meant, but I knew it meant something. Later that night, as I bobbed for apples and played traditional games with my parents, my Grandfather, who was visiting us, died. His heart attack was sudden and disturbing to witness and I was ushered away from the scene whilst the ambulance was called. I remember standing outside in the dark, in my pyjamas, remembering the bird. I understood its meaning then, but of course I had no idea of its significance to Hallowe'en. I just knew that it was a death symbol, and that my Grandfather would be dead before the ambulance arrived. I had no idea as a child that it was universally accepted as such a symbol. Only recently have I discovered its place in myth and folklore. The raven appears primarily as the bird of Bran, God of the Underworld and the ferryman between this world and the next. Ravens are said to remain at the place where Bran's head is buried, which is supposed to be the Tower of London. If the ravens fly then the city is unprotected from invasion.

The second connection with death for the raven is its association with the Morrigan, reputedly a Goddess of war. The birds are sacred to her as they always circle a battlefield, ready for the spoils of the dead, whilst She is at hand to transport the souls of the dead to the Underworlds. I think it is amazing that as an innocent child at that time of year, the time when the veils between this world and the Otherworld is thinnest, that I was visited by this archetypal symbol for death and the journey onwards. I was disturbed by the death, but intrigued by the unusual bird, which I thought was a blackbird! The next morning my Grandfather could be heard in my room, making the same unpleasant sounds he had made as he died. I think of this occurrence more as a psychic tape-recording than as a presence of the man in my room. He had departed with the messenger that had come for him, his spirit had not lingered. But it was, again, a horrible thing to hear a disembodied human noise in my vicinity.

The next time I saw the raven was as I came home from school one evening, some time later. I knew that on my return home I would hear of a death and I was prepared for the worst. No news came until the next morning when my Grandmother had passed away. I was protected from the news at first, although I knew she had gone the previous night, as I had seen her messenger. As mine was a small family, I became frightened of seeing that bird again, for fear of who it would take away. I made up simple chants to ward off its presence. I was not aware, as usual, of what I was doing when I chanted but I realise now that I was trying to create a spell of protection. Since those earlier times I have seen the bird again, and I no longer fear its arrival. Occasionally I have come across a dead raven directly in my path, a doubly powerful indication of a death, either spiritual or symbolic. The bird is still a messenger, certainly not an evil force to be warded off. It just fulfils its part in the dance of life and death and life.

As I grew into a teenager, I not only received my own visions through music, but I could also tune into my friend's lives through certain pieces I could listen to. I had a small but steadily growing group of friends who were very much misfits themselves. They were not entirely supportive of me and my visions, but sometimes curiosity got the better of them and I sat down to obtain guidance for them, using my psychism with a musical trigger to stimulate it. I was able to pick up events that had happened to them that they had never discussed with me, often trivial family matters and holidays.

I often perceived future events which I wisely kept to myself. Friends are not the easiest people to give predictions to as they often dismiss the claims they don't like, thinking that the predictor is being silly. Even now my best friends often look at my guidance for them with a sceptical eye. Most people expect things that I tell them to happen immediately.

I have found that guidance often appears a year after the information was initially revealed to me, and I always stress that the Otherworld's view of 'soon' or 'the near future' is very far removed from our own! Back then I did not know the time difference between me and my guides, and so I saw images that couldn't possibly relate to the person as they were then. I was convinced I was seeing future events, but how far into the future it was hard to say. People, then as now, expect specific advice and immediate information rom these psychic matters. Sadly, my guidance, either in written, pictorial or spiritual form does not work like that. It reveals signposts along the journey of life that an individual can choose to use or ignore. But I said enough of accuracy to get my acquaintances interested in spiritual matters, which was good for me as I could talk about my life a little less guardedly. From this stemmed their obsessive interest in gaining guidance, which lead to the ouija board.

For some reason, probably because it seemed safer than drugs, our parents let us use their front rooms regularly to practice the board. We managed to do quite a lot of sessions, in various houses, and it became our social focus. In my experience, the ouija attracts teenagers in each generation and my only advice to a parent or child would be to exercise the same code of practice that we ourselves forgot to use.

The basic tenet to use is "if a total stranger knocked at your front door one night, would you let them in straightaway?". Usually one can think of a variety of responses, the most sensible of which is a straight "no" but the most adventurous may be "only if I spent a long time checking out who they were and if I let them in I'd make sure I could defend myself in case they turned out to be bad, or a liar". This is ouija logic.

Everyone and anyone you encounter in spirit on the board will claim to be someone that once lived somewhere. This could be somebodies aunt Doris or Adolf Hitler. Now, if it is Doris then there are many simple ways for the person involved to test the authenticity. He or she could ask the spirit questions that only Doris would know. However, everyone knows a little of Hitler and so it would be easy for the spirit to convince the group on very basic evidence that he was that character. Everyone should be taken as being suspect, and even Doris should only be believed until she begins to utter things that are totally out of character.

The more lurid and famous the 'guest' the more likely it is to be a fraud. Even Doris could be a mischevious spirit who fancied a bit of harmless fun pretending to be someone's Aunt. It is a risky business opening the door to strangers, because spirits will call them if you raise enough group energy, in the tried and tested ouija ritual. It does work and is not a toy, unless you seriously believe that inviting strangers in is not a problem for you. Even if they don't wish to leave afterwards, which a lot of spirits don't want to do. As a group we went in blindly with no protective precautions and we got told many lies.

As we were all sensitive teenagers to one degree or another, we all suffered somehow as a consequence of doing ouija unprotected. My poltergeist activity upped in volume, and my closest friend suffered dreams and headaches. He displayed bizarre switches of uncharacteristic behaviour, from sleepy to violent, and he claimed that a man kept talking to him in his head all of the time. I was having a lot of trouble with things moving about once I had put them safely away on many occasions. My mother eventually noticed this too and was so uncomfortable about the phenomena that she burned the offending article. This occurred all through my life, but at that point it was not helped by the spirit contact we were engaging in so haphazardly. My own sleep was disturbed by apocalyptic dreams and terrible images of the sky turning black at midday, with signs and symbols which I did not understand appearing in the darkness. Much later, I discovered that the images I had dreamed were directly out of Revelations in the Bible. I had no biblical learning and so the images must have been coming to me from a particularly potent spirit with his own message to convey to me. At the time, the images made no sense, but haunted and disturbed me. My later contact with the Church was part of my spiritual quest, but at that time I thought that religion was irrelevant to what I was experiencing.

Some people began to feel frightened by our 'games' and dropped out of them. One girl had lived in a house that she thought was haunted as a child, and she had been plagued by floating heads and brass bands and footsteps when no one was in evidence. She had suffered no other phenomena when she had moved house, but she was afraid of the ouija. I hoped that once I left home, my own phenomena would cease. Perhaps our family home, a modern semi-detached, was haunted? I certainly suffered as much, if not more, phenomena when I moved and I moved many times in my adult life to escape the events. I could never escape myself until I finally confronted the phenomena with knowledge and understanding.

Unlike my friend, my 'hauntings' were because of who I was, not where I was. But she dropped out and we continued valiantly. I am slightly reluctant to recount our most startling ouija happenings, which included Henry the Eighth who turned into Satan claiming our souls for his own and an alien who claimed he was called Xommy Jehophret from the planet Vuts. I do not wish to make the ouija sound like a bit of harmless fun. Two things I will share are our stupidly attempted 'black rite' to contact the devil (why stop at aliens and kings when you can have the really big contact!). It was all inverted crosses, the Lord's Prayer backwards and a lot of black clothing. I have no idea what we were trying to achieve, but to us it looked impressive. I was still incredibly messed up from my own experiences which occurred almost daily, so I had no idea what was right or wrong. In shadow of watching lurid horror films we wanted a drama to make our lives more interesting, I suppose. I hardly needed any more psychic intrusion than I already had, but I couldn't bear to miss the excitement.

What came of that event was the knowledge that spirits will try to 'get inside' a person's sphere of influence if they are so disposed. The cunning entity told us all to be quiet and to listen. We all sat silently waiting for a revelation. Suddenly one of our circle yelled "everybody start singing!" which seemed a rather odd request, but we obeyed, as he was our unofficial 'leader'. He had known that the spirit in question was trying to influence, and gain access to, our 'heads' as we sat silently waiting. This seems as viable today to me as it did at the time. The spirit concerned was furious to have been stopped, and refused to leave the circle.

As we had always observed the rule of bidding the spirits 'hail and farewell, with thanks' we hadn't a clue how to deal with one which did not have a desire to go peaceably back to its own realm. The result was that we had to break the circle and leave the spirit present in the room we had been using. Consequently, the person whose house was being used reported poltergeist activity for a while afterwards. This was not uncommon, and reports of black-clad figures and strange goblin-like characters were also reported in connection with the ouija.

As for our foolish attempt at contacting the Devil, we wanted a show and we certainly got one. None of us were Satanists, or even Christians, but we just thought we would see if anyone answerable to the title Devil was out there. We were treated to a display of five inch long candle flames, a glass which moved unaided and the letters on the board which all reversed themselves. Undeterred, we went on to perform our final ouija later that week, which proved to be an extra-terrestrial spirit who wished to discuss armageddon and the planet.

We were too young to really want to converse in such serious and philosophical terms, so we urged the communicator to speed up a bit. With that the glass whizzed around the table at lightening speed and then promptly imploded. I recall letting out an unearthly scream, after which we all cleared up for the final time. We were slow to realise the very real power of spirit contact through ouija, but I believe that our ultimate experience showed us, once and for all, that we were dabbling in something too powerful for us to control.

At that point most of our group went on to fill their leisure hours after school with the use of recreational drugs. I did not feel inclined to join them, although I have since had experience of a limited nature with the soft drugs which seem to permeate even the most 'normal' of middle class social situations in the nineteen ninetys. I find that I am opened up greatly by their use, and although I am aware that many psychics use them as part of their spiritual practice, for myself I do not get along with any drug which alters perception. I find that I hallucinate immediately, and have been to ancient Rome and to other past lives quite spontaneously whilst under the influence.

I feel that the level of openness that drugs afford to me personally as a psychic make me vulnerable to all sorts of influences that I may not be suitably clear headed enough to deal with. I believe that the majority of drug experiences, most notably 'trips' are merely journeys within the human-created, rather than higher, astral, where one is vulnerable to thought forms and collective human entities. Therefore, one is as likely to meet a human thought form of a Christ figure as one is to meet an almond-eyed evil alien, a six-foot two blonde-haired Goddess or a talking unicorn. I think that our ouija contacts were to entities from the human astral and I believe that to receive true guidance, one must go deeper into trance or meditation to reach out further into the astral 'proper' which is less influenced by our manifest hopes, dreams and projections. Hence the ouija hauntings taking the form of easily recognisable spooky figures, the Death image in a black cloak, a *'Lord of the Rings'* style goblin etc. My preferred way to engage in any spirit contact will be discussed later. Personally, I reject the use of drugs and alcohol as a psychic, as I do not wish to find myself dealing with troublesome human projections, which are real and valid in themselves, in an unprotected way. I like to be prepared, and will share my 'psychic green-cross code ' in a later chapter.

I believe that I was, in my teenage years, acting as a beacon on the astral to attract plenty of floating spirits, be they those of the dead who have not been able to free themselves from their earthly links, or of those who were 'created' by some human or a group collective. I believe that certain individuals glow like a flame to those entities and souls who operate closest to the manifest and so they are the ones to which 'weird things' repeatedly happen, whilst others never have anything but the odd strange experience in a whole lifetime. I do think that everybody is psychic to a greater or lesser extent, but certainly some people shine brighter in terms of attracting 'astral flotsam and jetsam'.

This does not mean that these people are to be venerated as a guru, but it does mean that they should understand their role as regards helping lost spirits of the deceased and clearing away astral junk, like unwanted thought forms. Obviously as a teenager I had no idea of this concept, and I felt victimised and strange. I wished to be like my so-called 'ordinary' peers, but any attempt I have ever made to be 'normal' has ended in disaster. I could not accept that I was going to have a life filled with voices and noises and moving objects, but I had no idea how to tune-in to the contacts, how to control my psychic glow or how to be myself. The entities and spirits involved usually needed to communicate for some reason, although their methods of attracting my attention could be frightening. I am certainly able to distinguish now between an external influence or contact which I can approach appropriately, compared to an internal feeling or message, i. e. about past -lives. As a teenager and young woman I was unable to grow, to make the right connections and contacts, or to break free from the influence of the spirits. I spent many years running away from myself. Using the ouija had not helped me one bit. It was rather akin to my walking into the jungle draped in fresh meat.

Whilst I was embroiled in all of the usual psychic intrusion, I was witness to an extraordinary event above my parent's home, which was in a densely populated town setting. It was to be the first, and lesser, of my two major UFO sightings. However, what I saw on that evening, although it did not compare to the later sighting, was amazing in itself. I was in my nextdoor neighbours attic bedroom when we opened the window for some reason. Outside, directly above us, we both saw a vast nuts-and-bolts craft, hovering with a ring of flashing lights underneath it. It was classic in its shape, the metallic disc with a dome on the top.

The craft then began to move off over and above the roof, so we rushed to the front bedroom to see where it was going. However, it had totally vanished. Absolutely amazed and a little shaken, we reported the event to my neighbours parents, knowing their response would be dismissive. However, the girl's mother admitted to us in private that she had almost been struck by a pencil-thin beam of blue light whilst in her garden a few days previously. She had not wished to share that fact before as she felt a little foolish. I would say that somebody else must have witnessed the phenomena, although we found no such report. On such an evening, most people are sat in front of the television, not gazing out of the window.

We may have been the only ones to see it, and maybe it was a joint-hallucination which we experienced in the most exact detail to one another. I do doubt that, as we were totally unprepared for such a sight and were certainly not talking about strange craft previously, as to prime our imaginations. Two girls who had been drinking orange squash and chatting inconsequentially were hardly likely to have suddenly slipped into a hallucination. However, I do not know why we saw it, or how we saw it, but I do know what we saw.

By that UFO, I was reminded of the many dreams I had had in my youth in which shining beings would appear in the night sky. I would interpret them as being Jesus as he was the only cosmic figure I had as any kind of reference point. One night I had a terrible nightmare that the being in the sky had cavernous slanting eyes, a tiny nose and a thin line of a mouth. It hung in the air over my parent's house and I woke from the dream with a terrible fear of the malevolent intention that the image had made me feel. I tried for many years after that dream to recapture the singular feeling of evil that the face had. As an artist I was always transcribing my dream imagery onto paper, and that face had been a particularly stunning example.

I could never capture the exact look of the face. However, many years after I had the nightmare, I was startled and unnerved to see that very same face on the cover of Whitley Strieber's best-selling book 'Communion'. The face belonged to an alien which Mr Strieber claimed had allegedly abducted him from his bed to perform unpleasant tests upon him. Mr Strieber only recalled the details of his alien abductions during a session of hypnosis. As the image has now been widely popularised and accepted as 'the alien face' by the populace, I would not be surprised had I encountered the haunting image in dreams. However, at a young age the book had not even been conceived of and no such popular image existed to my limited childish knowledge. I wonder if I myself encountered a similar being, the details of which I cannot recall?

I am open to explanations of how I dreamed that face many years before it graced the shelves of all major bookstores. I had a fear which was almost a phobia as a child, and well into adulthood, that someone or something would come into my room whilst I was alone at night and nobody else would know. I had many recurring dreams where I could hear the intruders approach but I could never see their face. I recently heard another psychic talking about very similar experiences that he had as a youth. He had an almost identical history of paranormal events and visitations which happened at night in his room, except he actually had a clear memory of so called 'alien contact' as well. The man himself is a popular speaker on modern UFO contact and he works in the Wiltshire area where he runs workshops and sky-watches to introduce others into his strange world of space ships and energies. He, as myself, seems like a rational chap without the ego or the desire to win converts or extract a great sum of money for the pleasure of his supposedly 'superior' knowledge. He and I share the goal of making information available to all.

I would by no means state that I was an alien contactee, as is the fashion, especially in America since Whitley Striebers revelations. Even after my initial UFO sighting I did little to research the subject and merely added it to my list of weird phenomena. It was only after my second encounter that I began to read books and research the subject.

My encounter happened on the 24th of November, 1990. This was some time before it was fashionable to be 'into' UFO's, owing to the 1995 showing of the Roswell film in which a supposed alien autopsy was carried out. The Roswell incident is best described in many specialist UFO books, and I would recommend a look, as it makes very interesting reading. Subsequently, the blockbuster film 'Independence Day' has graced our cinema screens, with its alien invasion theme. There seems to be a current glut of magazines, programmes such as 'The X Files' and Internet Websites dedicated to UFO-logy and all of its attendant myths and mysteries. When I had my second UFO encounter, my head was free from book-learning or preconceptions as to the nature of alien life and space craft. I had grown up with *Star Trek* which had no overtones of reality whatsoever and so I was certainly not out looking for spaceships or aliens.

My 'interest', enforced as it may have been, was the psychic, earth-level of the unexplained. I was increasingly the focal point for a maelstrom of whizzing, crackling psychic energy, which could have been a beneficial thing, had I learned earlier to wield the mighty sword that the energy was. Instead of the sword being an instrument of truth and clarity, it slashed and hacked its way through my days in an attempt to attract my attention. I either walked with my head down and a frown on my face or else I was running away from myself and my true nature in terror. Had somebody been able to lend me a book similar to this one at that point in my life it would have saved me many more years of misery and confusion. As it was, after my second UFO encounter, I came across people who wished to 'tell me how it was' without actually helping me to find out 'how it was' myself. I will tell the story of the encounter now, for the reader to make up their own mind as to 'how it was'.

Chapter Two

It was the evening of Saturday, November 24th, 1990. An evening that was progressing in a pleasant, ordinary manner. I had, as ever, gone to Wiltshire with my then partner, Tim. We spent each weekend in a village with his parents, although we were temporarily living in London while I completed my degree course. For some reason on that weekend we could only stay for the Friday night and had had to drive back to London on the Saturday evening. Tim said, as it was a clear night without too much of a bite in the air, he would drive back slowly and show me Stonehenge. It was a monument that I had long since been pestering him to see and as he hadn't visited it himself since his youth, he decided that a quiet winter's evening would be as good a time as any for us to view the stones.

Tim did not feel much inclined to visit the monument during the day, alongside many other tourists. He had absolutely no spiritual interest in the site but he still had a curiosity to see what people found so mysterious about the place, and why myth and legend noted it as an incredibly magical place. I was sorry to have to drive back from Wiltshire early, as I loathed London and was sorry I had ever started my teacher training course there. I had less than a year to go on my course, and the regular trips to Wiltshire inspired me enough to get me through the next week in the capital city. When I completed my degree, I intended to move to Wiltshire, as I found the area generally much more amenable.

Tim was a Wiltshire lad, but he was not entirely au fait with the wealth of ancient sites in his area, and I was encouraging him to take us to as many of them as possible. I was still searching for an answer to explain my psychic experiences, which proliferated during my time in London as a student. I rather saw Wiltshire as a break from my frenetic existence during the week, and generally because I was so happy at weekends I did not get pestered by the persistent poltergeist activities of my student residence. I now see that it was my closer proximity to the things I was drawn to, the magical, restoring sacred sites and the greener environment that made me better able to fend off the psychic intrusion of my London abode. Tim's parents were used to us leaving on a Sunday with great reluctance, and arriving on a Friday with great relief. London was a nightmare for me, being trapped on a crowded tube train on the underground, with all those human vibrations, was enough to jangle my psychic sensitivity for days. I was not aware of why I got ill so frequently, but I was walking around absorbing vast quantities of human energies and losing my own etheric, or life-force energy in the process, by them 'leeching' it from me. I was basically so psychically open at that point that anyone could have a little bit of me, in terms of my energy. What with the overcrowding of people and the strange occurrences of my flat, it was no wonder that I found the green energy of the earth restored me somewhat at weekends. My experience of living in London and working with my own energies and that of others is another story in itself.

Tim and I had departed in his old Ford Fiesta on Saturday evening with various gifts of sustenance for our journey from Tim's parents. I would not mention this if it were not vital to the story, but one of the bits of food we received was a banana. This banana ended up being the only physical evidence that w e had after our encounter had occurred. Previously, at the start of the journey, I placed the piece of fruit on the dashboard, as I intended to eat it after we had visited Stonehenge. The journey to Salisbury Plain began in a most unremarkable way, with the exception of it being a remarkably clear and beautiful evening. That was the reason Tim had chosen to show me the monument. We were driving along, listening to tapes and chatting, and frankly, we were not wishing to have a strange event occur.

Tim was a young man who had no choice but be a little interested in psychism, as he lived with my own insights and experiences on a daily basis. His own background was of the scientific/practical side of life. He was not closed minded, but he gave me only his understanding, he could not actively support me and help me come to terms with my 'affliction' as I still saw it. That was all I could expect of anyone, understanding. I had little hope, at the age of twenty four, of meeting anyone that was 'like me'. I usually felt sorry for Tim being exposed to the same psychic events that so annoyed and scared me. On that evening, I was glad to be a believer in the company of someone who was sceptical. It made the whole event seem more plausible that Tim, a man with little feeling for anything beyond what he could hit with a hammer, or explain in a logical way, could witness a UFO and attendant phenomena as 'reality'.

It was approximately eight o'clock as we approached the T-junction that would lead us onto the main road past Stonehenge. I was totally unfamiliar with the route and journey myself. As we waited in a short queue of cars waiting to pull out onto the main road, I was astonished to observe a huge orange ball of light hovering over a bank of trees opposite to the junction exit. As we waited to pull out, Tim confirmed that he too could see the massive luminous globe, which he said was hanging above a wooded area. He had to concentrate on the road, but I kept my eyes on the object. The cars we saw then as we pulled out were the last we witnessed for three quarters of an hour.

Tim was asking me "what the Hell is it?" and I was bewildered as I observed the light had begun to move off as we had moved off in the car, in the same direction. This was no flare, nor was it an aeroplane, helicopter or any other craft we know. It was an enormous sphere of orange light which appeared to be following us. At that point, Tim drew my attention to a strange band of fog which we were driving through, like a defined strip of mist across the road at chest height. Through the strip of fog the road was clear again and totally empty.

I noticed the lack of cars because I wanted to see if other drivers were noticing the ball of light too. The night was clear, as it had been specifically picked for the clarity of vision, and I could see the ball clearly as it paced the car to the left. As we pulled up in a layby next to the Hele stone at the famous henge, I noticed in awe and a little fear that the glowing object, if indeed it was a solid, stopped too. There was no doubt it was mirroring our movements. My feeling of fear grew as Tim got out of the car to see the object and for some reason I insisted that he kept the engine running. It felt reassuring to know we could drive off rapidly out of the strange scene.

Tim had told me of the omnipresent security guards which he had heard were at the site day and night to forbid anyone entering the monument. I wished I had seen any of them that night, but the place was deserted of human life I would have liked to have shared the experience with other people to have gained affirmation for the crazy thing I was seeing. I too got out of the car and watched the light, which hovered directly opposite to us over a field. Whilst I did this, I leaned my hand on the Hele stone which appeared to me to feel as if it magnetised my hand, with the sensation that when I took my hand away, my skin would remain stuck to the stone. There was a distinct tingling feeling from that stone, the likes of which I had not experienced from a mineral before. But I was too occupied with the object to concentrate on the stone. I noticed how its orange glow lit up the whole sky and I wondered how the nearby villagers in their homes could fail to notice its brilliance. Then I noticed I could see no lights, there appeared to be no houses in any of the surrounding areas. It seemed we were totally alone with the phenomena.

As I continued to watch the light, it continued to prove that it was 'not of this earth'. Its capabilities included shooting up vertically at an incredible speed, flying off at a diagonal, disappearing and reappearing in a totally different part of the sky and finally hovering over the ground again. I was mesmerised by the display, and was acquiring a curious feeling that I could stand there forever, as if all time and space were irrelevant. Tim was paying absolutely no attention to the orange ball and after his first cursory glance at the ball to acknowledge its

35

presence, he was going 'ooh' and 'ahh' at the beautiful tableau of the moon over Stonehenge. On reflection later, Tim could give no rational explanation why he wished to look at the far more mundane moon, compared to the unbelievable house-sized ball of light. He said later that all his attention was swamped by the moon over the stones. He had even said he was getting his camera out of the car boot, to take a photo of the Henge!! I could not believe his lack of interest at the time, but I was determined to absorb every twist and turn of the balls ariel display. I could only imagine that the thing was an extra-terrestrial craft of some sort, or else a terrestrial piece of technology so advanced that nobody in the public had been told about it. To see it zip about and vanish and zoom off at a tangent was utterly incredible.

Whilst I was held in thrall I heard Tim yell at me "get in the car!! Don't look 'round, just get in... now!!! His tone was urgent and brooked no arguments so I wordlessly and swiftly obeyed, which to be honest is very unlike me!! Yet I did not look back, and once I was inside the car Tim drove off at high speed, barely allowing me time to close the car door. My first thought was for 'the craft' and I looked for it from the window. I saw it moving off, just as we did, steadily pacing the car again. I began to point this out to Tim, when I finally noticed that he was rigid with fear and gripping the steering wheel. He said that he would tell me the story when he had gotten us far away enough from Stonehenge.

I lit him a cigarette and continued my vigil with the orange glow. At that point, three things happened. Firstly, we drove through another strip of fog, identical to the first one. Secondly, as we did so the craft stopped, and we began to leave it behind as we travelled onwards, until I lost sight of it, which annoyed me greatly. Thirdly I noticed it was eight forty five, even though we had been out of the car for a few minutes only and we had arrived at about eight o'clock. I began to feel incredibly disorientated. My growing discomfort was added to when I spied that the banana, fresh and yellow as it had been at our arrival at the Henge, was black, split and in an advanced state of rottenness. I felt very peculiar indeed. What was it that had happened to us?

After a considerable distance, Tim was able to divulge his side of the tale. We pulled in at a garage for him to relax a little, and we both realised that we could see other road users again, although Stonehenge had been devoid of traffic. The UFO had held little interest to Tim, he recounted, but the moon had. As he went to get his camera from the boot of the car, he saw a figure approaching, lit by the moon, on the Stones' side of the security fence. Tim thought this was at last one of the dreaded security force, and he continued to find his camera, aware that soon we would be approached. However, as he looked up again the figure was incredibly close to the fence, and Tim couldn't understand how he had moved so rapidly. Also, Tim was bemused, as although the moon was so bright as to see each other perfectly, Tim could not discern the approaching figure's face, for all its nearness. All I could get Tim to repeat was that the figure was male and 'big, black and horrible'. It had no face, no features, but was cloaked and entirely dark. He described it as being around seven foot tall and rather square in shape. Tim decided to abandon the camera at that point and closed the car boot.

On turning once more the figure had done the impossible and was on our side of the fence. There had been no sound of jumping or climbing (all the time this was happening the night was silent and still with no traffic. I had not heard a thing, although I was mere meters away). Tim said "he was walking through the deep leaves" which seemed impossible later as there were no trees around the stones, let alone a profusion of fallen leaves. Tim had no idea how the man had scaled the fence, and it seemed as if he had simply walked through it. He was standing directly behind Tim when Tim had yelled at me to get in the car. As Tim had finally pulled the car away, the man-figure had been outside Tim's car door. I had been frustratingly oblivious to this male entity form that Tim had witnessed, and he had been disinterested in the aerobatic, enormous light-form I had witnessed. We had both experienced separate phenomena within the same space, but we could both see the banana, and the time which had flown by for our (seemingly) short stop at the Henge. At least Tim had seen my orange light, I had no idea his giant man had been there at all.

I knew Tim and his clear-cut rationale. I knew he was scared enough to ask to sleep in the same room as my flat mate, who seemed refreshingly normal upon our return to North London. He and I curled up on her floor in a sleeping bag as we told her the tale. She made us write notes about it and we drew a few sketches to accompany the record. She appreciated that it would be hard for us to remember the whole truth of the incident in time, and those records did indeed prove invaluable afterwards. We felt so strange that we had been in that odd, silent space where several peculiar things had occurred, that we needed simple human comfort of another impartial, sensible soul. Our flat mate, Lis, often provided me with her commonsense and her support throughout my psychic storms. She was an absolute gem that night.

We reported our sighting the next day, or rather, I tried to. I phoned up the Stonehenge custodian to ask a few pertinent questions. The first was "how many security guards had been working the previous night at eight o'clock?" I was told that there had been several working in pairs who carried flashlights and who would have approached us if they had seen us there. I asked if they worked on the stone's side of the fence and I was told no, they did not and they always carried lights and moved in twos. More to the point, nobody had seen us. I was told that nobody else had reported a strange object or a giant figure on the previous evening. Indeed, I was categorically told that what I had seen was a flare from the military (a flare which could hover and then shoot upwards at forty five degrees? A flare the size of a large dwelling?). Not only that I was warned from visiting the stones at night ever again, and I was accused of being a drunken fool. As one who did not, and does not, drink, I thanked the man as calmly and politely as I could for his help and advice, and then I hung up. I was saddened that Stonehenge had to be kept in captivity by such terse and one-dimensional men, although, to be frank I didn't really see the appeal of the site after that encounter. It seemed to me a rather cold and hostile place, apart form its strange phenomena. But I supposed that millions of spiritual seekers could not be wrong, and that I was probably alone in finding Stonehenge a rather negative place. I was also probably alone in my experience of its 'other side'.

Because we could not gain any help from the custodian, Tim and I were almost tempted to drive back there that afternoon and see if we could find any clues as to what had happened ourselves. I had other things to do later in the day, so instead we puzzled over who else we could talk to on the phone. At that time we had no knowledge or information about UFO sightings hotlines and such. There are phone numbers to call in such a situation, which I give at the end of the book. We couldn't believe that our hugely interesting and baffling experience was to come to a dead end. We planned to return to the monument in broad daylight, on the next available occasion. During that week, we did look up in library books about the Stonehenge area and were pleased to discover that there had been other ariel phenomena, yellow and orange globes of light, seen in the area.

We were also able to discover that the Henge has its abundance of myths as regards giants. These are generally seen as site guardians. We considered the possibility that the man that Tim had seen, was separate from the 'UFO' issue. Perhaps the entity had been psychically placed at Stonehenge to guard it against intruders? Tim said it certainly seemed to move with enough determination to have been a guard, or spiritual keeper, of the stones. Even Tim could believe that, after all, he had seen it with his own eyes. As it had been 'walking through the deep leaves' that were not manifestly present, perhaps the guardian was in another time from us, where there were trees, perhaps an ancient place which still existed in some dimension of time, when Stonehenge was in a wood? Maybe when the guardian had been 'created' as an entity or thought form by the builders of the Henge, there had indeed been more trees around?

The figure Tim had seen was undoubtedly 'supernatural', i.e. created as a spiritual being linked to the manifest by human thought, albeit an ancient one. It was too tall, too featureless and too silent (to my ears) to have been an ordinary mortal, plus it was able to 'get though' wire fences without making a sound. From the limited information we could gain from the library, our hypothesis was that the figure that Tim had encountered was the guardian of Stonehenge, which would account for its menacing protective presence, and for the fact that I did not see it. My attention was not on the stones at all, therefore, I posed no threat. As Tim had never had a single psychic experience before, I was surprised and pleased that he had been able to perceive the figure which did not exist on the manifest level at all. He must have been more 'open' than either he or I knew.

I am now better acquainted with the concept of site guardians, as well as the thought forms and entities which can be put in place, for positive or negative purposes, in the landscape.

The works of Andrew Collins, respected author and researcher, have done much to enlighten me subsequently. Mr Collins works with his partner, a natural psychic called Debbie Benstead, along with various other 'sensitives' and seers. They engage in their own psychic quests, which entails the psychics picking up messages as to sites that need clearing of negative energies/thought forms or of artefacts which have been buried and lost which they can retrieve. Examples of the former, including site clearance and work with guardians can be found in his works *The Black Alchemist* (Arrow) and *The Second Coming* (Arrow). Information as to his finding of artefacts by psychic means can be found in *The Seventh Sword* and the contact address for his other works, plus information about an annual psychic questing conference, can be found at the end of this book. I admire the work and writing of Andrew Collins because he is someone who does not claim that he alone can engage in questing and he is a strong advocate of people doing it for themselves. He is willing to share advice and experiences, but he does not wish to gain converts to his way of doing things. I especially appreciate his taking of psychic matters out of conference halls and into the countryside. I believe that their use of psychism in the great outdoors is positive and beneficial. Having met the man and his partner at Glastonbury Tor in recent years, I was further impressed by their encouragement to 'do it yourself'. Hopefully with more works like theirs, people will feel they can be involved in their own quests, and approach the matter with safety and full control.

As we continued our research into our UFO encounter during the week which followed, we came across a man who had been a researcher in the field, and who had written many books in the 1970s. His name was Arthur Shuttlewood and I thought he sounded approachable as his work was neither overly sensational or elitist in tone. I was finding it virtually impossible to continue as if nothing had happened to me, when I felt that something rather monumental had occurred. The size and glow of the orange object alone was awe-inspiring and I felt I just had to tell somebody about it, preferably somebody who would understand me and not ridicule me. I wanted to have an official log of my sighting, and the only idea I had at the time was to try and contact Mr Shuttlewood. On our return home, we phoned directory enquiries and were actually given his number. We had known he had lived in Wiltshire at the time of writing his books, as the references to the area, especially Cley Hill in Warminster, were profuse. So by area and his name we got his number, but sadly once we got through to his household we were told that he was very ill and unable to talk on the phone. I was asked to leave my details and he would call me back when he recovered. He never did call me back, and I was not feeling intrusive enough to call back to see if he ever did get better. So, we reached a standstill as to our reporting the event with a specialist.

The following weekend, we headed off in the late morning to Stonehenge, for what purpose we were not quite clear. My hands were literally trembling at the prospect of seeing that site again. We decided to retrace our approach, so as to observe the area in the same way as we had before. We drove from London to Winsley in Wiltshire, where Tim's parents lived, and then we drove out to Salisbury Plain from there, a very long journey.

By the time we pulled up at the T-junction as we had on the previous Saturday, we could see the first anomaly. There was no forest, or dense wooded area across the road, where I had first spotted the orange ball hovering. There was nothing except for the odd spindly sapling in evidence. We confirmed over and over with each other that we had both seen many large trees at that spot, we had even written in up in our notes afterwards. Yet there were no large trees.

Puzzled, we drove on along the main road. It had been so clear that night that there had been no way the odd stripling could have been mistaken for a forest. We were to be further disconcerted as we pulled up in the same layby which had been directly by the Hele stone. The place was infested with the usual tourists but we got out of the car as we had before and I tried to put my hand on the Hele stone, as I had that night. I could not. The fence, which was not newly erected, but was the same fence, made it impossible to reach the stone, even by stretching. Yet I had rested my hand on the stone with ease, pressing my palm flat to it. The stone had moved?

Also, the henge itself seemed smaller and more distant than it had to us that night. Again I must stress that it was a bright, moonlit night and that it was still very fresh in our minds as to what we had seen. We agreed that it was impossible for me to have touched the stone with such ease, but not only that, the entire monument seemed more distant altogether, and not so big or impressive. Tim and I could only share the confusing thought that this was not the same Stonehenge we had visited together less than seven days previously. Whatever we had expected to find at the monument, the fact that it had somehow moved seemed to be the least likely of events. Yet we had seen a different place altogether.

I turned and received my final proof. Looking at the field over which the craft had hovered, I could see houses, and quite a few of them too. There had been enough houses for at least some lights to have been seen on that night, but I had seen no evidence of any house or building for miles around when I had watched the craft moving about. There had been nothing but darkness all around it. Finally, we confirmed that there were no deep leaves for the man figure to have walked through. Thoroughly disconcerted, we drove away from the scene, with a full shared certainty that it was not the same Stonehenge that we had seen on November the twenty fourth, nineteen ninety.

It was not until the following summer and autumn, when I was working as an artist in Wiltshire after leaving University, that I met anyone who could shed any light on our odd experience. Tim and I spent a lot of time reading up on UFO lore and the latest findings, but the majority of the studies were American, and were nothing like our very peculiar case which had three separate components. Firstly, the orange light, secondly, the guardian/possible alien figure and thirdly, the difference in the landscape as we experienced it. There was also the blackened banana, a point I shall return to.

Our research into the UFO subject interested us in the crop circle phenomena. The common thought was that they were UFO landing tracks and alien messages in code. Coincidentally, these circles and glyphs were appearing with great frequency all around the Wiltshire countryside. We were fortunate to have been in the area, and were lucky enough to be able to travel to new formations in the crops. Regardless of the circles cause or effect, I found it very stimulating and beneficial to visit the places of great beauty in the landscape where these things appeared. I was inclined to go along with the idea of some of the more rational folk that one met in farmer's fields whilst checking out the latest circle. They saw the crop phenomenon as 'crop art' and nothing more, to be enjoyed in the landscape as a beautiful, symbolic form of artistry. The huge, increasingly complex signs and patterns in the corn which appeared in the corn in 1991 could be beautifully made and wonderful to look at. I loved being out in the open air, surrounded by greenery, enjoying the new 'pictograms' in the crops. However, most people were desperate to know who or what made them.

There was a conflict over the origins between the two most fanatical camps, these being that the circles came from the sky or the circles came from the Earth. The former camp thought that aliens were responsible, and the more wealthy or well-connected of them fitted up fields with infra-red cameras, sonic detectors and other such equipment to catch a craft on film, or an alien in the act. Circles continued to appear in the very fields in which the chaps had been positioned with their high-tech gear all night, so proving to them that the craft were invisible and far too advanced for their detection.

The other camp believed that the glyphs came from Gaia, the Earth mother, and that they warned of planetary destruction. As if to oblige, the crops began to form typically new-age symbols like the dolphin (which was particularly badly made and obviously the work of humankind). Grown men waxed lyrical about the Hopi Indian tribe who used similar symbols and who had told that our crop circles meant that the world was crying out to us. I am convinced that the Earth is crying out, but I am not convinced that the crop formations were made by orgone energy, sound patterns emitting from the ground or ley lines.

I have no firm opinion as to who or what made the circles, which have, at the time of writing, moved from Wiltshire to Hampshire and beyond. At the time, I just listened to human beings bickering between camps as to what was 'the truth'. Some people even arranged conferences, made people pay to enter them, and then proceeded to say that they alone knew the 'secret' of crop circles and they were not telling the likes of the common punter. The debate was mainly over whether the formation was genuine (Made by extra-terrestrial of paranormal means) or if it was a human-made 'hoax'. Many people set themselves up as 'experts' only to be brought down to size on film. The typical way to embarrass a self-proclaimed crop-expert was to show them a superbly made formation and to have them declare categorically on tape that 'it was made by means other than human construction' i.e. it was genuine. Then they would show the film of some person creating the formation by the use of a flattening board and some string, hours earlier.

Some keen folk even entered crop circle making competitions, to practice their skills to fool the so-called experts. There was no doubt about it that the circles could be produced by humans. I have seen formations created by 'hoaxing professionals' which were wonderful, and I have seen circles made by Tim and some of his friends which were plausible. I have also seen supposedly 'genuine' circles which were so wind damaged as to look hoaxed. That is why I stuck to the enjoyment of the whole phenomena, which was turning into a terribly bitchy, media-circus, as crop art.

Although I have my doubts as to whether 'genuine' formations ever occur at all, there were several things that lead me to keep an open mind. Firstly, the scientific tests on the corn from 'genuine' circles which showed that the corn had a 'magic bend'. In clumsily made hoaxed circles, the corn was broken not bent. It is very hard indeed to create a circle in the dark with a flattening board without breaking at least some stalks, if not all of them. Most formations were made at night, of course, and the accuracy involved by the hoaxers in pitch blackness was staggering. The 'magic bend' corn from the formations thought as too good to be hoaxed seemed also to have been changed in their molecular structure, as if flattened by a force unknown to humanity.

This of course fuelled the extra-terrestrial theorists to a new, almost religious, fanaticism. It was indeed very difficult to bend corn without snapping it, but I believe that certain hoaxers may have perfected the art by patient hand-bending of the crop. The molecular change was a scientific fact, however, and it certainly made me curious. The other factor which kept my mind open was the video footage of light forms seen in the crop, and also a strange disc shaped object which hovered over the field near one formation. It was a tiny disc but it moved independently over the corn in a very odd manner, unlike anything else we have in England. As I myself had seen an unbelievable thing, I could believe the footage of the light forms and the disc. If only Tim and I had had the facilities to film our experience!

The crop formations may have indeed had non-human origins and they may have meant something important to humankind, but as yet this has not been clarified and the truth, if there is one truth, has not been revealed. Although the formations have become incredibly intricate in Hampshire, intensely beautiful and creative pieces of crop art, the general furore has died away in the face of many videos which show elaborate hoaxes and talented hoaxers at work. It seems that any message that the crop circles were meant to convey got lost in the deluge of capital gain, exploitation and discrediting of other humans. The only message that I personally heard was that people should spend more time outside in the landscape. My own experiences with home-made dowsing rods and with 'feeling' the sites of circles had come to nothing. I felt no energies in the circles other than the feeling of the land in that area. To me the crop circle phenomena just brought thousands of folk out of their homes, into nature. That was the most beautiful part of the whole thing.

For myself, it was interesting to finally come across dowsers, psychics, mediums and other mystical characters for the first time in my life. I had still not come across anyone who could help me with my dreams, visions and poltergeist activities and at the age of twenty five I was getting a little tired of living a life which was out of control. Instead of meeting people who would talk to me, and help me by sharing their experiences, I met egotists who wished only to promote their theories and practices. They were fine until questioned or contradicted and they had no time to hear what anyone else thought at all. As with anything in this world, a hierarchy of psychics involved with crop circles had formed. I was nowhere in the scheme of things and was not worth consulting with except as a possible acolyte for them and their cause. Without sounding too cynical about the whole affair, it attracted its fair share of people with problems, and the psychic atmosphere in the meetings that we all held would have given any really sensitive person a headache. I also pondered, if they were so psychic, why could they not tell that I was?I was a positive hive of psychic activity at the time, yet not one person picked up on it.

Similarly, I did not feel that they had any particular 'glow' about them, but I expect their attentions were more focussed on competing with other humans, rather than tuning in to the environment around them. I think that this is a dangerous way to be, without actually criticising them, simply because I saw them be discredited one by one. The way that the rest would turn against one who had been proved fraudulent by validating a 'hoax' circle was astonishing. The pub meetings were a sad reflection of human nature, condensed into one seething room. Tim and I always attended, although we were not particularly welcome or suitably important. I desperately hoped that one day a psychic would arrive whom I could talk to as someone on the same level. Meanwhile, we continued to go out to see formations in the crop and it was at a most spectacular crop pictogram at Barbury Castle that I had my first real insight into my life-long psychic 'problem'.

At Barbury, I climbed the hill to get a better ariel view of the pictogram in the crop. It was rather late in the evening, turning dusk, and I was alone. Tim remained below, inside the crop formation. Whilst I walked, I found myself in the presence of a spirit who wished to talk with me. This was unheard of at that point, nothing had ever occurred spontaneously out of doors before, and things happened to me without my consent. The spirit that was around me was not scary or demanding, and I felt as if I could open my mouth and that he (for it was a he) could speak out of my mouth. Curiously, in the house that sort of thing would have scared me rigid, but outside, in nature, it was fine.

I began to sing, in a series of noises that were not words to my understanding, but which I could understand on some level. I could think something in my head, and the sing-song male voice would respond to me from out of my own mouth. I danced round the hill, rhythmically singing quietly in the strange manner and it felt great. I was aware that the presence was my guide, someone who was making themselves known to me. All I could see was a middle-aged Native American Indian man in my mind's-eye. Now, I have always been someone with one foot in the Otherworld, and with my head full of dreams, but fundamentally I am a down-to-Earth person as befits my upbringing in Merseyside. I have what I regard as a healthy dose of commonsense and I prefer to regard things rationally as well as spiritually. The idea that I should have anything as clichéd as a Red Indian guide but amused and alarmed me. Was he fantasy? I was convinced of the fact that he was genuine, and not some flight of fancy, by the fact that he was the very thing that I would least expect to have as a guide. I was not drawn to Native American thoughts or practices, and I thought that one should be more in tune with one's own indigenous peoples of yore, and the myth and legends of one's own island than that of a huge country over the ocean. I also believed that he was a reality for me as I had not been thinking about guides, nor was I thinking of Indian men.

I was simply walking on a hill on a lovely evening. I believe that I had opened up psychically in that green and beautiful place, and as I was alone (which was rare when I went out with Tim looking for crop circles) he had finally gotten through to me. I had no idea of how long he had been my guide, or if he had simply appeared to help me at that point in time, but he was real to me. He felt real too, warm and protective as a tangible presence. He did not speak in words I could understand, but in those curious sounds and in pictures in my head. That was my first encounter with him. Subsequently he has never sung in such a manner from out of my mouth, and we communicate purely by thought and image. He does not speak using English and his pictorial conversations are often very symbolic and cryptic. I can see him only in my mind's-eye, he has never materialised. However, I was so jittery and afraid of my psychism when I first met him that it would have probably been the final straw if I had encountered him 'in the flesh'. I am now aware that he is more of a 'principle' than a man, more of a representative of his tradition than an individual.

The reason that so many Indian guides come through to people is not because there are thousands of dead Indians willing to be guides. It is because people can relate to the energies of the Native American peoples and so the spirit involved simply dons the identity and energy of the Indian with which to relate to the human with success. He is a part of that Great Spirit which the earthly culture represents. I will never be actively involved in the Native American tradition on

Earth, as my own path is of the Western tradition of the Wisewoman. However, I do have an affinity with that way of being, and my guide has been a source of much good guidance and comfort.

I know now that some people do not believe in guides, usually because they have never met their own guide. Others walk alongside their guide daily as a treasured friend and mentor. My guide is not a deity to be worshipped, nor is he a slave to be ignored or abused. He is a representative of the Great Spirit of Native American culture and practice and he is with me for as long as we can work together. I suppose that I would have imagined myself with a guide more along the lines of Robin Hood or Morgan Le Fay, or some other image that was more English by tradition.

Obviously the essences of myself and my guide blend well and I am now grateful to have such a friend who has shown me many marvellous things in meditation and image. After I heard his voice at Barbury Castle, I was not afraid of my psychism. I had the first piece of clear guidance that I had ever received on that evening. I was told that I should bend down and pick up the flint object at my feet, which I did. I had an excellent confirmation that my guide was not a figment of my imagination, as I would never have noticed the flint otherwise. It was unmistakably in the shape of a woman's head and torso, it reminded me of the Goddess figures I had seen in text books for archaeology, which I was interested in. It was crude but certainly female in shape. The find of that simple flint woke up something within me which was long sleeping, and feeling more at peace than I had ever done in this life, I thanked the great spirit and pocketed my find. I had solid proof that I had talked to a real force, and I felt more comforted than if I had spoken with any number of psychics or mystics. I was able, from that point on, to refer my problems to my guide, and I ensured that I made a system of testing the guide before I received communication, to make sure he was the 'true' spirit. I visualised him in his form in my mind's-eye and then I would point my finger at him, imagining a blue light emitting from the fingertip. When the light reached him, if it were the real guide, he would glow blue and then appear as he was. If it was a false spirit trying to gain access (as with the ouija) my command 'reveal yourself' would show the true form of the spirit, be it snake or twisted imp. The form would vanish and the true guide would replace the image in my mind's-eye. This was my first form of a very basic Psychic Highway Code, which I adapted from a very basic library book I had found on the subject.

Before meeting my guide, I had not the confidence in myself to try and deal with the maelstrom of psychic interference I received. He gave me the faith to try out my own skills, and I found I could control the images that I received. I felt safer in my head, but still the difficulties in my home environment reigned. I will discuss my improved, tried and tested, code of practice in a later chapter. It should be remembered that the astral is a busy place and it is not uncommon to find an impostor in a familiar disguise. One can usually tell by the feel of the image and communication one is receiving if it is 'genuine' to the true guide or not. If the guide is not forthcoming and the time has not spontaneously been right for the guide to reveal itself, then the individual can perform a meditation ritual to meet the guide which I will also describe later.

It is so valuable to know who your guide is, and preconceptions are worth little, as I found out! The guide can be a dead relative, an ancient spirit, a discarnate that one knew in another life, a representative of a compatible culture or belief system or a figure that means something personally to your own psyche. The guide can wear a suitable costume to be recognisable to you or it can appear in its last earthly guise. Whatever the shape or form, guides are invaluable sources of help and encouragement towards personal growth and harmony. They are not to be feared. Some people have two guides, some have several in a lifetime depending on how suitable they would be to a life phase. But everyone has a guide.

The stone lead me indirectly onto a new path, and one that I found increasingly hard to share with Tim. Although my life still revolved around UFO research and crop circle watching, my personal studies changed and I began to look at books about witchcraft and Paganism. At the time they made little sense to me, and I was a little scared of them as even then it was still possible to read an ignorant sensationalist expose of devil worshippers and covens. I knew I was drawn to the ancient traditions but I was still groping about blindly. I would stare at books on 'magical' Britain, sacred sites and strange traditions of England, and although I did not fully understand anything, or make connections, I knew I was being drawn to something. I had stepped onto my path, even if I was walking slowly. I got a feeling which was associated with my initial research. It was something deep and familiar, like a past-life recall.

Meanwhile, the noises and goings on in my room at night continued as ever. The crop circle group was dissolving as the seasons changed and the crops were harvested. The 'Doug and Dave' media hype had occurred, which supposedly proved two pensioners had created all the crop circles. It was laughable, watching footage of them methodically demonstrating how they flattened corn with a bit of old plywood. They were nice chaps and totally sincere, but it seemed highly unlikely that they alone had started the phenomena altogether. Also to be the perpetrators of each and every formation over the summer was physically impossible. They would have had to have been in two, maybe more, places at the same time on certain nights of the year. The public, I'm sad to say, accepted this as the entire explanation for the phenomena, and promptly all went back to sleep in their armchairs. I doubt if the 'powers that be' had been too keen on researchers sitting out in Wiltshire fields at night, sometimes near army bases and military operations. All the crop circle phenomena had attracted people from far and wide to tramp all over crops and sit up hills all night, awaiting alien invasion. There was too much happening for the military in Wiltshire for it to be entirely happy about a human invasion after dark into 'their' areas. Also, the media is always keen to trash a UFO or unexplained story. Perhaps to steer the public's consciousness away from anything that may expand them a bit and make them question too much about their lives. Or perhaps, as the few would have you believe, because they do not wish for the public to get too close to things like UFO's in case we find out what it is they like to keep from us. After my encounter with the orange light and the subsequent 'trashing' I received from the Stonehenge custodian, I can perhaps believe the former and the latter reason for trying to discredit all unexplained phenomena. The man I spoke to at Stonehenge wasn't politely dismissive nor was he just humourous in his disbelief. He was adamant. I had not seen anything. He was telling me, not asking me to believe that.

One such person who liked to provoke other people with other such inflammatory statements was a man called Ron who was involved at the core of crop circle politics in Wiltshire. He stalked people at the meetings with a dictaphone hidden on his person, and he played one person off against the other. He had a side-kick who was an American and the pair of them fell in and out of favour with the top echelons of the crop circle community. They infiltrated peoples lives, got them to reveal their findings and secrets and then promptly wrote articles and made videos to destroy the person involved. An evening at Ron's house would be interrupted by innumerable whispered phone-calls. He and his friend systematically dismantled crop circle groups and beliefs with apparent ease.

Both were intelligent and charming men and I mention them for two reasons. Primarily they are important because I and many others cannot believe that two bright, wealthy young men would have nothing better to do with their time and energy than to go out into fields to create fabulous hoax circles, fake lights in the sky, write defamatory articles, take paranoid phone-calls and methodically destroy people's trust and faith in each other and the whole mystery. One must remember that the whole thing was very newsworthy that year, with television coverage, newspaper features and books galore. Without being seen to be being too much of a conspiricist myself, I would like to suggest that it seems a little odd, especially when the two men involved did not work and yet had plenty of money. I have heard many far fetched things, including that one was a CIA agent and the other was a Government man. Even although I am not prepared to accept this, I do wonder why they were involved in the phenomena, and why they showed such determination to discredit it?

Ron's other relevance in this tale was that it was he who introduced me to Rose, a woman who bore the title of materialisation medium, a psychic who could make the spirits of the dead become manifest. I heard two conflicting reports of her authenticity. Firstly she had been proved a fake and secondly she had proved under scientific conditions that there was life after death. She seemed to be a woman in an advanced state of paranoia about being followed by persons unknown. She also claimed to have created crop circles by thought, including the fantastic Barbury Castle formation. She was an imposing woman, somewhat overbearing, who I wished to ask for some help. I needed some assistance with my recurring dreams and visions, which were getting nigh on unbearable and which were disrupting my life to an unacceptable degree. Although I had my guides presence, I could not seem to stop the flow of images, often graphic and unpleasant, which came every night as I retired for bed. I had rather hoped that Rose, with her dominant personality and air of authority, could help me directly but she was not moved to do so. She dismissed me and said that I should contact a man in Berkshire who dealt with past-life work. I do not think that she took to me at all, and considering the person she recommended me to go and see she must have ill-wished me considerably. In my naive and still troubled state, I contacted the stranger in Berkshire by post and I hoped that I would get a positive response. At least I had a link to being helped by another human being, at last.

I had no idea what sort of link it was to be.

Chapter Three

My contact with the man in Berkshire opened up doors that I had never expected, both manifestly and in terms of perception. As with such spiritual matters, as one begins to delve into the mysteries, another connection will occur and then another. One can be lead to the most unexpected places by a step in the direction of knowing and also up a few blind alleys.

My letter to Berkshire was responded to by a couple. My plea to them had been to discuss my psychic difficulties with them, especially the dreams, with a view to my learning how to cope with them. I did not wish for them to help me, but for them to give me the benefit of their experience on how I may best help myself. I also mentioned my Stonehenge experience and I believe it was that which interested them more than me myself. I was aware of what an unusual experience it was and I knew that someone, somewhere, had to be interested in it. The couple invited me down for the weekend, and added that I would be in the presence of both a male and a female, lest I feel uneasy about staying with strangers. I wasn't entirely convinced by this, but the tone of the letter seemed genuine enough and I decided to trust them and go with it. If the truth be known, I was becoming desperate to be freed from the endless cycle of dreams which ruined my every night. I was willing to risk the couple being axe murderers for the sake of some peace in my life.

I told Tim about it, warily, and he was very disapproving and would not accompany me. In many ways he was atypical of the small Wiltshire towns he grew up in, but in others he remained a rather bigoted and sexist individual. He did not like me doing things without it being his idea and so he refused to go with me, or to be interested in the journey. I had kept a great deal of my persistent psychic occurrences to myself, unless I was unable to hide them happening. When Tim and I had shared the house with Lis in London, he had been party to some hair-raising events. Since our arrival in Wiltshire he had been sheltered from the majority of my psychic interference because it was happening more and more in an internal, rather than external, manner.

In London Tim and Lis had lived with all the psychic things that I had lived with for years. For some reason, the house we were in seemed to facilitate the events even more than usual. Never before had I been able to show anyone what it was like to occupy my world, albeit involuntarily, of poltergeists and such. Tim and Lis saw the same shadowy figures on the landing as I did, accompanied by the candles that ignited on their own, the objects which moved as they wished, unaided, and the noises which were perhaps the most scary aspect. The objects were one thing, shoes appearing under my pillow, toilet rolls balancing themselves on top of lampshades, keys constantly vanishing without trace or worse appearing inside kitchen appliances, but the noises were worse.

One night there was a sound like a wardrobe being pushed down the stairs, a sound which kept being repeated as we hid in my bedroom. The same wardrobe then sounded as if it were being slammed at full force against the wall. I was driven mad by the sound of a squeaky bicycle being ridden round and round in the attic above my head by an invisible person. In the lounge I discovered that one seat I sat on turned hot as I sat there and I began to smell burning until I leapt up. One evening I heard an invisible woman weeping pitifully in the corner of the same room, which again was witnessed by someone else. A previous tenant had left because she felt oppressed and suicidal whenever the shadowy figure appeared on the landing. Nobody actually blamed me, but no one else had ever suffered such strange phenomena, whereas I had always lived alone with the fear of an 'attack' by the unseen forces.

Tim and Lis took my unusual self in their stride for most of the time and we had many interesting discussions on the subject of phenomena and the possible causes. Neither of them could help me though, and I did need to talk to someone with experience, expertise and sensitivity in the field. Taking the advice of an inexperienced person on the matter could be very risky and I knew I was dealing with a serious and determined force. I had to grab at the opportunity in Berkshire no matter how Tim protested. Tim didn't know that I had the same dream every night which was driving me halfway around the bend. I really did need help.

The dream consisted of me running through arches, perhaps catacombs, underground. From there I would run into a small stone room and I would close the heavy wooden door behind me. I was panting and scared in the dream and I was obviously fleeing from somebody or something. I looked around the room and I found to my dismay that there was only a small wooden shutter in the room, half way up a wall. It looked like a miniature door. I opened it, using an iron ring handle, and I found that I could see the outside world, trees and bushes, through it. However, I knew that I could not fit my body through it and I knew that I had trapped myself in that room.

There was a dreadful feeling of panic in the dream, I knew that someone would come and find me trapped in the room and I dared not leave it to escape another way. The frustration of seeing the world outside, but being unable to get to it,

51

was utterly awful and I began to shake and sweat as I heard footsteps outside the door. As I was not a lucid dreamer I had no idea that the dream was not real. Once I was dreaming it, I believed it was my reality.

At the moment the door opened I would awake, terrified. It would take me an age to recall that I was in bed, not in that room. My sleep was interrupted by that dream and other images that were not connected but which felt relevant. I was constantly being chased and then killed in a bloody manner. Although one is not supposed to die in a I dream, I died many times, by being shot or stabbed or disembowled. No matter how hard I tried I could get no more clarity on the dreams than the fragments that I saw time and time again. The theme repeated itself over and over; the chase and the murder.

The hiding in the stone room was the most unbloody of the dreams, but the panic it made me feel was equally horrific. The stone room dream felt very close and familiar, deeply personal. I knew it was part of a past life, and one that I needed desperately to recall, if only to rid myself of my tormented sleep. I had only ever tried once before to be regressed into a past life recall by means of hypnosis. I had seen an advert for a man in the West End of London who would do a session on past lives for twenty five pounds. When I had paid up, in my innocence, I was approached my a dirty, crude middle-aged man who worked through a supposedly 'new age' organisation (an umbrella term which I find covers a multitude of suspect practices which are offered in exchange for cash by ill-equipped, badly trained people). I was not convinced by the man. He claimed he could read my mind, which indeed he seemed to be able to do, but he did not believe in formal hypnosis and he thought I could access my past lives if he played me a tape of the sea and put his hand 'reassuringly' on my breast. I left in all haste, too frightened to approach anyone again, until I was told about the people in Berkshire.

I was feeling depressed and tired due to the dreams, and as it was Autumn, the time when I have even more psychic interference, I was dealing with other feelings too. I really did need help. I now see that my subconscious was simply bringing the past life memory to the surface as I had an important lesson to learn from it. I believe in regression as a tool to access far memory, and I will share my methods and experience of this technique shortly. However, I also think that memories surface of their own accord if the Self sees the need for them to be recalled in this incarnation. In the case of the my dreams, I think the prompting I was receiving to delve further into the past life was overwhelming. I really did need to use regression to find out the root cause of the haunting memories. As the recall was so painful and of such a difficult memory, I needed to be relaxed enough to cope with the images that would come up.

Regression gives a distance between memory and subject that trying to access the dreams yourself cannot. There was no way that I could have dealt with the pain of those memories in any other way than regression at that time, as I had no personal means to cope. Had fate not presented me with the Berkshire couple at that point, I suppose the dreams would have caused me physical and mental distress. However, as my psyche had thrown the images up, it was clearly important to realise the message contained within them and so the obvious conclusion was that my guide would wish me to find help in order to learn and grow from the message. I believe my guide was instrumental in helping me discover the Berkshire couple at that time.

I travelled to Berkshire on the train, without any idea of who or what I was to expect when I arrived at the address I had been given. I eventually arrived on foot at the front door of a town house and the door was opened by a dapper little chap in his middle thirties. A neat, trim man with a clipped beard and a warm manner, Richard invited me in to meet Shirley, his partner. I was frankly astonished by the woman who sat in the living room. She was a large woman with jet black hair and dramatic clothing. What was most extraordinary about her was that I could see a large golden halo effect around her head. I had never seen an aura before and to suddenly be faced with one which was so magnificent was a little disconcerting.

The woman was about twenty or so years older than Richard, and a charming hostess. Immediately after shaking my hand she told me that she knew I had been burned at the stake in a previous life. Nowadays I would have taken exception to such a remark, thinking it rude to tell a total stranger that they had, allegedly, had such a life. Back then I was fascinated and glad of her candour. I had waited a long time for someone else who was psychic to pay attention to me. I had no idea whatsoever about the life I had lead as the lacemaker in France at that point, but I had been told by two other people that I had been burned in a past life. One was the horrible man who I paid to regress me in London, and the other was a gypsy woman who literally stopped me on the street in London to tell me many truths about myself, including the burning. As her other predictions and insights were all correct, I have no reason to believe that she was lying to me about the past life revelation.

Shirley was the third person to tell me this information. Up until then I had been sceptical about such a possibility, having a past life as someone who was burned alive was as 'fashionable' as someone who had a guide who was a Native American Indian! Obviously I was guilty of having both the past life and the guide! Until Shirley told me I had been burned, I had dismissed the idea, although I had had to acknowledge that I did have a phobia of fire which was totally irrational and which had no links to any incident in this life. As a teenager I had always had to have a pint of water next to my bed, lest I somehow caught alight during the night. Also I had almost fainted when I had first seen the exhibit in the London Dungeon which showed a heretic being burned at the stake. I was not squeamish about other, gorier, exhibits, but the burning made me petrified.

Another pointer I had had was when watching a video with Lis and Tim, a scene featuring three burnings for witchcraft came on screen. I had an irrational urge to withdraw my feet up close to my body and I found tears coursing down my cheeks as I watched. Somewhere inside myself, even then, I knew I had suffered a burning and instinctively I was trying to withdraw my feet from the flames below, even though I was in the twentieth century watching a television set, and I was not part of the film. I had not dwelt too heavily on these points as they were minor when compared to the poltergeist activity that occurred around me, but when Shirley revealed that she too thought I had been burned I had to consider the matter with more seriousness. As I had been visiting the couple to share my Stonehenge experience, and my poltergeist phenomena, I cannot say that Shirley picked the thoughts of 'burning' out of my head as a mind-reader. I was not focussed on burnings but on my dreams and the related material that went with them. Shirley continued to pick up information psychically from me as the weekend wore on. I thought she was an amazing woman, and I later discovered that she was part of a practice called Wicca.

Over tea, myself, Richard and another researcher called Clifford discussed my Stonehenge incident. I was questioned and my responses were treated as genuine. Richard shared his own experiences, when he and Shirley had encountered a huge man-shape similar to the one Tim had seen. They both had many tales of incidents with some correlation to my experience at the ancient monument, although our experience seemed to be the only one with a 'time slip' or 'Oz' factor. Many UFO witnesses had experienced this missing time, but few people had had so many phenomena all occurring at once, as we did.

Richard told me of the 'Philadelphia experiment' in the USA which occurred between the years of nineteen thirty nine and nineteen forty. This involved a vessel called the 'Eldridge' being partially, or totally, de-materialised by use of a massive negative charge of energy. When the ship did totally vanish, only to reappear in another location several moments later, the crew had gone mad, or died in the interim. Wherever the ship had gone to in its missing time, it had sent the crew to the limits of their sanity. In their book 'The Demonic Connection' (Badgers Books, 1987) Newton, Walker and Brown cite an incident where a hitchhiker was picked up in the vicinity of Stonehenge who appeared to be totally insane. The reason for the man's apparent madness, it transpired, was that he had been a crew member on that ship, and was one of the few survivors. Such information is not science fiction, but a factual event. Therefore, I would suggest that this tear in the fabric of this material realm which gave access to a place where time is irrelevant and past and present overlap, is exactly the cause of what happened to Tim and I in November nineteen ninety. Inadvertently, we had slipped through that tear, and then returned to the present. Perhaps the 'barriers' of fog were in some way involved as they denoted the entry and exit points of the whole experience?

Looking back, I find the notion that Tim and I could have been trapped in some alternative space and time quite a terrifying one. Furthermore, I would suggest, hopefully without being accused of being another conspiracy theorist, that if the government and military were capable of creating time/space experiments (the Eldridge) in the 1940s, then what could we have stumbled upon in the 1990s on Salisbury Plain, a notoriously military area? 'Technology' in such areas must have improved tenfold by this late point in the century. It is a chilling thought for me to imagine having disappeared into such a reality.

I wonder if there would have been any witnesses that night to have seen our Ford Fiesta suddenly de-materialise, if that was what happened? This concept also made me ponder on the way articles actually moved around my rooms without being seen or 'caught in the act' of being transferred. Perhaps the psychic energy field I was creating around myself at that time was one in which such tears in the fabric of this reality occurred more frequently? I still have no satisfactory answer as regards the Stonehenge time slip, or, indeed, my moving possessions.

Richard wished to interview both Tim and I separately for the cover story of his next self-produced UFO journal. When Tim finally consented to this interview he was angry to discover, after all reassurances, that we were misrepresented as 'alien contactees' and the description of Tim's male entity encounter had been adapted to suit Richard's theories. I certainly did not like the idea of being contacted by aliens, nor did I want the sort of publicity which goes with such claims. However, on that first occasion of meeting Richard, he was rational and interesting and seemed unlikely to exploit me or my experiences. Although I was naive, which I will admit for the sake of any other innocent person who feels a fool for being taken advantage of by so-called teachers or spiritual leaders, I could not be blamed for seeing Richard as an intelligent and interesting man on that occasion. This did not remain the case on subsequent visits, and I shall share the warning signs that I got, and ignored, from the man who had claimed he wished to help me to help myself.

Initially, Richard wished to have every detail of the Stonehenge story, after which he was willing to work with me on my troublesome dreams. It was wonderful to be able to tell sympathetic people, at last, about my recurring nightmares, visions, voices and moving objects. Richard confirmed what I had suspected and was too underconfident to believe of myself, my psyche was crying out for me to acknowledge a past life memory. Richard was a regression therapist (I never did check his qualifications, but he was a skilled regression facilitator, anyway) and he insisted that I had a free session immediately.

In the cosy room as darkness was falling I felt safe enough to agree, with Shirley and the mild-mannered Clifford sat in attendance. Instinctively I trusted them all, and I was promised that at no time would I be 'out of control'. I would be free to stop the session as I wished, or to get up and walk away. I was uncertain as to the viability of this as I had assumed that in regression, one was totally hypnotised and was susceptible to another's suggestion. This is not the case at all, the regressor is a guiding voice but the person being regressed is not at their command. The method that Richard used was very pleasant and it worked well. I have since used it on friends and they too have had positive results from it. I will describe the method here for personal use and adaptation.

The main fact that must be remembered before entering into hypnotic regression is that the person is not a victim to be manipulated by the fascilitator. The person is in control and is simply accessing deeply buried personal memories. If one considers the trivia, emotional baggage and information that a soul carries with it from life to life (imagine it, people, places, feelings, shopping lists, for many lives)then it is easier to understand why one needs to enter a relaxed trance state to go deeper within to 'find' a lost memory. In the case of my haunting dreams, my memory had risen to the surface of my psyche for a reason and I had only to be regressed to be able to see it the clearer. Regression removes the fug of twentieth century worries and knowledge in order for the person to delve into their well of far memory. In regression, one should be aware of the eternal Self and not the current 'persona' that the Self is wearing. Incarnations are merely suitable masks that the Self dons, appropriate for the learning the soul must undertake. The Essential Self is doing the work, the regressor is only the guide on an inner journey.

In this respect, similar methods can be used in personal meditations in order to 'see' distant memories. At first, I believe it is safer if possible, to use the guided technique. Not everybody is able to have access to a willing friend or partner and so personal regression in meditation can be undertaken. One must be aware that it is possible to experience deeply emotional feelings and scenes in regression, which can make it hard for an individual to leave or withdraw from them. This is only natural, after all, it was your life, albeit a different one. Feelings will be experienced in a real sense. It is beneficial to enter into the process with a distance between yourself and what you see. Memories cannot hurt you but the best way to recall any past trauma is by pretending that you are watching a film. Films can affect you but they cannot directly harm you and the 'watcher' is at liberty to turn off the film, or to end the session of regression, as is appropriate.

I believe that the Self will protect itself from seeing horrific or unnecessarily painful imagery when a person is regressing themselves alone. If my words seem a little daunting, do remember that the majority of lives are peaceful ones which occur without too many major incidents. A friend once told me a tale of an uncle who was regressed by a professional. The session consisted of the man being asked, by an increasingly frustrated regressor, "and what are you doing now?" to which the uncle replied every time "I'm trimmin' the 'edge" in a broad West Country accent! The man's life appeared to consist of trimmin' the 'edge and sexual intercourse, a simple life indeed! So do not be put off by expectations of dire memories, but be prepared for emotional responses.

Whether one is meditating alone or being guided by another person, I must stress the vital importance of being protected before beginning any psychic work. Psychic protection should be used AT ALL TIMES. My preferred methods of protection vary but have the same principal. I cover myself in a bright blue shield, I may visualise this as putting on a full-sized blue plastic romper-style space suit, complete with helmet, or I may prefer a suit of blue armour, again with a plumed helmet and chainmail gloves. The whole person must be clad in shiny light blue. I know people who step inside a blue egg, which works well for them. No part of the person must be outstanding from the protection, remember hands, feet and the head should be covered.

At first, the protection should be visualised, in the mind's-eye, methodically i.e. with the 'romper suit', pull it carefully over one foot, then the other, draw it up to the knees, past the thighs etc. The more clarity and focus the initial protection has, the more powerful it will be in practice. I like to 'seal' my protective suit with a symbol that suits me, which I place at the top of my head, at my third-eye or at any other 'portal' I think needs special protection.

I do not wish to describe the traditional view of the chakras (the energy points on the body which I refer to as portals) as there are plenty of marvellous volumes which cater for this topic in far more depth. I tend to adapt information to a system which feels right to me, and although I was taught about the chakras in the accepted sense, I could not get along with the concept myself. I prefer the word portal, a place where energy may leave, enter or build, which is more in keeping with my traditional, western approach.

I see my own body as a form which is similar to the landscape. Many, many people accept that there are places on this Earth where the portals/doorways between this world and the Otherworlds are more accessible than others. These areas, where the veils are thinnest and the energies are strongest are commonly regarded as sacred sites and areas where leylines meet. These points in the landscape are those which can be influenced for good or ill by anyone who encounters them. For example, an energy hotspot and 'portal' like Avebury stone circle in Wiltshire can be planted with negatively charged crystals which will disturb the energies as they pass back and forth, around and around, the area. A sensitive individual or group could tune-in to this energy imbalance and work with the site guardian to cleanse and restore the land.

A person must accept that they must be the site guardian of their own body, and when entering the astral realms of meditation, magic, trance etc one must protect these delicate areas from attack. The seven 'weak spots' which are also powerpoints to be charged with positive energy, are as follows. Firstly the crown portal which is the one associated with the spiritual 'higher' Self. The next portal is the third-eye which represents the psychic Self, (which could be attacked by somebody wanting a person to 'see' things their way). Next is the throat, the communicative Self, (this area can be under attack by someone who wishes a person to express themselves in a way which they would not ordinarily wish to do). Fourthly we have the heart portal, which would correspond to an attack on someone wishing to influence the emotional Self, then the solar plexus which is a portal of creativity. Finally we have the portal at the abdomen which would respond to 'gut-feelings' as well as affecting the conception and birth of ideas and dreams and then the genital portal which governs the physical aspect of the Self, the vitality and energy. This portal is easy to observe as if one's sexuality does not hum in its usual manner, one can assume that there is an external influence which is upsetting this sensitive portal.

To shut down, seal or protect ones portals before entering into psychic work depends on the personal feelings of the individual. Perhaps it is best at first to cover one's self by protecting every portal with the chosen symbol, be it a cross, a pentacle, a crescent moon or a silver rose. Silver is an excellent colour as it reflects back all ill-wishes and unwanted energies on the astral levels, so I advise imagining your protective symbols at the portals in silver.

When one is more used to working astrally the protective ritual should be followed by selective protection of the portals. I usually cover my crown and third-eye portals as they are most easily influenced in the astral realms. I may then cover my throat portal if I feel someone manifestly wishes to make me express a different opinion to the one I have expressed to them previously. The astral is a place where aspects of people's souls can go without them even being aware (whilst their bodies are busy and their 'monkey' minds are occupied). It is easy for an astral influence to reflect an earthly one and therefore if one is aware of someone sending out thoughts to influence ones communication then it is best to protect the portal.

One can do this as a matter of course throughout the day as one encounters people with whom there is conflict or disharmony. Imagining the protective 'suit' and protecting the appropriate portals (heart and genital for unwanted attentions, third-eye for someone who wishes you to change your mind etc) can work marvellously on a manifest level as well as astrally.

I have a friend who erects a protective blue egg of light around herself when she works with a particular surgeon in a hospital theatre. He is totally unable to exert his usual influence and pressure on her when she is protected and no doubt this has him very perplexed! Once 'erected' the protection stays and will only fade gradually if not re-affirmed in the mind's-eye. The more time spent on the initial visualisation, the longer lasting the protection. When one is well used to this protective pattern, the ability to imagine it on the instant is achieved. The protection is strong and instantaneous because it has been made a reality so many times that it only needs a boost or refresher for it to spring back. These protective gestures do not impair second-sight. They do not keep everything out, only what is naturally undesirable to your energy field.

Once protected, the next step in any psychic work, regression or otherwise, is to relax. As with all the stages involved the key is to take ones time. I think that Richard, in my first regression, took about an hour to make sure that I was fully relaxed. There is little point in setting an unrealistic timescale to the proceedings, psychic work must be given the level of time and attention which is appropriate. Constant thoughts of 'but I should really be doing the ironing' or 'this is self indulgent' won't really be very beneficial! Working with the Self to aid growth and personal understanding is one of the most valid things an individual can do in this life, do not feel guilty about spending 'quality' time on it. The point of relaxation is to be aware and not 'out for the count'. In my first regression I could hear the dulcet tones of Shirley snoring in the background as she had nodded off by the fire! I was aware of noises but they were unimportant. Some people do fall asleep before they get to do the psychic work they intended to do, but I believe that that is nature's way of telling you you are too exhausted and you should return at a more appropriate time. All is not lost if one does fall asleep, I have always thought that the meditation or other work continues on astral levels while the physical form slumbers.

Others may believe they have fallen asleep, such is the state of relaxation, and the images accessed appear as dreams. This is a rare state of deep trance and I do not know of anyone who has fallen into such a state. The intention of a good regression is for the person to feel in control. Richard did not suggest that I was getting sleepy, he allowed me to tell him when I felt relaxed. His technique was to suggest that I, the participant, got into an imaginary elevator. He calmly stated that I was to travel in this elevator deeper down inside myself to access hidden memories. I began at the top floor, and then began to travel slowly down into my inner realms as Richard counted down 'ninety nine, deeper and deeper, ninety eight, deeper and deeper... ' and so on. As I passed a floor I would see a coloured number flash on the elevator control panel 'Eighty five, deeper and deeper.. '. At this point I had never done any visualisation and so I was just using my imagination. Fortunately they are one and the same thing, using the imagination to visualise the required 'image-tools' to access information. Note that the participant is going deeper within and NOT going outside to the astral levels. Therefore any information accessed will be personal and not from external, astral influences. One can be sure that the information is a memory, or a personal story. However, rely on gut feelings and if instinctively anything feels wrong then do just stop. It is not dangerous to stop at any point as long as one relaxes back into the 'real' world of the present day. One can shout 'CUT!' like a director of a personal film project.

If things are going well, then at certain levels the regressor should suggest that the participant stops the elevator to see if they are deep enough into relaxation to want to open the doors. If not, the count down continues. I myself took the elevator all the way down to floor one before I wished to 'get out'. When the person is ready then they should focus on the elevator doors in front of them with the desire that when they wish to open them they will see the scene from a past life which is most relevant to them at that time. As one opens the doors there is often a blackness outside. Patience will reveal shapes in the darkness and the regressor should encourage the participant, gently, to 'see' whatever is there and hidden. Other people can see clear images immediately.

Obviously, visualisation practice helps. One can try imagining all sorts of simple, familiar objects in order to strengthen this faculty. For instance, try 'seeing' a red teapot with the mind's-eye, or a blue and white stripy cup. See the stains, the cracks, the subtle markings that make it an individual item. The person guiding the regression should gently suggest that you may see images that are familiar to you if there is no clarity outside the elevator doors. The more

Richard said this to me, the more frustrated and disappointed I became that I could not see anything at all. I realised that I was getting too agitated to let the images simply flow and so I relaxed again and tried to let the pictures come to me. It is important not to get too worried if this lack of imagery occurs, as the more the logical, rational mind intervenes, the less is likely to occur. The images come from somewhere deep within us all, a place which we seldom access by an act of will. The only key is total relaxation, by which we can be far enough removed from ordinary concerns like 'am I doing this right?'.

I spent a long time groping about in the darkness, and the first clarity I had was that I simply realised that I was standing in a room, and from that feeling I began to see the accompanying pictures. Richard kept up a gentle flow of encouraging questions along the lines of 'look down at your feet, what do you see?' or 'describe your hands to me'. From there, more revealing questions such as 'what are you doing?' or 'what do you see around you?' can be asked. Having a tape recorder running as the regression takes place is the best idea. If one is engaging in regression via a self-guided meditation, an attempt to speak aloud would be an advantage, as taping the results gives far more clarity than trying to remember all the details later on.

In the regression Richard did for me, I was male, with sandals on my feet and chubby, pale hands. I had bare legs and a hessian style garment on my body. My only adornment appeared to be a simple ring on my left hand. I identified myself as Brother John, a monk who was doing his duties, which included lighting the lamps.

As soon as I fell into my 'role' of John and began experiencing the scene which unfolded for me in the first person, Richard began to guide me to a point in my life which was relevant to the dreams I had been having. As he suggested I 'see' any relevant event, I found I was in a sunny chapel, arranging flowers on a simple altar. I knew that there were two men outside the chapel door, as I could hear them discussing a matter which related to me in some way. They did not see me, but the chapel door was ajar so that I may hear them. When asked about this I could find no specific answers to questions like 'who are they?' but I had a name in my head which was Chelbeck or Welbeck, which was the place where I was. I also repeated the name Charles, who was one of the men in charge. I knew I was in England but I couldn't say if Charles was a king or a superior of the monk's order.

I was struggling to come up with further names and places when I was flooded with images relating to the two men talking. Some time previously, I had discovered the abbot in his chamber with two young girls. I had been horrified and disillusioned. I was a very pious man and the discovery had shocked me to the core. I had continued at my daily duties but was filled with a deep inner turmoil. I recalled sitting at a wooden bench at a table with the other brothers, with a wooden bowl of food before me which I could not eat. I felt intensely alone in their company with my awful secret. Coincidentally, I also discovered, as the chronicler of daily events, that there was a huge discrepancy in the orders monies. It appeared to me that the abbot was a corrupt influence upon the abbey and that I had to reveal his misdemeanors somehow.

I was a very simple man who spent a lot of time writing at a desk, which I loved. My life was safe and enjoyable until I had discovered that truth. I was foolishly filled with the courage of the righteous, naive as I was, and I decided to approach the king himself with news of our unholy abbot. I realised that several of the more influential men in the area were dealing with the abbot financially, and that I needed to go to the highest authority to escape the local hierarchy. I gave a note, revealing all, to a messenger boy who came on horseback every Tuesday to the abbey to take communications elsewhere. In my unworldly state, I had believed that the note for the king would remain unopened until it reached him. I was an honourable man, and thought all should be like me. Obviously, the note did not reach the king, but it fell into the hands of the local lords, who passed on the information of my dissent to the abbot. The conversation outside of the chapel had been about my 'disposal'.

I waited until nightfall before I decided to take flight from the abbey. Stupidly, I made an attempt to 'cleanse' the building as I went, by trying to set fire to it. Of course, this alerted people to my departure. I was unfit from hours sat at my desk and I knew I could not get far before the guards sent after me would catch me up. I did not cover much ground, and as daylight came I found a derelict building which looked a lot like a disused church of some sort. I then entered the place of my dreams, the inside of the church-like building, and the same story continued. I ran until I reached the small stone room, closed the door behind me and saw the same small wooden 'door' in the wall that I had seen night after night. Although my twentieth century Self was still calmly looking at the dream images, understanding at last their relevance, the John-Self was frantic, opening the door in the wall to see the outside world that he couldn't escape to. I saw now that I was too large as brother John to have ever gotten through the small space.

In my dreams the scene had become blurred at this point, but in the memory I sank down to my knees and began to pray. I reflected upon my life, a happy existence as a chronicler and before that, life with my parents. I saw myself watching my father working with wood outside of our dwelling, working with my brother whilst I was fussed over by my mother. It was never assumed that I would be part of my father's woodcraft as my mother had taught me all she knew in order for me to be accepted by the monks into a life of study and contemplation. She wanted me to learn to read and write and to be a religious man. She knew my sensitive, quiet nature would never fit with my fathers rough and ready physical work. I had missed my mother, but my life with the monks had been pleasing to me.

I had been convinced that I had been right to expose the abbot, whatever the consequences and so I was able to be at peace with myself and with my God. I was still praying when I heard the men who had been pursuing me bang on the door and come through it. At this point, I became emotional in the regression. I had fully assumed the character of John, I was John even although the twentieth century 'me' was aware of lying on a couch in Berkshire. As John, I saw the men standing over me with long wooden weapons which had oddly shaped metal points. Even although I was a sitting target for them, I refused to call out for mercy. I would die believing in my act of righteousness and I would not beg or plead. However, as I watched them smile cruelly above me my reserve broke.

"What are they doing now?" I heard Richard asking me, gently.

"They are going to run me through, " I replied, my voice cracking and my eyes streaming with tears.

I felt the points of their weapons go through my throat and then all was dark around me. I made a choking sound and I felt very distressed. At that point, Richard guided me back to my elevator which was waiting for me, and he counted me up from floor one to floor one hundred, bringing me back to the present. When I returned, he let me lie still for a while as the tears came for the poor man that I had been. It is important after any meditation or psychic work to fully 'ground' oneself to the manifest by taking a little food and drink. This makes the earthing connection between body, soul and the manifest. It reminds the participant of the physical and breaks any astral links. I sipped tea as Richard said how pleased he was with me. I had the whole event on tape to listen to at my leisure (not exactly easy listening) and I had the answer to why the dreams had been haunting me. Or did I? I knew what had happened to me, which was a relief, but I did not understand why it was so relevant to the present day as to keep recurring as nightmares. Richard did not go into this aspect of the regression. To him, it was all sorted out and done. He was very pleased with himself.

Poppy 1996

The rest of my stay at the house of Richard and Shirley was uneventful until I was walked to the station by Richard. I was alarmed to observe that Richard kept vanishing from my sight and reappearing under my nose without seeming to have moved. I did not mention this strange happening to him as he continued to talk as if nothing was amiss. I liked him and his partner and did not want to jeopardise my chances of visiting them again. I had a lifetime of psychic occurrences to discuss with them, if they were prepared to see me again. I had the feeling that perhaps they were not telling me everything about themselves. They too appeared to have no discernable source of income, yet they lived in a very large house filled with possessions. I was intrigued by them, especially the charismatic Shirley, and even after 'seeing' Richard do his vanishing trick I did want to see them again. Perhaps he was testing me out, as he saw it?Whatever he was doing, I am adamant that I witnessed him vanish and reappear.

Later in the week, on my return to Wiltshire, I checked out some of the 'facts' I had gathered from my regression. It is vital for the regressor to encourage the participant to reveal as many details of place names, dates, costume, housing etc as possible when the regression is occurring. This enables the participant to check the information in a historical context when they have returned to the present. It is so important to feel one can 'prove' that whatever it was that one saw was 'real'. With a life like John's, which was very insular, it was hard to get too many worldly reference points.

My first stop was a weaponry book. I was not someone well acquainted with medieval weapons, yet I discovered that the lance-like item I had seen with the funny shaped blade was precisely the sort of weapon used for a limited period of time in the mid-fourteen hundreds, which was the broad time period I had given for my life as John.

Elated by this obscure discovery which I would never have known of as my current Self, I progressed to checking the name Chelbeck or Welbeck Abbey. The latter name proved to have existed in Nottinghamshire. There was precious little information about the Abbey of Welbeck, I knew that I would never have known about such an unimportant place unless I had been a researcher of such matters. However, I was excited to discover that the abbey had had several corrupt abbots in the fourteen hundreds, who had given money to the lawless Barons of the locality. I could discover very little else about the institution, but what I did discover gave weight to my own tale of woe. The death of one renegade monk was hardly going to have been noted historically, yet the place had existed and the corrupt abbots too. Because the majority of lives are unnotable in the scheme of things this will be the case with researching most regressions. It is the smaller details with which one can verify an incarnation.

I was amazed, as a coincidence, to discover the real use of the wooden 'door' half way up the wall, in the stone room of my recall. Tim took me to Lacock Abbey as a treat after my regression. Lacock is a medieval village near Chippenham in Wiltshire, which retains a lot of original features. Sadly the Abbey was closed in the Winter, but I was thrilled to see a 'door' in a wall there. Having grown up entirely in modern towns and cities, I had never seen such a thing before, and it was only seeing it in context that I realised that the door was not a door, but a wooden shuttered window! I had not realised in my ignorance of medieval buildings, that the wooden door-style covers were for windows. The image was the same as the one I saw in the dream, down to the iron ring-pull handle, so I had another unexpected authentication that the wooden 'doors' were a feature of that time.

As my historical knowledge was mainly gained at school in the study of Hitler, Stalin and twentieth century politics, with the odd bit of the Saxons or Tudors thrown in, I could hardly have remembered such a detail from a history lesson. I doubt I would have been taught of a specific weapon used in the fourteen hundreds, nor of an abbey with a corrupt abbot. It was clear to me that I had not made up the story as an elaborate fantasy for myself. If I had, for what purpose?

I do believe that sometimes the psyche will come up with as recall of a life which is a fantasy, but I believe that they are valid in their own right. If one considers the 'fantasy' recall as a complex historical psychodrama, one can understand how it is that the psyche wishes to be seen. Even a fantasy recall can have a relevance to the Self, to explain some facet of personality or a way of being.

If it can be validated as a factual far-memory than obviously it is more relevant to the Self as the Eternal Soul actually chose to incarnate in that manner, for that purpose. By looking at past lives we can gain an over view of our lives today, giving new clarity to current ailments, relationships and phobias. I feel that the more lives we can know of and understand, the better the overview of the Self is and the more understanding about the present life can be gained. I believe the overview to be valid not just in our lives but as a way of understanding the lives and deeds of others with more sensitivity. To be another person in another life, to actively experience the soul acting out another role in a past life recall, is to gain a better idea of what it is like to walk in another's shoes. With an overview, we can see the way people's decisions and actions affect others, spreading outwards in waves from the person. Regression and our knowledge of our other lives broadens our understanding of ourselves and our fellow humans. Even if some of the lives 'recalled' are fantasy that cannot be verified historically, they fill in the gaps and tell us more about who we really are, how we see our real

Selves, what it is we need and how we should relate to others. I would not advocate that anyone make sweeping judgements about themselves or others based on one isolated recall, which may not even be verified. As with all things, gaining the broadest picture, having the most information possible and being open to new input is the best way to access 'truths' of a personal nature.

After my recall with Richard, I had hoped the dreams would cease. Of course, although I knew what they were about I had no idea what they meant, nor did I understand why I had started to have them in the first place. They continued, with variations including even gorier murders, more alarming chase scenes and new images involving Roman centurians, mass executions and arenas. I was baffled and deeply disturbed by this fresh wave of imagery. Richard was my only contact who could try to help me a little. I wrote to him and was duly invited to Berkshire again.

Clifford was not in attendance when I arrived and I found that Richard was not the chirpy, quick little man I had met weeks previously. He snapped irritably at Shirley and looked suspiciously at me. He was my only hope of stopping the terrible dreams and so I decided to bear with his mood. Richard claimed to have many strings to his bow, including healing and spirit rescue. He appeared to give my story much thought as I sat in their front room.

Eventually, using his intuition as a spirit rescuer, he came up with the solution that I had not been John the monk but that the monk was the poltergeist spirit which had always been attached to me. For some reason, the lost spirit of John was tormenting my dreams, as well as moving my objects, in an attempt to get me to notice him. Richard declared that John should be 'removed' or exorcised and sent on to the spirit realms. I was very bothered by this assumption, but I was still hopelessly helpless unless I had Richard's assistance. The dreams were sapping me and making me close to snapping. I knew that I had been John, just as much as I know that I am Poppy now. I knew John was an integral part of my Self. Yet Richard was convinced, although I felt that to have a part of ones Self exorcised was somewhat unpleasant.

Richard had an almost religious fervour about his ability to rescue spirits. He was being a bully, and not displaying the modus operandi that I wanted and favoured. I wanted empowerment by his explaining to me what he felt was wrong, but by him suggesting methods by which I could check for myself if it was appropriate. I felt it was instinctively incorrect, both to exorcise me and to tell me that this was the only right way. But I was alone and frightened by my psychism, so allowed Richard to play psychic surgeon rather than insisting he told me how to tackle things sensibly myself.

67

Richard obviously liked people to be reliant on his 'superior' knowledge and power, he adopted an air of secrecy and made me believe he was testing me to see if I trusted him before he revealed to me some bigger, better truth. I would strongly advise any budding spiritual seeker/psychic worker of any type or path to steer clear of any one, male or female, who wishes to keep one in a state of reliant disempowerment. Even if the person is not charging you financially, they will charge you spiritually by cording your third-eye and crown portals, if not others, making you see and feel things as they wish you to perceive them. Anyone seeking mentor status will claim some payment, usually the removal of will in the 'victim' or a sapping of their energy for their own use. They need not appear as a sinister, black-cloaked fiend; Richard was an ordinary, diminutive man who did not dress like an occult fanatic.

Obviously there are great teachers and communicators out there who genuinely wish to help newcomers and to provide a sharing of knowledge, but it would be folly to assume that every person with 'spiritual' status is either caring or wise. The attention some psychics receive can feed the ego to monstrous proportions, resulting in further power-trips and the acquisition of either money or energy.

I let Richard exorcise my monk-Self. I had to help by visualising him vanishing 'into the light' which was very hard to do as I did not wish for him to depart from me. I began to cry as I saw the image of John shrinking away. Richard said that I was not allowed to think of, or mention, John again, otherwise he would return to haunt me again. Richard was adamant that from then on I would have no more dreams or poltergeist visits. He convinced me that he only wanted to help and that he knew it was for the best. Perhaps he thought he did, but my gut feeling was to be upset.

After the exorcism, Richard told me of his psychic happenings which made my life seem distinctly dull. He spoke with such authority that it was easy to believe him. Now I realise that he had corded my head with astral links, I know why I found him so plausible. He wanted me to see him that way, and so I did. I knew nothing of astral cording then, or of protecting one's portals psychically, so I believed all I saw and heard as the truth. When Tim met Richard on one occasion to be interviewed for the UFO. magazine, he saw the man clearly, as Tim himself was not corded by Richard. He saw him as a creepy little man who he did not trust and who he thought was rather seedy. He felt sorry for Shirley, his patient partner. She was the one with the real gifts, I now realise, but then, Richard was the one who liked to appear the powerful one.

Richard told me that he too had a Red Indian guide (much to my distaste, I was rather fed up to discover I had acquired something so common!). His guide had put him through several 'initiation' tests including having goldfish swimming in through his bedroom window which then proceeded to 'swim' through the air around his light shade. He had also apparently seen a dinosaur in the road outside his house. Richards 'test' was to prove he knew no fear of these inexplicable events. Richard claimed that his initiation was for a purpose not yet revealed, but he added mysteriously that things with him were 'not as they seemed'. His guide was preparing him for some 'great work' or other and it was all very 'hush-hush'. He may tell me next time I visited.

At the time I was suitably open-mouthed with interest. In retrospect I can see that many people, from the mentally ill, to those seeking guru status, all claim to be involved in some 'great work' of a secret nature. Lois Bourne, in her marvellous book '*Witch Amongst Us*' (Hale, 1989) cites an incident when she was visited by an acolyte of a 'master' who claimed to want Ms Bourne's aid in his own 'great work'. She did not discover what the masters work was, but I was told of Richard's great work in a coming visit. Frankly, I wish he had stuck to his tales of goldfish. Also, Shirley told me that she had been abducted by a UFO in broad daylight whilst walking a dog in the local park. As this was before the absolute wave of abductee claims I was more inclined to believe her, as I liked her and she seemed to believe herself. Richard kept chipping in with reminders of details and such, which I found annoying. Perhaps Shirley's alleged abduction experience had been somewhat added to by Richard, in order for him to slot it into his own theory of the phenomenon? I thought this as that is precisely what he did with my tale of the strange light at Stonehenge.

Shirley was also paranoid about being pursued by 'men in black' (a concept which began in the 1950s, of suited, faceless men who would silently harangue anyone who claimed to have spotted a UFO) I found it rather bizarre that men in black should be haunting a town house on a busy road in a largely populated area, because one woman had told a few people she had been taken by aliens. I sincerely believe that Shirley had psychic powers and a gift of clairvoyance that was truly amazing. But I think she was a woman who had been totally corded by her partner in order for her to see things as he wished her to see them. She was the more powerful psychic, but he was the more cunning. As she was his partner, I presume she did not wish to accept that he was doing this to her, and as she was exposed to him day and night she did not get any freedom or clarity from his constant input and influence.

Once at home after that second visit, I was horrified to find that I was being sent different images by Richard, which troubled my sleep further. I think that my original dreams only ceased because Richard bombarded me with his thoughts and feelings, long-distance, having adequately corded me astrally on my visits. I knew it was his doing, even in my ignorance, as the images were alien to me and involved him, in various future situations. I appeared to feature in these dreams as a sort of assistant for Richard's work, which seemed to be happening in the desert.

During the days, when I spent time alone working on art projects, I was treated to different types of poltergeist occurrences... whistles, moans and shrieks in the empty house. Items moved about, especially keys, as usual. Nothing had really changed, but the dreams were different. Richard had succeeded in eliminating one set of memories and replacing them with his own thoughts, but he had also opened me up psychically to many other far-memories, which came flooding to me at all hours of the day or night. Most of these correlated, in a disjointed manner, to the French life I have already described, but at that time I had no idea as from where the images came. I had simply lost one problem, to have it replaced with others of equal unpleasantness. To cap it all, I was receiving distinct messages from Richard that he was John the Baptist, reincarnated.

I tried phoning Clifford, to see if he could help me with Richards unwanted input, which at least I was able to discern as external and not internal, like my far-memories. Clifford, however, was like Shirley and was in awe and totally corded by Richard. He was willing to defend him to the last. That was the general message that I got from my dreams about Richard, that he would like me to defend him with my life. I did not see Richard as evil, nor did I even regard him as particularly deluded at that time. Foolishly, I just thought that he was more powerful than me and that he knew more than I did. I did not want to be in his power, as such, but I was still reliant on him for help, and he knew it. He knew how isolated I was. I never did come to think Richard was evil, but I did come to see his delusion and his terrible abuse of my isolation and fear. Never once did he tell me how to work with my own guide to get my own inner worlds and beliefs in order. Never once did he teach me the rudiments of psychic protection. He let me walk around as vulnerable as I ever was, only having made me more 'open' spiritually than before.

My final visit to Berkshire threw me into a panic. I was faced by a decision, either to accept Richard and all of his outlandish ideas and influences, or to be cast out alone into the middle of a spiritual wilderness where fear reigned. I wondered at the time why I did not meet other people who could have helped me more appropriately. Now I realise, and accept, that I had many lessons to learn myself, so as to make me a better, stronger, more sharing person. My being alone, with only Richard for help, forced me to learn from a bitter mistake.

I did chose to return to the wilderness but only after Richard revealed his 'great work' to me. I, apparently, was a chosen one to help them when the world ended in the year twenty twelve. Only he and a small group of followers would survive in the desert (which fitted with my dreams). He thought that the world would slip on its axis, and that the desert we would be in would have been an icy wasteland previously. How we would survive was explained by the fact that a great spaceship would descend for us chosen ones, just before the world's great shifting. We would be returned to Earth by the craft, when the shift was over, and most of the population would be dead. It would be our job to save the planet.

Richard, of course, knew this because he was, in fact, an alien. Not an alien spirit in a human shell, but a shape-shifting alien who could appear to look human for all of our benefits. He could prove this, he claimed, as ordinary men had seen him as he really was, by accident, in the street, they had been shocked at his 'natural' appearance, apparently. Sadly, I did not know of these men, but of course, Shirley and Clifford verified it for him. He also said that he had the ability to disappear, which I had in fact seen him do, unwittingly. That aside, I saw no proof that the small, bearded man before me was an alien of any description. A feeling of unreality and dread filled me up. He appeared so rational and ordinary, yet he was telling me things which meant he was not altogether a well person.

In recent months I have worked closely with people suffering from schizophrenia and related mental illness, and I have to say that Richard could easily have been very sick indeed. At the time, I thought perhaps he was a tad eccentric, or worse, perhaps he was right and I was too dense to grasp such an amazing possibility. One can imagine that I was very confused indeed, poor innocent psychic that I was. More so when Richard intimated to me "you know who I am, don't you?", referring, no doubt, to his messages as to his John the Baptist claim. I pondered in my confusion how he could be both an alien and a biblical figure at the same time? This was the same man who had laughed at another 'spiritual' chap who claimed, as many do, to be Jesus Christ. He had gone from being the kind, calm, helpful man of my first visit, to a raving preacher of apocalyptic doom spiced up with alien interaction, in a space of mere months.

His final word was that he was going to do a lecture on the matter, when the time was right, and he would reveal himself on television as the alien form he really was. I would not have dreamed of rubbishing his dearly held beliefs, but at the time I wondered what source he was tapping into to pass on such bizarre ideas. I did not consider the possibility that the man was ill at the time, as I did not have the knowledge about mental health to comment, and besides, I thought he was a spiritual man. I decided that he was someone with a message far beyond what I was willing to accept or take on, and part of me felt foolish for doubting him. His influence over me was undeniable, and I felt the inevitable guilt and pressure, even doubts as to my own ability and sanity, as I pulled away from him.

What decided me further about dropping Richard as an advisor was my contact with a man called Albert Budden. I am using the man's real name as he came to see me to interview me for his then-proposed book on UFO's Ironically, it was Richard who put Albert in touch with me. At that point, I had foolishly moved to London, partly to escape Tim who would not tolerate my involvement with Richard and partly for other reasons which I will disclose shortly. Albert came to see me on Richard's encouragement, to hear my recounting of the Stonehenge incident. Mr Budden eventually used my story, once again slightly adapted to fit his own theories, in his interesting and well-written book *'The Electromagnetic Indictment-UFO's -Psychic Close Encounters'* which was published a few years later in nineteen ninety five by Blandford.

The book should be consulted as to the authors scientific theory of UFO and lightform phenomena which I could accept to a degree, but was reluctant to take on as the sole explanation of our strange Stonehenge encounter. His idea was that Tim and I had hallucinated the whole experience due to exposure to electromagnetic energies at the site. The blackened banana had obviously responded to some blast of energy which must have affected us also as we were right next to it. However, I found it hard to totally believe that such a structured, shared experience was hallucination. The boundaries of fog and the solid appearance of all objects, even if they were in the wrong places, was incompatible, I felt, with it all being an hallucination. Yet, on the side of Albert Budden's theory was the banana, the strange buzz of energy I received from the Hele stone and the orange glow of light which could well have been a UAP, or unidentified ariel phenomena, which are associated with electrical energies.

Albert suggested that I was electro-sensitive after I told him of my experiences such as making kettles switch themselves on as I walked by, and my breaking of stereos and other equipment without actually touching them. It was something that had always bothered me, but I thought it may have been other forms of poltergeist activity around me. I found Mr Budden very reassuring and down-to-Earth and so listened when he told me that he had gone to visit Richard on a matter related to more UFO research for the book, Richard had yelled at him that my story was his property and that Albert could not use it. I confirmed that the story belonged to me and of course Mr Budden could use it as he wished. I was only too glad to see it being analysed as to its meaning. I wanted the story made public, so as to help anyone else involved in a similar, isolating experience elsewhere. I used a pseudonym in the book as I did not wish to be hounded by people seeking to exploit me. It was the story that was important, not myself. Richard's outburst annoyed me intensely. How could he own my experience? It proved to me that he actually believed that he owned me. Mr Budden did suggest that I sever contacts with Richard, as he was behaving in an odd, unstable manner.

I wrote to Richard and Shirley, severing my alliance by expressing my annoyance as to his belief that he could claim a story that was not his own. I did receive a written response in reply which confirmed my fears. It suggested Mr Budden was 'the enemy' and was the last straw for me. I could no longer give Richard any credit, of the two, Albert was by far and way the most approachable and 'normal'. Albert 'felt right' and Richard did not. I was not so desperate as to continue with someone who I felt deeply uncomfortable about. I was quite right to follow my instincts as later I was informed by a reliable source that Richard believed that he was Adolf Hitler reincarnated to destroy the Jews. Sadly his cords to Clifford had been so strong that the young man had become deeply involved in this dangerous fantasy, and had got into a great deal of trouble over it.

Shirley, I was relieved to hear, left Richard before the dreadful concept of his being a fascist dictator reincarnated had appeared. I would love to speak with her again, free of Richards hold upon her. I did feel gratitude for Richard's initial regression session, which he had performed for me at a time when he was 'well'. He had helped me, at that point, like a true Wiseman, or Cunning man. He had performed the task without prejudice or influence and he had asked for nothing in return. I would not have missed the experience of Richard and Shirley for the world, they were a part of my learning and of the inevitable pattern of my life.

Shirley was undoubtedly a true Witch, apparently a High Priestess of Wicca, and a great example of her Craft. I see her glowing aura as it was in the beginning when she was less corded by her partner and I remember her skills at psychometry. She could hold a personal object and divulge a stream of information about the owner. She taught me how to use my skills as a psychometrist, in our quiet moments alone together.

The method was to use a personal item, a watch, ring or necklace if possible, something worn close to the person and to immediately begin speaking as one saw images with the third-eye. The secret was not to let the rational, logical Self intervene before the images could come through. Some imagery would appear odd to the psychometrist, but everything must be spoken of straight away as the image is received. If it is not, then the likelihood of the everyday Self stepping in to say "that doesn't seem right" or "hang on, that mightn't be true" is far greater. Voices and images should be relayed with trust, as the ones which pour out of the personal item as the psychometrist first holds it are generally the strongest and most relevant. The key was not to strain, nor to rationalise. One should open the third-eye and simply see the story which the item holds. All of our personal items store our energies, rather like houses which appear to be haunted, but which are only revealing their stored imagery to certain sensitive people.

Everything and everyone has a personal set of energies, which can be seen as the aura using the third-eye, or by use of kirlean photography. As with all divination, the best way is to respond to the energies and go with the flow. It is far easier to tune into the energies by simply relaying what is 'seen' by the psychic, than it is to stop and think "will this make sense to the person I am telling?" This intervention of the rationale is partly based on ego, the desire to be seen as a good psychic and someone who is always right. The best way is to be a channel through which energy and information can be swiftly translated to the person seeking advice and guidance.

Usually, the person for whom you are getting the imagery will pick up on an aspect of what you see and that can be taken further. One can ask one's guide for help if the imagery is not clear, or else one can always admit that it is impossible to get information on some occasions. For whatever reason, personal tiredness, illness, worry, or simply a clash of energies in the situation, it is not always possible to be 'clairvoyant'. A good psychic will admit this. The aim is not to be infallible, and not to involve the ego. You are not relevant in the situation, save as a means for information to come through, and so all imagery should be passed on without one's personal interference. As with regression, had I stopped in my regression, where I became John, to ask incredulously "This isn't right, why am I wearing sandals in winter?" then my flow would have been interrupted and the images would have either stopped or been warped by the intervention of logic.

By all means, be a questioning person who assimilates new information into old ways of being. Be someone who is willing to check facts and discard any rubbish in favour of change and growth. But do not bring cold, hard scientific logic into the realms of intuition and guidance. The material world should not intrude upon time spend in communion with the guide and the Otherworlds. I will discuss later the benefits of creating 'sacred spaces' in our lives, but for now

I will add here that it is a waste of time if one keeps one foot firmly in the material world whilst engaged in psychic work or meditation. This letting go (obviously with having taken safety precautions like protection of the portals etc) is a vital part of learning to be a better psychic, it combines with relaxation to ensure a deeper and more accurate source of guidance. I think 'letting go' is one of the greatest of all personal lessons, and perhaps one of the hardest.

Shirley was the first person in this incarnation to introduce me to the art of 'seeing' in a controlled way. I believe now that I once knew these arts in my French incarnation, and they were not so much freshly taught as remembered from the depths of my Soul. It was wonderful to be able to channel some aspect of my whirlwind psychism into a useful, creative role. If Shirley was a representative of the 'Craft of the Wise' then she was a far cry from the ludicrous images of Witchcraft, or Wicca, that I had seen in library books. There were no wax poppet dolls stuck with pins and no dancing naked around a dead chicken. Instead, she was a caring woman who I believe could have brought my psychism under even greater discipline if it had not been for Richard's looming presence. As my first example of a Wisewoman she was inspirational.

It is a tragedy that Richard was suffering from a form of mental illness, but then, perhaps mental illness is just a sensitive person tuning in to the human astral? The human astral is full of the images that humanity creates and thinks about, including the public's insatiable interest in murder stories, true life crimes, horror films and violence. Perhaps Richard had tuned into this level and had been willingly, and falsely, influenced, by a particularly nasty thought-form or aspect of humanities collective unconscious?

Perhaps his 'illness' was no more than this unfortunate connection to the astral, as all such deluded people may have? I do not know, nor do I claim to have an ultimate judgement on a man who had once helped me, only to want to take me over. Perhaps, as a final suggestion, that is just human nature, the stronger absorbing the thing perceived as weaker?

I do not regret what happened in my life as I left the orbit of Richard and Shirley, yet I was to walk into some of the hardest times and most difficult lessons of my life so far. Although there are instant solutions to certain problems, I would always recommend good, hard graft when it comes to understanding psychism. There is nothing like personal experience, and learning by ones mistakes, to make one grow. "I have learned more from my mistakes than from my successes" says Sir Humphrey Davy in the book of inspirational quotes 'Begin It Now' (In Tune Books, 1987). The aim of incarnation is to know ones Self. What use can one be in the world if one is not striving to understand the Self better? I was terrified of my Self when I knew Richard and Shirley, and so any chance of my positively influencing the situation was limited. Shirley's guidance as to me channelling my psychism into psychometry, as a place to begin disciplining my energies, was the first step to personal understanding. Without the 'mistake' of the encounter with Richard, I would never have learned this discipline, and furthermore I would not have had first-hand experience of how easy it is for a deluded, or ill-guided Soul to influence and cord others. It would have been easy for me to have de-corded them using visualisation and meditation, if I had understood at that time. However, if I had had such knowledge of psychism then I would never have gone to them repeatedly for help anyway.

Recently I have seen another example of this cording, on a much bigger scale. There is a popular 'new-age' book doing the rounds which involves psychically channelled material from supposedly highly evolved beings. The beings speak through a trance medium and they claim to be the highest authority in the universe, denouncing all other channelled material as the work of the mediums' 'higher Self'.

Such lofty and exclusive claims alerted me to read the volume, which is a mixture of revelation and guidance for humankind. When one has realised that the book reveals nothing that could not be created by an intelligent person who has an average understanding of environmental, historical and religious issues and information, then it is clear from an uninvolved and lucid perspective to see that the channel is either accessing her own higher Self or is being spoken through by a rather arrogant entity from the lower astral.

The ignorance is shown in the lack of credence given to eastern spirituality of any kind, the references to God as being a He, the obsession with Christian topics... hardly appropriate for a cosmic being who is supposedly many times removed from humanity. Surely a less Euro-centric, less-patriarchal, more globally holistic view should be achieved? The arrogance is shown in the declaration that only that particular channel tells the universal truth. The people involved could see no flaws in this, and there were many flaws that I will not list here. The people involved were corded into fully accepting the whole illusion, unquestioningly.

It is so easy to sit back and let a leader tell you just how it is. But it is not so easy to get away once your gut feeling has finally alerted you to the fact that you no longer accept the wholesale theories of your teacher. We live in a lazy society and we like things made really simple, given on a plate to us in easily digested pieces. The road to really knowing Self, the true path of the Wise, is littered with sharp stones, potholes, and pretty, glittering things which tempt one away from walking onwards. To ignore the Self, and the way to understanding Self, is to stagnate, or in the case of the natural psychic, to court disaster in one's life. I speak from experience.

I had moved to London to part from Tim but also because I had given up art to become a teacher in a suburban school. I had chosen to do this in a desperate attempt to shake off my psychism by denying my real needs. I thought if I tried to be like other 'normal' people and fit into society as a teacher, something I had never wanted to do in the first place, then I would lose the psychic events that made my life so strange. I thought I could run from my troublesome Self into the headspace of 'straight' society which has no regard for the spiritual in the face of status and money. I really, sincerely believed that it would be an end to my psychic isolation if I fitted into my job and settled down.

I did not bargain for three things that happened. As I had only accepted my place at teacher training college with the hope I could transfer to an art course, I was not exactly committed to the profession. I was, and am, an artist first and foremost, and my art had always been expressed daily. In Wiltshire I had painted leather jackets for a living, which I had given up in order to go into the classroom. I hadn't realised that by denying my art, which was a huge, integral part of me, I had blocked a vital expression of my natural energies.

As a consequence, the second thing that happened was that I got ill. All the pretending in the world couldn't disguise the fact that I was different. I did not fit in at work, the other staff were wary of me and the parents knew I didn't 'smell or feel' like a teacher. On a primitive level, my scent was wrong and everyone knew it except for me. I believed that, with the right clothes and attitude, I could be a teacher and I could forget all the art and psychic stuff.

All that happened was that I was off work constantly with ailments that reflected my blocked energies. I had stomach problems (my gut reaction to the situation) headaches and migraines (my spiritual, psychic reaction) and I had emotional problems like depression which was debilitating in itself. As it was not a physical ailment, I felt it was untreatable, so I suffered it. On the physical side, my throat swelled up and hurt (I could not communicate how I really felt about teaching) and my sexuality shut down as a profound response to unwanted energies. I was totally out of sorts.

Worse still, the psychic events did not stop just because I had tried to repress myself and who I was. I will describe the continuing phenomena in the next chapters. I understand now that there is no place in society for someone like me, a concept I have only recently come to terms with. Society has no need of the seer or Wisewoman, unless she is willing to be exploitative, charge huge fees and hire a flash office somewhere. Then the Wise one can fit into society's expectations and everyone will be less frightened of them, expecting them to be a clever charlatan or at best someone who can dispense harmless quick cures and advice.

There is a way of thinking which says that unless something, be it actual or spiritual, is paid for with hard cash then it is not worth anything. The bigger fee, the better treatment. I have heard a Reiki teacher use this as an excuse for charging her unreasonable fees recently. My response has been to charge by donation only if I ever work for people, and this need not be a financial donation but one which is a skill which they have which we can trade. My basic role model of behaviour still comes from Shirley, who invited me into her home, gave me as much free training as she was able, cooked for me and lent me a non-judgmental ear. She was the inspiration that I had once I finally dropped all the efforts to fit into a norm that was never meant for me. Once I had left teaching behind, in order to pursue my creativity, I returned to Shirley's Wicca and to the Goddess-shaped stone which I was given by my guide. They held the keys to my future. But before I was to realise this, I had many other lessons to be learned.

In order to reach my Self again, I first had to learn what I was not.

Chapter Four

"You must believe that it is possible to change, you must want to change, you must work toward change. "
(Quote from my Book of Shadows and Light)

"Things do not change, we change."
Quote from Henry David Thoreau

I find it fascinating to observe how the fates, combined with my own determination, have lead me to the place where I am at present. At times, it had seemed to me that I would never reach a place of greater understanding. That perhaps I was simply cursed to stumble blindly through one disaster after another, pursued by my own true nature, forever.

From where I stand today, given the overview of the culmination of all those events which seemed at the time to be isolated, unpleasant and meaningless, I can see that each one was a lesson and a part of the process of 'bringing me back'. I do believe that I was being returned to my natural way of being, and brought back to being someone who I had been before. Somehow, because of the pains and circumstances of other life-lessons, other lives, I had lost touch with the true essence of my Self. I believe that each and every one of us has such a pattern in our lives, and I hope by my revealing of my own overview of my pattern that I will help others consider the implications of the patterns in their own lives. It is unlikely in the extreme that I should be unique in having past life connections and that I alone have a personal reason and purpose to my incarnation.

I will not subscribe to the opinion that anyone with the gift of 'sight' is somehow chosen and that anyone lucky enough to reach an audience with their story is somehow special. We all have our various patterns, connections and links, and our own ways of returning to the essential, Eternal Self. It is my hope that in reading this, the reader will feel suitably inspired to look at their own intricate Dance of Life and Death and Life.

Long before I really understood the meaning of Wicca or Witchcraft, long before I had heard of neo-Paganism, long before I had considered my path as a Wisewoman, I had been a Born-Again Christian. Considering my fear, my

80

innocence and my desire to be 'cured' of my psychism, I can see now why I wished to hand over my free will to the United Reformed Church. It was not an isolated event, nor was it a mistake, but an understandable part of the process of learning to Be.

The Christians I encountered seemed more than willing to 'cure' me and to end my struggle with myself, to bring me peace. They meant well, each and every one of them, as they all held the belief that they must share the marvellous Good News they had received themselves. It was their purpose to save me and I desired their salvation. I had long since connected Jesus to the glowing beings I saw lighting up the sky in my childhood dreams. I saw Jesus as a kind, gentle Hippy-type man who, with my Euro-centric, 1970s education, was the only spiritual figure that I knew of who seemed accessible and nice. I grew up with television programmes which reflected the Hippy-Christ image, and I was happier seeing the intensely bright and glowing figures from my dreamscapes as Jesus, rather than aliens, or worse. Jesus was a familiar, safe figure in this life for me to latch on to.

I was brought up, with the best of intentions, to be terrified of the unknown. Although my mother was, and is, a superb psychic, it was her fear of anything she could not explain away in relation to religion, especially Catholicism, that I picked up on. Not only that, but my life as the Monk John meant I also had connections to relating to Christ. I became a Born-Again Christian before I had any idea that I had ever been John the unfortunate and pious fellow of the fifteenth century. As a final factor, when I was first at University, I found it hard to make friends with the majority of students who seemed very immature and interested in little except alcohol and drugs. The Christian contingent were more at peace with themselves, or so it appeared, and I found them friendly and trustworthy. I had never intended to get involved fully, but with my characteristic naivete I thought they would help me with my psychism and be my friends. However, this was not to be the case as their group energies were very persuasive, and although they all had their own problems and inner turmoils, collectively their 'healing' energies sucked me in.

The event which really sent me scurrying into their open arms was the result of a culmination of many weeks unrest in the room I was occupying. I lived in the Halls of Residence on campus at that time, and I occupied a room which had the worst atmosphere I had ever come across. I thought I might shake off the phenomena if I immersed myself into study and 'normal' studentdom, but as usual this was impossible. I had not wanted to attend the University to do teaching, and a twist of fate ensured I was trapped on the teaching course and unable to obtain the transfer I had wished for. I was very unhappy about this and not very comfortable about fitting into an organisation such as a structured college degree. I had no difficulties with the work, but my natural desire for personal autonomy and creative freedom rebelled against the antiquated methods of conveying information.

It was probably not the fault of the college, but it was one of my lessons that I could not try to force myself into a 'normal' space in order to change who I essential was. The more I ignored 'me', as I have said before, the worse the psychic activity got around me. I should have learned by this first experience of how trying to operate in a mode which did not suit my true Self would make things worse, not easier, psychically.

However, I still went on to teach, as I have previously described, again with disastrous results which I am yet to mention. So, in the Halls of Residence I was deeply discontented and angry with myself, but outwardly desperately trying to blend in with the other students and be accepted. Consequently my room reflected this conflict and the energies of the place were appaling. The room appeared to sap any visitors of their life force, or etheric, energy, and they often left complaining of feeling tired, headachey or depressed. I did not think it was me causing this, as when I related to the people outside of my room, all was well. However, it is obvious with hindsight that it was my energies which doubled when on home territory (the place where I spent the most time dwelling on my feelings etc) and it was not the only the room which was strange. My energies, combined with the energies of the room/building, made for a disturbing combination.

At the time, I believed the room had a 'presence' which made people feel that way, and so I began to get frightened as to what was 'haunting' the room. I also felt victimised, why did I have to get another 'haunted' room? As a psychic who was denying this aspect of Self, one can see that if there had been a 'haunting' then obviously I was sensitive enough to attune to it, even if I did not wish to, where as other people would not notice it. If it was not 'haunted', as I now suspect it wasn't, then I was simply experiencing the outer manifestation of my psychic denial, which was 'fed' by my fear of what I was actually creating. I do think that I was interacting with the group energies of the Halls of Residence as well, and I know that some fairly unpleasant things occurred in that block, from suicide to ouija boards. (More recently, I have lived in a residential block for elderly people, and I found that there too I reacted to the group energies of the block. In the case of the elderly, I often picked up their energies of loneliness, defeat, despair and sadness. Fortunately, I could recognise the cause of these effects and could protect myself accordingly).

Back at the Halls of Residence I was unaware of my guide, and the only spiritual people I had met were the 'God Squad. 'I suffered the usual disturbed sleep in that room, listening to pots and pans move about on their own at night, watching posters all fall off the walls at the same time and worse, dealing with the embarrassing stench of human excrement which came and went in thick blasts. Guests could be seen frantically checking their shoes for dirt as the smell manifested, but it would go as soon as anyone noticed its presence, which made every one very confused and me totally embarrassed. Once again, I felt out of control and helpless. The Christian contingent believed the smell of human waste to be associated with Satan's appearance, which did wonders for my getting to sleep at night. All my reading of sensationalist books as a teenager, trying to find a spiritual answer, had left me in fear of Demons and Devils.

The smell could be associated to my being as an astral 'flame', capable of attracting all manner of passing discarnate rubbish. I have a very refined sense of smell and am now often alerted to a spirit presence by its aroma. I have since lived in a flat which regularly announced its many spiritual presences with smells of rotting meat, cordite and spices. My husband's guide presents himself to me with a waft of alcohol! The smell of excrement was perhaps the least attractive of all the smells which could have been used as a psychic 'calling card'. I would associate this with a particularly unpleasant human thought form or entity and as the Halls were home to all manner of human life, including ouija-board meddlers, I expect that there was a traffic of unsavoury thought forms passing through. Had I have known then what I do now, I would have used the following methods for dealing with astral intrusion from the lower end of the spectrum, humanities unwanted thought forms and entities.

Firstly, I would protect myself in my chosen manner, as described before, using the blue light in a suitable form, and protecting the portals. This would stop me feeling any fear that I was feeding the entity with my etheric presence. It could not enter my 'sphere of being', either astrally or manifestly, and so it would not be able to gain power by extracting fear or energy from me. For further sealing down of the main energy portals, one can imagine the symbol to be used as a silver rose, whose petals close up tightly against unwanted intrusion. Be calm and unhurried, as usual, about the protection process. It is easy to forget a small part of the ritual, and to leave a hand uncovered by blue light, or a vital portal unprotected. Obviously, the participant can consult with his or her own guides or sources from the Otherworlds as to the most appropriate courses of action to take. As I am fully aware that not everybody is au fait with their sources of guidance then I feel it is ethical for me to suggest a 'leg up' onto riding the horse of psychism, which can then be ridden with greater freedom and control as confidence increases. (This protection ritual is also useful when entering crowded places, especially a gathering of other 'sensitives', as with the popular 'Psychic and Mystic Fairs'. One can use the protective steps when one feels jangled by the vibrations in the air in a group situation. At one of the aforementioned 'fairs', imagine all the wills of the so-called mystics flying around in the air, trying to gain custom above their neighbour! It is amazing how well the protection can make you impervious to such directed acts of will, but then, visualisation works. The more simple and focused the act of protection is, the more effective). The next step after personal 'sealing' is to protect the environment against further intrusion.

To seal the building/room/locale/environment, one must sit in a comfortable position, with arms and legs uncrossed, and visualise a tongue of blue flame. With the eyes closed, imagine the room, or wherever, around you. This is using the third-eye for visualisation. See the tongue of blue flame before you and spend time with both making the flame brighter and more vivid and also seeing the room in more and more detail. Once the flame and the room are a reality to you, seen clearly with the mind's-eye, then one may proceed by imagining the flame spreading out across the floor in a vivid, bright blue sheet, this is not a burning flame but a cold-fire of protection, until one is sitting in a sea of flame. From there imagine it spreading up the walls and across the ceiling, not devouring, but covering as it goes. If flames do not seem appropriate, then cover each surface with bright blue polythene sheets, or even a blue skin. I use flame for its properties of cleansing, transformation and strength. It is important to know why one has chosen a particular form of protection, and if one works with an element, like fire, then one should be prepared to spend time understanding why it is, or isn't, appropriate.

For this, book learning is adequate, but not the best way. Ideally, the participant should tune into the elementals of fire, the salamanders, in meditation, or else ask the guide to reveal to you the essential nature of the element you wish to use. Visualise various manifestations of the element and write down the key-words which seem appropriate to it. A little personal work goes a long, long way and such questing and learning is never wasted and can only enhance the whole process. To think that the blue flame looks effective is not enough, although the protection will still work it will be less effective than if it is rooted in inner knowledge and imbued with the power of a personal reflection and connection.

One could also choose to encase the entire area/building in a blue egg, lined with reflective silver. Additional acts could be to cover all portals(in this case, doors, windows, chimneys etc) with the protective symbol. Lighting a black candle, if possible, attracts negative energy to it. Similarly, salt can be used to collect up the negative vibrations. Following the ritual with a salt bath is recommended, as it is known as a purifier. Sitting within an actual circle of salt is a good way to ensure protection when one is visualising the blue light etc. This circle is a simple way of creating the sacred space which I will return to later. The salt alone will not keep away negative influences and manifest acts must be backed up with acts of focussed will, and vice-versa.

When these protective acts are done, then the participant must do a little psychic wandering as to find the entity, thought form or other influence which is causing the disturbance. Do not be afraid to do this, as your protection has followed the universal rules of psychic safety, the barriers cannot be crossed by even the most persistent being. However, if one does come across a particularly large, unpleasant presence it is best to retreat if one feels it is too stressful to try to remove it alone. Just as one's act of will is a powerful tool to be used, so can the acts of will be that created the thought forms originally. The most sensible approach is to call on the guide, unknown or known, to assist with the problem. Guides are further removed from manifest realms that we are at present, and so they are far more capable of seeing the best course of action to remove a particular kind of entity. Guides have an overview of situations that we cannot have, hence why they are vital beings to talk with for a wider perspective. I have never come across an entity which cannot be removed with the protective measures and process I will now describe.

In one's mind's-eye, continue to see the property or room in which the problem lies. 'See' every inch of the area, and be alert to any being who may be lurking therein. Do not be alarmed by its appearance, big or small, but do immediately draw a circle of blue fire around its base. This will bind it so that it cannot move. You may discover that the being you have captured is a discarnate, i.e. the soul of a human being which has become trapped, for some reason, on Earth. I believe that this occurrence is the rarest form of 'haunting' and that most such disturbances are caused either by the person involved having personal energy problems (i.e, my poltergeist phenomena) or else the problem is an entity/ thought form. I believe this latter idea to be the most common as there are billions of humans alive today, all thinking thoughts, all dwelling on things which are not always sweetness and light. Beings can be created for good or ill, on the lower astral, by consistent thoughts and sometimes deliberately by magical means. These entities do exist and they float about when no longer needed by their 'owners' until they fade out. However, if they can find a new 'host' human to feed off by scaring them and tuning-in to their compatible thoughts (an entity of greed finding a new greedy person to feed off, for example) then it will continue to grow and sustain itself from fresh energies.

In the Halls of Residence such things could have been let loose through inadequate ouija sessions, or they may have been created by countless students, either by the use of drugs or by their thoughts of competitiveness, isolation or worry. Teenagers have a lot of energy to channel and deal with as they move into maturity and I'm sure that the Halls were a hotbed of entities and energies which I attracted.

Usually then, if one has had to perform a ritual to find the cause of a 'haunting', the captured presence which will be kept in a circle of fire will be such a thought form entity. On the rare occasion that the catch is a human soul, then deal with the situation as you would by talking to another live person. Ask them why they are still on the manifest. Do they know they are dead? Are they tied to living loved ones by guilt or longing? Are they tied to that particular place for fear of moving on to the Other Realms? (One can encounter disincarnates who lived life as Catholics and who are too scared to leave the manifest, lest they travel to Hell.) Most souls leave the manifest willingly under the empathic, reassuring protection of their personal guide.

On the rare occasion that you may meet a 'lost' soul use tact, kindness and sensitivity when talking to them, and ask for personal guidance. They need to be asked if they will let you send them on to the place where they should be. With respect for them, you can make an invocation by extending the ring of fire up around them until they are standing in a glowing cylinder. Imagine this tube of light as turning to white energy, a column of white light. One may ask that he or she may be taken to that place in the Universe where they belong, by right, at that time. At this point, they will be taken up, or down, inside the column. There is no harm in them being taken downwards. This is not a sign that they are descending to the Christian Hell! Nature and time are not linear, and top and bottom meet in the great circle eventually. Up and down are bound to meet on the vast wheel where January is not opposite to December at either end of a stick, but it is next to it. As above, so below, each becoming connected. So do not have any fear that the person has been banished to somewhere 'bad' because of you. Just as darkness is not evil, nor is moving downwards.

Proceed with any entity in the same manner. If at first it is hard to locate the presence, and they will hide from you, then simply cast the circle of fire first and then summon them into it. Do not give them any emotion of anger or fear for them to feed off, but know that you are the one in control, after all, entities are nothing without human thought and emotion, although they may have a very much more inflated sense of their own worth! Be aware that the creature will appear a certain way in order to gain a human response from you. The thing you capture may be rather hideous, or it may appear charming in order to try to appease you. Do not spend time in contemplation of its acquired form but simply draw another circle of fire adjacent to it and summon the person responsible for the creation to appear. If nobody appears then one can safely assume the entity is not personally directed at you and is just an astral wanderer who has bumped into you and taken a shine. This is the most likely event. However, one may discover that the creator is somebody familiar, who had malicious intent in creating the entity. Or it may be a stranger who did not realise what they had done by careless, repeated thought. They are then at liberty to banish their own creation into the column of light, with the invocation about the place in the universe most fitting for the creature. Everything belongs somewhere!

Without feeding, the entity will fade quietly away in time. Remember that you are only dealing with part of the soul of the person you have summoned up. You will not have taken them physically nor will you have possession of their full soul. Part of them will have come to you in the astral space you have created to work in, this cannot harm them if you behave with responsibility and care. One can only reason with another soul, but if all else fails, you are in control and you may banish their creation and send them back into their manifest Self. Generally, the part of the soul which comes to talk to you from another human will be far more amenable then their actual integral human Self! This is the Higher Self which comes to you, and will, no doubt, be far more wise and reasonable. But souls come in all types, so do remember to act ethically at all times, and with respect, but also remember to remain in control. This soul summoning can also be used if a person needs absent healing, but it is usually more appropriate to ask the manifest person first, before giving healing astrally.

The personal protection/portal sealing/house protection/house portal sealing/summoning of souls or troublesome entities/sending of soul or entity in the column of white light ritual or procedure is one which can be adapted for many uses. Had I have had access to such procedures when I lived in the Hall of Residence, then I could have 'cleared' my room of any astral hangers on which had been attracted to me by my psychic glow. Then, if I still had problems in my room, I would have had to look at my own energies to see where the trouble lay. It is easy to think of what I should have done, when I now have the knowledge. I have nothing but the greatest sympathy for my poor troubled, 'haunted' Self who spun in hopeless circles back then. If I had a time machine now I would not go back to rescue myself, however. I needed to learn my lessons.

Back in the Halls of Residence I had no knowledge, no protection rituals and no contact with my Wisewoman Self. I was deluged by umpteen troublesome occurrences a day, my keys being the worst culprits. They disappeared constantly, providing maximum inconvenience for me. I never did see them vanish, but I still lived in fear of catching them in the act. My Bible vanished consistently also, appearing one day under my nextdoor neighbour's bed, as if it had simply passed through the wall. I was not to happy with the Bible the Christians had bought for me, so I did not mind the vanishing, although I knew they would see it as the Devil trying to confuse me. Half the time I guessed they thought I was possessed by Satan anyway.

I had discovered that for people who were spiritual, they had had no spiritual/psychic happenings at all in their lives. Anyone who did, according to them, was filled with evil spirits. Anything that did not come from the manifest Earth, anything which they could not understand, they deemed as bad, which did wonders for my Self-image! Far from telling them my psychic woes, I was unable to reveal my problems lest they too rejected me as being the 'daughter of Beelzebub'. which wasn't as far-fetched as it may sound. Their spirituality was nice and uncluttered by Otherworldly occurrences, totally of the Earth in its origins. Their spiritual outlook was based on one book, feelings and actual experience did not come into it at all. This contact with the Christians convinced me in later years that book learning on spiritual topics is fine and good, but is only a part of the overall process, with personal interaction and experience being paramount.

Secretly, I found it rather dry and uninspiring, the Bible was out of date, incomprehensible in parts and sexist in others. It said nothing to me about my life. No matter how much I desired their acceptance, and to be as blithely accepting of the Faith as they were, I could not, deep-down, stomach the teachings. The Christians had stock, unsatisfactory answers for every question that I posed for them, everything from the immaculate conception to the incestuous relationship of first-lady Eve with her own sons came to my mind, and they managed to somehow have some reason for it. The very fact I dared question 'the truth' as they saw it, made me feel I must be a tad evil myself. I was not utterly convinced that they had any idea what the Bible was really about, but as my Self-esteem was so low, I would have listened to them above my own intuition every time. With my Bible constantly absent without leave, their growing belief that I was indeed possessed grew, as did the strange atmosphere in my room. I lived on my nerves and prayed to my Hippy-Jesus for help. It did not come.

The culmination of events was the night I had a friend, Keith, around for a coffee. As was the way of any visitor to my room, he quickly became maudlin and listless. I was attempting to jolly the proceedings along, as I did not wish him to leave, when he began to look very uneasy. "What is it?" I asked, not wanting to really hear his response. But I knew what it was... the 'presence' was in the room, the temperature dropped rapidly even with the radiator blasting out an unhealthy amount of heat, and the curtains fluttered in breeze that should not have been there. The atmosphere had congealed to a consistency of a thick broth yet my perception was pin-sharp. In such a state, when a presence enters my space, I see things in a state of 'hyper-reality'.

Keith bolted for the door, and I ran after him. I decided that I should go and fetch Marcus, a huge, jolly Born-Again chap from down the hall. I believed he could help me, I had ultimate faith in his Christianity, if not my own. Marcus was duly found, and he came with me, smiling indulgently at me as if I was a silly little girl. He had his Bible with him and he intended to sort this matter out alone. His manner was very condescending. He said he would not be long. Keith and I waited outside while he entered my room. Exchanging worried glances, we waited for the few minutes it took before Marcus emerged, looking considerably less blase. He asked if I would join him in ridding my room of the presence of Satan. With Born-Again people I discovered that everything was black or white. It couldn't have been some lesser Demon in my room, it had to be the Big Cheese Himself.

With Keith left knock-kneed outside the door, I entered with some trepidation. The room was even more hostile than it had been upon my departure. I stood and held hands with Marcus and we faced the wall as we began to recite the Lord's Prayer. Now, everyone knows that prayer by rote, but as we began we both petered out, unable to recall a single word. As I stood in silence, perplexed, I found that I was staring at one of my posters on the wall, an image of a girl's face, smiling. As I continued to stare, transfixed, the picture contorted before my eyes in a manner I had not seen before, nor have I since. before my eyes the girl began to sneer, and pointed teeth sprouted over her lips. The girl in the picture began to laugh at me with her fang like teeth showing. I stared in horror for a few seconds longer and then I let rip with a piercing scream. I ran from the room, leaving poor Marcus standing aghast, and I raced down the corridor, still screaming. I ran full pelt into Dean, a big lad of the rugby playing variety, who was running in the opposite direction, also in a state of panic. Doors along the corridor flew open at the sound of this commotion and faces peered out to see Dean and I clutching at each other in fear, Before any one of them could utter a humourous remark or an insult, the lights went out.

In total darkness Dean and I stood amidst cries of "What the Hell's going on?" By this time Keith and Marcus had joined us and we huddled together. Some clever soul had lit a few candles in their room and we found our way to

Marcus's room in the flickering half-light. We borrowed a candle and we all sat down inside, shaken and scared, hoping that someone else would speak first. Dean was the first to brave telling us of an experience which seemed ludicrous at best but chilling at worst. In the dark, a darkness which seemed too inopportune to be a coincidence, we all seemed to have lost our sense of reality. Nobody seemed to know why the lights had gone out, as there was a secondary generator, in the event of such a loss of power, apparently.

As we sat in silence in the shadows Dean stated that he had been trying to make a phone call on the upper floor. He could not seem to get through, and just as he was about to give up a voice had said "Hello Dean, I know all about you". It had taken him a second to realise that there was a voice on the dead phone line, that he hadn't spoken to inform anyone on the other end of who he was, and that the phone was temporarily out of order. He had become suddenly petrified and had ran back downstairs away from the phone, which was when he had bumped into me. Then the lights had gone out.

I then told my tale, much to Keith's alarm and Marcus's growing unease. He flatly refused to admit that he too had witnessed the event in my room, although I could tell by his face that he had. Why couldn't he have carried on with the Lord's Prayer? And why had he stood, staring transfixed at the same wall as me? I was disappointed with this supposedly 'spiritual' man and annoyed that I had wasted my time trying to get his help. He didn't really seem to want me in his presence, and as the night wore on he withdrew his favour from me altogether. I had seen him as a representative of Christ, someone who should selflessly help others. I see him now as a very scared young man whose rigid beliefs and restrictive version of faith had been challenged in a way he was not prepared to tackle. The rules as to 'how life is' had been crossed. He saw me as bad and refused to even offer me a floor to sleep on, as I couldn't be allowed to return to that dreadful room alone.

I see Marcus, in retrospect, as I see the thousands of people in England and beyond, who do not wish to see or hear about the destruction of the landscape by road building, the terrible abuse of animals through experimentation, or the pollution of our air and water. I see him as I would see any frightened, insecure person who is not prepared to look away from the narrow channel which they have dug for themselves. That is one reason why I refuse to ever state 'how it is' as a truth. To refuse to see is to refuse growth. To accept that 'to know is to understand that you do not know' is to accept change. I know that all Christians are not so blinkered, and that such denial of things outside of what affects our normal lives is an affliction which knows no cultural or religious boundaries. Sadly, though, at that time, all the Christians I met could be held up as an example of those in denial. A girl called Sally, who was fanatical in her belief, did offer me sanctuary in her house for a while during my exodus from my room, but it was on certain terms. The college had agreed to transfer me to another room the following term, but in the mean time I needed temporary accommodation. With hindsight, I should have left the Halls altogether at that point, as it was not the room, so much as the entire block, which I interacted badly with. I could not live in the other room again, and even the college wardens understood when they saw that in my brief absence, a large puddle of urine had manifested on the floor. I watched in disbelief from the college refectory window as the lights in my unoccupied room turned on and off. I had obviously opened the floodgates in there.

The other room I was to occupy eventually was not so bad, being on the end of a row and less surrounded by other people's energies, but I suffered some unpleasant feelings there. In the interim, between this room transfer, Sally took me under her wing. I had a safe place to stay, providing I went to her church, her prayer meetings and that I underwent a personal exorcism. This was not to be the bell, book and candle affair, but a simple laying on of hands by the 'friendly' people at the church. Besides the vicar, who was a genuinely lovely man, I did not meet any friendly souls at Sally's church. It was not warm and welcoming unless you were like Sally, totally happy, without complaint and utterly convinced without question of the validity of the Bible.

Two of Sally's church buddies came around to see the empty room in Halls which I had vacated in all but personal objects. They declared solemnly that the Devil had gone (probably into me!) but that Christ was absent. Not exactly reassuring stuff, but then, is any of the churches teaching supposed to make the participant full of self-confidence and free of fear?

Back with Sally's exorcists, I underwent several sessions, during which I felt nothing at all, although I did lie to save Sally's face afterwards. I said I felt much lighter when in fact I felt more gloomy and alone. Christianity was failing me. I even went to be baptised in a plastic swimming pool, which was pleasant enough, but a spiritually 'dead' experience as far as I was concerned. Nobody expected anything to happen to them, except for me, as I was used to things happening to me, and found it odd when they did not.

Sally then went through my possessions and made a ceremonial bonfire of my incense, any music caseates that she disapproved of, and a tarot instruction book which I used for a reference for my artworks. She had made me 'clean' and so her job was done. We remained casual friends and I saw her at church where I continued to go, trying in desperation to find hope or help among the people who sang and danced in praise of a Christ who was far more distant to me that my own Hippy-Jesus had been.

I can understand what I was looking for now, some of my monk's experience of the devotions of the Church perhaps? Or else total acceptance, and a being swallowed whole by some greater force. I wanted to be controlled, to have an explanation of my circumstances which would absorb me lock, stock and barrel. However, this would never have happened as it was my destiny to discover my path through other means. I was the lone Spiritwalker, a solitary practitioner, my soul would not allow me to be part of the establishment. And of course, although I had 'joined the other side' as a poor monk, my soul recalled the burning and injustice I had received at the hands of the establishment/Church, even if my mortal Self did not. Try as I might to integrate myself by giving up my will, I could not. The fates had other things in store for me, although when I finally walked away from the church in North London, I believed myself to be cursed.

Three things came out of my experience with the Halls and the church organisation. Firstly, I discovered that many others had seen things within their rooms, including faces on their walls. The building was erected in the grounds of an ex- prisoner-of-war camp and the lake on the site was filled with barbed wire from those days, to stop the prisoners swimming away. Such a site would be highly inappropriate for building on without extensive psychic work having been done on it first. The anger, frustration and pain of the prisoners would have provided strong energies to be stored on that plot of land. The land did record some of the images of that time, as it was not unusual for a student to report having seen a soldier walking in the air, on guard duty on a wall which once existed. Of course, we were not told of this fact before we moved in. I was informed by more honest wardens and by other students who had left the University years earlier. This, had I have known then, would have made me feel less victimised, less inherently cursed and bad, and would have explained a lot, even then. Looking back, the combination of this site, plus the energies of the students, plus the energies of my denied psychism, made a lethal brew which was bound to cause problems.

Secondly, the chap who had so blithely stepped into my rooms tenancy, once the term of my letting was up, had met a very unpleasant end. The lad, a young American, over on an exchange, had been full of scorn and ridicule for my experiences and had said that he could cope with anything. I am not wishing to draw a connection between the room and his fate, but when he vacated the Halls, (after using the room as a place to use, and deal, soft drugs) he boarded the aeroplane which went down over Lockerbie in Scotland. I do not know this as a fact, but I was told by different people that this had been the fate of the poor chap.

Thirdly, I gained a curious 'gift' from the time I spent trying to assimilate myself with Christianity. I had often heard people at the church singing in a strange variety of languages which they called 'speaking in tongues'. They took this gift as being a spiritual blessing, and it was their one concession to Otherworldly intervention. The 'languages' were all different, and some of them had proved to be of the Earth, ancient or tribal tongues which were inaccessible to the average Christian.

I was spending a lot of time focussing on spiritual enlightenment, and I prayed daily to understand my plight. Perhaps this focussing was more like meditation, although under the safe umbrella of Christianity. All 'new-age' practice, to Sally and her chums, had been of the Devil. This list included meditation, vegetarianism, divination, clairvoyance, reading science fiction or horror stories, venerating nature and all manner of other innocuous and positive pastimes.

I was regularly handed tracts on the dangers of thinking of anything which wasn't strictly of God and Christ. My focus was not away from Jesus, but nor was it strictly on him, as frankly, he was so distant and pure that I could not connect with him. However, one evening, in 'meditation' (prayer) I discovered that I too had a secret language which came out of my mouth at will. It was very beautiful, and I could understand why it was referred to as angel song. Its sound moved me profoundly, connecting to an ancient place within me which was long lost, or so I thought. Since leaving the confines of Christian explanation, I have had my language analysed. My favourite explanation is that it came from the Egyptian-Celtic cross which occurred centuries ago in Scotland. The person who defined it as such, a respected psychic, said that it was a race memory of that language, and that I could well have been of such a lineage of descent.

I personally place little store on bloodlines and ancestors as I am more inclined to favour soul-lines and links. I believe the people to be the important ones in our lives are those whose bond is of the soul, past life links and loves, more so than of the people with whom we are related. Of course, this connection can be one and the same thing. It is nice to know your bloodline, and I certainly have the look of a meditteranean or Egyptian, and my mothers maiden name was Scottish. However, I do not put any more store on it than that and I certainly would not declare myself Egyptian-Celtic!

The language does not use any recognisable words but has a pattern, repeated sounds and words which give it a rhythmic feel. Speaking in this manner does not sound like gobbledygook, and the rhythm and sound is suggestive of a much simpler, more expressive means of communication. I do not know if the accessing of such a language is an exclusively Christian phenomena, but I doubt it. I would be very interested to hear of another person who has experienced a hidden, second language inside of themselves which they discovered outside of the Church. The impression I get when using it is of a primitive, magical language, but I do admit that I am ignorant of its origin.

Until 1992 I had not been associated with any spiritual creed or group but Christianity. The word Paganism had not come into my sphere of experience, save in references by Christian books as to its inherent evil. Paganism was something I could only categorise in terms of the sensationalist approach which screamed 'Satanist' at anything it did not understand. Strangely enough, it was my being called a Pagan which opened the next door in my life. I had moved into yet another rented room in London, my constant moving of home reflecting my ongoing need to escape myself. Each room brought about fresh waves of dreams, noises and poltergeist activity. The room I was in when I met Kathy was no exception. I was woken at three thirty six each morning, without fail, by voices whispering in my ear, electronic whirring sounds and footsteps.

I was constantly ill, and was in danger of losing my job as a teacher by my absence record from work. I would suffer inexplicable sickness, stomach pains and exhaustion. I can understand this now as being a manifest representation of the fact that I could not stomach what was happening in my life, my gut feeling was bad, and so the ill health merely mirrored the internal conflict and discomforts I felt. I was being physically threatened at work by parents whose only gripe against me was that I was too young to be teaching their children. As I was one of several young graduate teachers this did not explain their hostility. At one point, the headmaster offered to install a panic button in my room, so real was the threat. Despite my constant illness, I was good at my job and I got along famously with my students. I can only assess that the parents resented me for reasons they could not put into words, i. e. I 'smelled' wrong, or did not fit in with their pack mentality.

Many of the other young staff were Born Again Christians, and so were able to appear safe and 'normal'. No matter what I did to fit in, I stuck out like a sore thumb on an instinctive level, both to the parents and with myself. The children, who I formed a strong bond with, often asked me questions such as "are you a witch, Miss?" or "are you a gypsy, Miss?" which I found very peculiar as I did not reveal outwardly any sign of being 'different'. On some level, they too knew I was not like the other teachers, and they pointed it out in the only language they understood. Obviously, children of primary school age still retain their innate sensitivity to 'see'. My energies felt wrong, and I felt wrong. I was incarcerated in my room in the rented house for many hours, often so ill that I was hallucinating. As it was a typical shared dwelling, the occupants paid little attention to each other and nobody noticed that I wasn't about much. On one particularly grim occasion, I recall 'seeing' the Titanic sinking in my room. I was taking part in the hallucination as a woman called Edna-Mae, who was on board. I believe my sickness put me further in-tune with my capacity to 'see' and the whole experience was vivid enough to make me believe that there may actually have been a woman on the Titanic by that name, who did experience the things that I saw.

It was because of my delirium that one of the other residents, Kathy, came to notice I never came out of my room, and she eventually came to see me and did my shopping. During this time she came to notice the rings I wore, which were an unwise collective of just about every arcane symbol one could imagine. I was so confused about my spirituality that I thought one of the ankhs, celtic crosses, runic inscriptions and so forth must mean something to me, and so I wore all of the rings at once! Kathy noticed, and exclaimed "oh, you're a Pagan!" Not wanting to disagree with her, I replied in the affirmative. That simple exchange lead me into the next stage of my quest. Kathy was an intelligent, happy-go-lucky young girl, who seemed as sane as the next person, and so I did not believe that she could be involved with anything as ridiculous as Satanism, when she declared she was a Pagan too. Kathy's energies did not lend themselves to being a devotee of evil.

Since my encounter with Shirley, I had been able to 'read' a person's aura, totally instinctively, and Kathy possessed a totally bright and healthy one. I didn't really know what I was doing as regards knowing the exact colours of how the aura should be, I just 'knew' which shades reflected which states of being. I saw the halo of aura around human beings totally spontaneously. I could be having a conversation with someone and suddenly a burst of colour would shoot out from the side of their heads, which was very disconcerting! Now I have the ability to switch this vision off, and I understand why it would not be good to have the mind's-eye open all of the time. The prospect of seeing auras all the time would be distracting in the extreme as they are fascinating to watch, constantly shifting and dazzling.

In basic terms, the muddier the colour, the less happy or healthy the individual at that time. Anything from red to black denotes an ailment or unpleasant state of being. Similar to bruises on the body, the aura reflects the same shades to show where there is hurt or harm. It is possible to scan the whole person for signs of a damaged aura, but as one is generally focussed on the face, that is the area which reveals the first signs. The aura is just a sign of a person's etheric, life force energy. I am now a firm believer in the fact that everything comes down to energies, be it health (the reflection of unhappiness, anger etc as can be illustrated by my teacher-Self displaying outward signs of internal upsets) or be it how one reacts to people and places.

Someone once taught me to see the energy I produced by rubbing my hands briskly together for a time and then drawing them apart. I could indeed see the energy which was generated between them, before it faded back into each palm. If one considers that everything, scientifically speaking, is made of moving energy (protons, electrons and neutrons) then one can accept more readily the fact that our own personal energy field (for we must generate one, if we are living energy) may respond well, or adversely, when exposed to the energies of other things and situations. So, as has been proved, the energy of electricity in pylons and sub-stations can adversely affect our health. In the same manner, other human energy can affect our well-being. Hence one of the reasons for an irrational, instant dislike to a person or place, the other being a difficult past life link. The energies of a person can be rejuvenated by exposure to the energies of 'greenery' in woodland, or it can be sapped by needy, ill people who need to 'vampire' one's energy, subconsciously, for their own benefit. Our energies explain a lot of our instinctive likes and dislikes. With Kathy, I instinctively knew, for all my spiritual ignorance, that she was good. With an overview, I can also see that her introduction to me was essential to my growth.

Kathy said that she woke at three thirty six a.m. also and that she had heard the voices too. She had a disturbing side effect of waking up paralysed for a time. She had also seen the phantom cats and an old woman that I had seen on the stairs. For the first time in my life, another sensitive person was experiencing exactly as I did. Moreover, they were not afraid. I knew that we were both reacting to the house's energies, and that this time, it was not just me. Realising this helped me a thousandfold and even when I heard footsteps pounding down the stairs to stop outside my door in the middle of the night, I did not feel my usual terror. There had been nobody there, and the reason that I had heard the steps was not that I was mad or bad or a victim of a curse. It was because I was a sensitive. Like Kathy. She, like Shirley before her, was an excellent role model for me.

Kathy was a Wiccan, a witch who belonged to a small group, or coven, in Buckinghamshire. She agreed to take me to meet them, which I felt trepidation and some residual fear about. One cannot be a Born Again Christian without carrying a great deal of fear and anxiety about being filled with the Devil for a long while afterwards. Before I went with Kathy, she introduced me to the art of brewing herbal teas for relaxation and minor ailments, and she also taught me how to meditate on a candle.

We would sit in her room, in a darkness which would have previously frightened me, with our focus on a single candle flame. With counted breathing I learned to unfocus with my eyes but to focus with my third, or minds, eye. I let the pictures and images come unbidden, without fear. Kathy and I discussed what we had 'seen' afterwards, and I realised that there was no shame in admitting that I saw pictures and images which I could not explain. She introduced me to the idea of writing down these memories of images, lest I need to refer back to them, and as a record, perhaps of future, or past, events. She wrote hers down in a book called a Book of Shadows. I thought this was a bit too 'dark' and scary for me, so I added 'and light' to the title and began my own record of thoughts, dreams and visions. I also found that meditation on the candle flame aided my relaxation after work, and improved my health. A regular time set aside for such contemplation made me feel that it was special and important.

Other, trivial, things could be left undone, but Kathy set great store by keeping up the meditations. I found that such discipline sharpened me up and made me feel more in control of what I 'saw' and when. Because I had finally given in to my ability to 'see' and was giving the sight time and space to come through, I found that the poltergeist pestering, which I had had since youth, finally ceased. It was wonderful! Although I did not wish to subscribe to another religion, and although I was enjoying having a little personal control at last, I decided to meet Kathy's High Priestess. Wicca could not be all bad, if Kathy was a part of it.

The story which follows was unexpected, and an odd one. However, it was a vital key in opening a further, denied part of my Self. The Priestess had an air of composure and serenity which I admired a great deal, and her energies revealed to me that she was very psychic. I did not trust her as much as Kathy as she appeared to wish to keep her rank of being 'the boss', and she met me on this level. I do not know if she wished to bind me to her group, or if she inadvertently locked into a need in me, but she immediately claimed that she had known me in another life.

This time, I was not surprised when she too told me I had been burned at the stake. She calmly told me that she had been my sister, and she had got away from being captured, whilst I had perished. A great alarm bell went off within me, although I was too polite and nervous, and in awe, to speak up. I recognised the scenario that she spoke of, but I had no recollection of her at all. She drew a total blank within me. She then spoke of a man who had come to help me in the woods. At this, my eyes filled with tears for a man I half-recalled, but when the Priestess pointed out a friend of hers and told me it was him I recoiled inside. The story felt right within me, but the man before me did not seem quite right. He almost reminded me of the 'man in the woods', who I half-remembered as having mousy brown hair, greenish eyes and a slim build. This chap was very nice, but he lacked a certain something which would have made me recognise him. In my dreams I had met the man, who I called Julien, and I thought that if he had existed then I would simply know if I ever saw him. The chap, called Charles, was not him, I was sure of it. But he and the Priestess told me categorically it was so, and if they knew that I had been burned and that a man had helped me, then they must know that they were the people who had been there too.

I felt as if my psychism wasn't as powerful as theirs if they could remember and I couldn't. My memories at that point were still fragmented. I was so naive that I went along with this story. The chap Charles believed that he and I had had a passionate relationship in this other life, and so it was expected of me to continue it in this one. He believed that he had been a monk who had sheltered me in his monastery, whilst we engaged in sexual relations in secret, and I had been a practicing witch. He had felt intense guilt when I had been captured and burned, and he wanted to make it up to me in this incarnation.

One must remember that up until then I had met very, very few folk who even believed in reincarnation and so it was tempting for me to go along with the charade for the company of being taken seriously. I did not want to lose the friendship of like minds as I had spent long enough searching for it, so I accepted their scenario. My gut feeling was that it was wrong. For some reason, the more Charles and I met, the more validations I received that the story was true. He told me of events in the 'lost' life that I had dreamed about and I thought there could be no way that he would have known those events unless he was indeed Julien. Once, a total stranger came over to chat with us in a pub and the stranger asked if Charles's name was Julien. It all seemed to add up logically, if not emotionally. However, as I was gaining in personal enlightenment and strength, through meditation and reading the books that Kathy showed me, I decided to find out what my 'truth' was, not theirs.

I sat down with a pen and a piece of paper. I had read a little on trance, or automatic, writing and I believed that all I needed was a method to channel all of the information which had been trying to come through me for so long. It was as if that finally turned a key within me, after years of remaining locked up tight with fear and ignorance. I entered a light trance state through relaxation and controlled breathing. I held the pen with a loose grasp and I waited. I was still a little afraid that a passing spirit may come through me and so I made an invocation to my guide (who I knew was there somewhere!) to only allow the information I was seeking to come through me. It was internal information which my 'higher Self' would know. I did not need spirit guidance, but access to far memory.

I did a rudimentary protective visualisation for myself, a scanty forerunner of the full 'blue suit' I use today. I did this through lack of confidence, not laziness. I have never dared be lazy in my rituals, protective or otherwise, as I have full knowledge that there are things 'out there' which are less than pleasant. I do not wish to give them access. Also, if one is a psychic one should be a good psychic who has respect for the energies one encounters and uses. A Wisewoman who has no respect for the energies is just as dangerous and irresponsible as an electrician who approaches his or her work haphazardly. Back then, I did my best with the confidence and knowledge I had no doubt with my good intentions my guide made sure that he did the rest!Had I have been silly or careless, he would have probably let me learn my lesson the hard way!

I sat in my trance state, still aware of the pen in my hand. Laurie Cabot in her work 'The Power of the Witch' (Arkana, 1990) describes this state as 'alpha' and describes a method of achieving it both instantly and with the required steps. I use a breathing pattern of 'in, two three, out, two three' or 'in, deeper and deeper, out, deeper and deeper'. As I do this, I try to relax each part of my body, from the toes upwards. This is achieved by clenching the muscles, if possible, and then releasing to the count. Some areas will need more time than others, as we all have our key places, dependant on our work or regular activities, which store our stresses and tensions. I would not recommend the use of relaxation tapes for the purpose of achieving a meditative state. For the practicing psychic, it is a little impractical to believe that one will always have a tape recorder to hand for entering trance.

With the automatic writing it is necessary to remain impassive, unhurried and free of extraneous thoughts. Easier said than done... but it takes practice. As with riding a motorbike or with working with a powerful tool, one must take extra time and care until one feels capable of using a motorway or tackling a difficult piece of do-it-yourself. At this point, words, symbols and pictures may come through.

I have known other psychics to use this ability to draw psychic portraits of other peoples guides. Naturally, these present themselves as the usual array of Egyptian Priestesses, angels and, I hate to admit it, Red Indians! (I do think that my guide must have an extraordinary sense of humour to present himself to me in such a way, knowing how I feel about cliched imagery!) I think that this portraiture makes the person involved accept someone else's vision of their guide. I think, personally, that it is better to discover one's own guide, for ones self. Recently two women have asked me 'Do you think my guide is such and such?' I will not answer, as I do not think that it would be beneficial for them to take my word above their own experience. Who is to say that I see the energies of their guide in the same way? As with humanity, appearance is only a surface matter given far too much importance, and it is immaterial what a guide looks like, compared to their guidance.

I have produced psychic artwork, but more readily I produce writing. I find this is put onto paper with lightening speed which cannot be read as it is being transferred. I am often amazed to read back what my hand has written with such speed. Another way of gaining written guidance is to use two pens, not one, by means to have a question and answer session. By this, I mean that if one has a black pen in the usual writing hand, and a red pen in the other hand, the black pen (you) can ask a question, and the other hand (guide) can use the red pen to answer.

As one is unaccustomed to using the other hand, the results will be shaky at first, but the idea is that the passive side of the person will allow the guide to come in and communicate more readily than the active hand which is used all the time and which one can control more easily. It is astonishing to read back such communications, to see the very different styles of language and speech the two beings use. Even if one is merely having a dialogue with the higher Self, the information which can be accessed in such a manner can be revelatory in terms of Self-knowledge.

A simple invocation before attempting any writing, be it automatic or left hand/right hand, is useful to focus the need and aim. For example, 'Dear Spirit (insert name if appropriate)I ask that you be here to guide me as I write, with love, wisdom, truth and understanding. I ask that I may receive the answers to the questions I ask, if it is the right time for me to know. May I have your blessing as I now seek the truth. So may it be'. As with all such practices, the art of communication requires patience, practice and regular discipline. As I have said before, should we feel guilty about giving time to the quest for inner wisdom and personal understanding for the good of the Self and so for the All?

Priorities need to be given, and in our modern lives it is all too easy to switch off from busy schedules and hectic days by watching television or drinking. Thus our true needs and desires always remain buried under a list of more pressing, 'important' things. We are so wrapped up in 'surviving' financially that we suffer emotionally and spiritually which reflects into the way we treat others and the Earth. Everything we do, or don't do, reflects outwards and influences others and the environment, as well as damaging our Selves. As one can see from my exaggerated example, my denying Self was destructive to me, and if I was no use to me then my use to the All was pretty limited. We are encouraged not to be Self-indulgent, but to 'get on with it' with no time for reflection and contemplation. It is strange how in business it is unthinkable for there not to be assessment, planning and recording. Yet, in our lives there is no incentive, it seems, to do the same, whereas in business the incentive is material gain. Our spiritual gain has never been more vital, as our personal inner well-being reflects into the World. The less focus on personal gain by wealth and acquisition, the more by inner peace and personal (so universal) understanding. It is an old message, but one the Western world has yet to fully understand, it seems.

In such a modern life it is easy to have good intentions to meditate daily or to take a walk in the greenwood before breakfast, or to learn a divination technique. Yet, all to often there is ironing to do, or a television programme to watch. One must be 'Self-ish' to continue on the path and put the Self first, not above others, or at the detriment of the environment, not to gain anything but Self-knowledge and harmony which can only spread out in waves from the Self, and benefit all. I have chosen the path, after a hard slog and many, many mistakes, of personal growth and creativity above financial security. It is the path less trodden on and it is a hard one, yet one need not to go to my extreme to have a magical existence. The goal is to know ones priorities and make all daily rituals special and 'indulgent'. "To be what we are becoming is the only end of life" said Robbie Louis Stevenson.

With my pen in hand on that fateful day I began to receive my first channelled message from my hidden Self. It was written with such speed and flow that I did not have a chance to logically or rationally interact with its construction. Thus I was given this poem by my Wisewoman Self. It changed my life.

> And as the corn is taken in,
> And darkness becomes the better friend of our waking hours,
> Those who are blessed are travelling home,
> As once I did, aye, even I!
> Now 'tis mine only to recall,
> Dreams that I dreamed aside my fire's glow.
> Know ye of fear? Then heed me well,
> For though I'll run and I'll not stop,
> I will not weaken for their cause,

Or drink then from a lesser cup,
'Til my body will my soul betray,
And so it will, be sure of that,
As surely as the moon doth rise,
they will not catch me 'til I drop.

My shelter here, it grows the less,
Amongst the slender, dripping trees,
My shroud of mist so cruelly thins,
Clad now in solitude, revealed.
And here he came, here in the wood!
Truly! Can ye hope, lest believe,
This man, defenceless, brave none the less,
Seen here in this place with me!

This man, defenceless, brave none the less,
Seen here in this place with me.
His face, like the purest winter star,
His silence, gentle eloquence,
His are the tears I cannot shed,
Fashioned into dew-clad diadems.
And I be touched by his simple grace,
By his true faith they do not know,
His hands flutter, pale December moths,
Useless against their savage lusts.
His lips of milk that sing, O sing,
He speaks not of futility, this gentle Prince,
Says only unto me... "are we not then sure,
That we have conquered such loss before?"
Indeed... in morning I find strength.

Together then, aside the lake,
A shining bliss ne'r to know,
So cruel an age... my fleeting life...
O n'er to possess those sacred bones.
He slips away, our time is done,
He goes forth shining into a barren world,
That safe passage may be granted to me,
Past silver birch, the larch, the oak,
I stumble on... bereft.

And when they come, I fight, too late,
No safe passage, no escape,
Thrown onto a horse and bourne away,
And taken, feigning death, feigning bravery,
I lift my head high before the man,
Around who I spy the Light of Truth,
Appeal then do I to his soul,
Alas, he cannot bow to that,
He follows through as his God feels best,
And so do his men take me unto Hell.

This room, in which I stand... then fall,
Around me chaos, madness,
The fools, they think they can escape,
They climb the walls, they scratch, they moan,
I stay now, still,
For has my life not reflected peace?
My mind goes back beneath the dripping trees,
I keep it there, safe, sacred, untouched by this,
And when dawn comes, my body is taken,
To look injustice in the eye,
Midst my screams and cries of anguish,
And then, indignities and jeers,
And their accusations cannot reach me,
For my mind is a cold and distant star,
The anger and pain are burning far away,
My body... a dry and distant desert plain.

Alone in a stone room waiting for death,
I had been, chained with bonds not of my own making,
I can sense that all I be,
They seek to disperse, scatter, cast to the four winds,
For none shall access that part of me that flies, untethered Whole,
Searching across the centuries for another time,
Another life, where freedom reigns,
And those so gifted, shine, revered,
So pitiful they cannot, will not, see!

Outside then, 'tis another case,
When I see what is prepared for me,
And... not that walk, not yet!
Simple human fear I feel,

And so I have divided myself, let the spark of spirit free,
For I cannot comprehend such pain,
The nature of such travesty,
The pain... more than I have words for...
And,
As I harken to my own screams,
As my blood sings softly in the flames,
I rise from ashes unto light,
Leaving charred remnants of a life,
Moving swiftly now, untamed,
Lest I be tethered by grief or hate,
I make once more that familiar journey,
Unto the Light, unto the Lady.

But, one pause.... one pause I shall allow,
For the loss of body, bodily love,
And shall we meet, perhaps in death?
O sweet St Julien be gone!
A thousand winters I shall search,
All moments they shall be as one,
Until I find the place where we,
Can love without a fear of wrong,
And freedom be rejoiced in there,
In thought, kind word and song.

As I read those words, that poem committed to paper by the Wisewoman within me, I remembered. One cannot just remember logically, but with feelings. I felt as if I knew, not only where I had come from, but also where I was going, but I knew that the explanation that others had given to me was not my truth. After all those years, I understood what I was, who I was, because of my own revelation, a personal illumination which I could trust on a gut level. I understood that everything has a season, a precise moment to be revealed. I had stepped towards the moment, trusting my Self, without fear and my manifest action had been reflected astrally.

The revelation of my automatic writing, its eloquence and the accompanying images and feelings, showed me much more than the fact that I had been a Wisewoman. It showed me the truth of 'who I be', and in so doing, all my manifest struggles and problems fell into place. If "Your goal is to find out who you are" as it states in the work 'A Course in Miracles' (Foundation for Inner Peace, 1983), then I had begun the true quest, finally, by identifying who I had been. In this respect, I could see who I was and who I had to become more fully, realising only the potential of who I could become. I could no longer battle against my true nature.

I could see clearly that my next life, the one as the monk, which had directly followed the burning experience, was my first attempt to mould myself into another way of being. The lesson that I had learned as a Wisewoman was that if I was myself I would be tortured, ridiculed, persecuted and killed, all for simply being who I was. The monk-Self had learned to hide who I was under the guise of the respectable Church. My soul, I believe, had chosen the monk life to reveal to me a valuable lesson. My attempts to hide who I was also ended in disaster, as try as I might, I could not stop my single-minded belief in truth, honour and justice. In many ways, the monk's life was fitting, it was quite solitary, interned and creative. However, I was part of an organisation which expected me to be a certain way, and to accept the hierarchy of corruption as being part of the way of things. I was not able to accept my position within such an acceptable, powerful organisation when I could see it to be unfair and dishonest. My monk incarnation was my first try at 'blending in'.

If one can imagine, after suffering the hideous death of a witch, the memory of the 'punishment for being one's own Self' scars the soul badly. My subsequent attempts to compromise my Self made for more chaos and pain in the long run. It had taken me many centuries and many lives to come to this conclusion. The simple fact was that I had energies which would not fit into certain shapes or forms, no matter how hard I tried to make them. My attempts to disguise my true form as a teacher, or as a strict Christian, in this incarnation just made others suspicious. I 'smelled wrong' on an instinctive level. If I was fully my Self, the Wisewoman Self which was calling across the years, loud and clear, then people could respond to me honestly. There would be no confusion for them or for me, who I was would be clear. It did no good, for anyone, to pretend. I had been a soul in confusion and torment, ashamed of who I was, frightened of the consequences of being disliked, or worse, for being 'me'. I knew that the poltergeist activity and haunting dreams would stop when I accepted my Self. And so they did.

My recalling my monk-Self had been part of the process of understanding what could happen if I tried not to be me. The memory of the Wisewoman, which had followed, was a clear message of how I should be, to be happy, despite popular opinion. The next step I had to take was to find out what being myself meant.

How was I to manifestly behave in this life, in order to live harmoniously with Self? How did I see my role in the world as it was now, and how could I best

105

realise my Self? Obviously, I could do this by accepting my creativity as a gift to be used for its own ends, not for financial gain or recognition. My Wisewoman Self had not had anything in the French life besides her own pleasure in lace craft and the arts of healing, etc. I had to first sacrifice the material bonds which bound me to working as a teacher. I cannot deny that I gained valuable experience and many transferable skills when in the classroom, but I never had time or energy to create when I was 'a teacher'. The words of George Bernard Shaw had always rung in my head as I forced myself into school each day, I decided to be 'one who does' rather than 'one who teaches'. Obviously there are many souls who are well suited to such important work.

Looking at the signs, my dislike of societies' values, my reluctance to perpetuate certain myths, my rejection of success being represented by greater acquisition of material things, my discomfort with being a part of an institution where I had little or no choice but to accept higher decisions, all of these matters meant that I could not morally or spiritually enter another school again. There were many things which I found hard, such as the telling of 'his-story' in a patriarchal, Eurocentric, Christian sense, which my voice alone could not change... and I met with little or no support. Just because I squirmed under what I perceived to be the dishonesty and immorality of the status quo did not mean to say others did. Before, I would have thought that they were right and that I was mad or bad to disagree. As I had done before the men who had supposedly put me on a fair trial in Avignon in 1326, I tried to hold my head up and to stand firm in my beliefs.

I did attempt to teach art, as a compromise, to older children, but the same problems existed for me. I could not support a system which had no time for small groups to communicate or express themselves openly, without judgement or punishment. Staff and students alike were broken en masse under the relentless wheel of achievement and progress. The message for us to all accept, fit-in and not question was strong. We were all working towards one great big material goal in order to survive. Worse still, there was a veneer of democracy, a lie. This suited the majority, and they were contented to soldier on but I had to leave, walking with confidence into an insecure future. With this decision came fresh clarity and power.

My non-conformist spark of Self would no longer be restrained in such circumstances and it burst through like a hot spring through mud. I had learned too much to allow my manifest Self to get ill, and my blocked energies to erupt in bursts of uncontrolled psychism. However, knowing who I was, accepting that, was in many ways much harder than trying to walk with my eyes closed, with my head down. It meant that I was awake, and alive in a way that I had never been before and with this realisation came responsibilities to Self and Others.

With my new-found methods of meditation, I connected more and more with my inner Realms, my guide and other 'bigger' beings in the Universe. I will describe, at length, the personal processes which I evolved to contact and work with my inner Realms and the Otherworlds. I will give a section to such techniques, as I think their worth to the individual is vast. As with all of my spiritual work, it is simple, uncomplicated and accessible. At the time of my discovering the Wisewoman Self through my own experience, I was still, in psychic terms, a novice and so my means of contacting Self, guide and Otherworlds reflected my simplicity. But they worked, just as my Wisewoman spells and spirit contacts had worked in medieval France. I learned that back then I had read no books, attended no workshops, and seen no teachers other than my mother's wisdom, the trees and nature, and the belief that spirits existed, everywhere.

My way, which was not the only way, but my way... my way was of the type described in books today as the 'Kitchen Witch' (an American term used to describe a woman who worked with the tools around her instead of the often complicated ritual items of today). The Hedge Witch has also been used to describe the solo magical/spiritual practitioner and I would relate to this in its more traditional sense, as the hedge was used as a delineation between the Worlds, and so the Hedge Witch was a 'rider twixt the realms'. My rejection of the word witch has already been explained, and so I had to decide what the Wisewoman Self stood for, what the tradition meant and how I was to continue with it.

I recently heard a speaker at a UFO conference referring to a quote from the Bible, in the chapter of Ezekiel. It may seem strange to have a Wisewoman, traditional 'enemy' of the Church, quoting from 'the Opposition'! I do not disregard any other faith or fact, and wisdom can be found anywhere and everywhere, often in the least expected places and ways. This Bible passage referred to those who spend their time on Earth using their gifts to help others 'out of the darkness', and blessings were bestowed on those who were brave enough to live in this manner. I believe that with great effort and practice that I can re-access my knowledge gained in medieval France, my soul-memory, to continue my souls tradition of helping others. As I have stressed before, I wish to work as a channel for knowledge, guidance and healing, and I do not wish to have any loftier ideas about myself than that. Being a Wisewoman is just as valid as being a plumber, we are all called to our different tasks. It is the recognition, acceptance and joy of realising our purpose which is divine. There is power in the realisation and acceptance which can be further used for the good. As I am incarnate, I intend to keep my head in the clouds of the other Realms, but my feet firmly planted on Terra Firma.

The Wisewoman role, as I perceive it, is not about being airy-fairy and disconnected to the manifest in any way. As I began to understand my definition of who I was, I began to look into other peoples' versions, other peoples' truths. In my search, partly triggered by my interest in the other 'witches' I had met, I did read many magical handbooks and volumes of advice to the newcomer to the path. I do not read magical texts to copy ideas, ritual suggestions or rules, but I do enjoy comparing notes, as it were. I would suggest a broad reading around all traditions, all paths, plus their historical context and background.

I must stress that my initial Becoming a Wisewoman was focussed entirely around my guidance, spirituality, meditation and memory. My pull towards modern Paganism was a separate, but connected, issue. I had not considered myself Pagan in my past life in France, and the idea that I had been a coven member or part of any form of organised witchcraft cult was totally abhorrent to me. I was grateful to Kathy for her introduction to witches and a modern coven, but I had to leave their confines once I had discovered, finally, my own identity. I was not, and could not be, part of an order. It was not through vanity, but through an understanding of how I functioned best. I could accept the path of the solitary witch far easier, and I sought the company of other such folk, but my path was still different, I felt. Until I really understood the meaning of being a Pagan I could not fully update my past practice into today's world. Whether or not my French Self had needed to understand Paganism or not, I realised that I wanted to know more about this umbrella-term which sheltered many traditions beneath it. Witches were Pagans, I knew. Could the solo Wisewoman be one?

With the original term being used to describe the rustic person who stayed away from church and who communed with local spirits or deities (*pagus* meaning locality) it seemed entirely feasible. I had left Kathy's group, and the members were displeased. The departure was not openly hostile, but my rejection of the scenario they had put upon me did not best please them. I think that they actually believed that I had been the Priestess' sister, and Charles's lover, in some dark past time. No matter how lonely my path ahead was to be, I could not go along with a fantasy. Their truth was my fantasy, if they were genuine then no party could be accused of being in the wrong. I had to leave them.

The 'true' Julien was out there somewhere, that was, if he was incarnate at that time - and I meant to find him. It seemed a cruel trick for me to have remembered Julien, only to discover he was not alive on Earth today. I always held out hope that I would meet him, through my journey into understanding my path. As part of my reaching out along the way I met Jack, a Druid, Bard and fellow artist who taught me more about Pagan thought and practice than any book or group could. I knew that he was not Julien reincarnated, and our relationship was purely platonic. He worked spontaneously, as did I, and he had many strange tales of psychic happenings to tell me. He too had experienced the problem of frequently vanishing objects. He had actually seen his belongings de-materialise in front of him, which made me shudder. Had I seen such a thing at the time, my fear would have been unbearable, with my new understanding, I realised that this was the precise reason why I had never witnessed the vanishing of my objects. Even in the turmoil there had been a rhyme and reason to everything.

My guide, and my higher Self had known what I could take, in terms of phenomena, and what would be too much. Everything had a lesson. Jack was not afraid of his phenomena, nor was he undisciplined in his approach. I feel that the psychic occurrences which courted him must have wanted his attention for different reasons, I had no intention of transferring my story onto him in order for him to make sense of things. He was very similar to me, he too affected electrical items, he too had far-memory, but he was not me, and he did not walk in my footsteps on the same path. I found I could tune into him as easily as I did to myself, and I clearly 'saw' his other lives and memories. I was able to discuss this with him, and our stories correlated. I did not fall into the trap of telling him what his past lives were. I knew the confusion that such an assumption could bring.

Jack's Druidry stemmed from his belief that he had been a 'Merlin' in another time, a seer and diviner working for a Tribal Chief. Whether this was true, or a psychodrama to explain a part of his Self, Jack lived an exemplary life, being true to his instincts but harming no one. He was an active road protester and he worked with nature and the elements to create positive magic for the environment. His personal belief in his own past lives did not matter to me, but his modern Pagan practice did. I never once wished to call myself a Druid, it was not my way, but I could share in his way.

Jack practiced divination by stick casting, using sticks cut from trees which he believed had certain properties. These sticks would be carved and seasoned, further empowering them with his will for them to be imbued with certain energies. He would engrave corresponding runes on their surface and he would meditate holding each stick, visualising further the essence which he wished the tool to represent. This, to me, far outshone the mass-produced tarot packs and runestones which could be purchased. I came to understand that it is the will of the person, working with the natural forces or materials, which create the real magic. Jack's time and effort gave the sticks great power and connection, far more so than opening a box or packet, no matter how beautifully produced it was. Never once would Jack cut a tree for his own use without communing with the tree-spirit. He used a special magical knife which was kept specifically for cutting natural resources. His gentle Paganism was my starting point for growing on my path.

I then produced my own divination kit by visiting a beach and collecting stones which I felt particularly drawn to. I then meditation each stone, casting out those which did not 'sing' to me of some particular energy. These could represent love, creativity, dreams or worldly wealth, health and housing. I devised a system for reading the stones as the person layed them out, according to how they saw fit. Because I had tuned into the stones, held them and focussed my will upon them, according to their natural energy, they worked as divination tools. I did not once have to refer back to a manual or instruction book, as I felt was fitting. The traditional Wisewoman craft I was attempting to attune to, would have little use for written guidelines, compiled by another. Devising one's own way, using creativity and focus, is a pleasing thing to do, whatever the path or tradition. It is a confidence boost for the practitioner to know that their system works, but it is also a 'green' way to practice. The more natural forms of divination we use, the less mass-production there will be of yet more 'things'. I felt this was in keeping with my old Wisewoman Self. She was not a consumer, she used what she had to hand.

Jack's knowledge of folklore was wonderful, and I enjoyed his storytelling. I began to understand the actual timeless message behind the 'fairy stories' and to comprehend humanities' use of archetypal figures and scenarios to describe a particular type of energy, or way of being. By this, I came to realise why it was that Witches, Druids and practicing Pagans related to Gods and Goddesses, as well as to nature. Paganism, as I understand it, is a term which describes those who see the whole of nature as divine. Certain aspects of that divine energy can be best described in the form of Higher Beings who represent that principle. Further, the cycles of nature and the natural world, which Pagans hold as divine, can be described by the interaction of Gods and Goddesses, be they local or of the country involved. Much of this thought and practice still stems from the folklore, traditions or legends of the place in which the Pagan person lives in this incarnation. His or her definitions of divinity and the natural world will reflect the connection they feel with the area, its tales and old ways.

However, there is some speculation as to whether there is an actual, provable direct line of connection between current Pagan belief and practice and the

110

supposed survival of actual old traditions. The blend of what we know factually from past practice and belief in our area or country, plus our own spiritual interaction with it, plus our own past life memories of the way we used to practice as Pagans are the sources of what Paganism is today. It is more of an organic thing which is growing, reflecting nature and modern needs, as well as reflecting our hidden traditions, memories and heritage. People such as Gerald Gardner and Ross Nichols have done much to re-weave the old information and traditions which still remained, into the accepted faces of Wicca and Druidry today. It should not be overlooked that it was only in the latter half of this century that the Witchcraft Law was repealed, and that others did a great deal of work and ground breaking for people on their spiritual paths today.

When I first met Jack, I was fortunate to be experiencing the new wave of interest and acceptance for Pagan practice, belief and paths. I am indeed fortunate to be able to compare the way I was treated for my life and works in 1326, in contrast to how my thoughts are received in 1996. Although there is a long way to go to be accepted, and the new surge of interest and understanding is only just beginning, I believe that the old souls have incarnated again with enough faith and strength to share their way of viewing nature and the world, without fear of extermination.

I do not subscribe to the belief that each one of the thousands and thousands of folk who died accused of witchery and heresy were coven members or actively magical people. I do believe that those who were different, those who wished to be left alone, those who could not condone corruption or lies, those who lived in tune with nature, not humanity, were those who met their ends at the hands of the Church and others. The simple reason was fear and ignorance, and the dispelling of this fear and ignorance still continues.

But those who have incarnated again, at this time, are stronger and wiser than before, and their understanding and faith will not be quashed by threats or insults. I do not believe that such souls are the chosen ones, but I do believe that there is a need for people who give nature reverence and divine attributes. Such beliefs are obviously needed on Earth at this time. The Earth is crying out for help, and a growing number of people are trying to heal the planet by direct action and magic, as well as through kindness and understanding.

There is no need for everyone to become Pagan, or a Druid or a Wisewoman or a Witch, there is no need for anyone to become anything other than who and what they are. But the voices of the Pagans and the old souls should be heard, at last, for the sake of the Earth, as a balance to those who have been heard louder and longer, throughout the centuries.

I will reiterate my belief that souls are not better than each other, but different. I do not believe that one type of soul can be forced to be a different way that is perceived by another as a superior way. I do not believe that a Wisewoman, Pagan, creative-type soul can suddenly thrive in a life as the manager of the Department of Transport who has extra-marital affairs and supports fox-hunting. Or vice-versa.

Some folk may have a purpose to inspire, to educate, to create or to grow things. Others may have a life which causes destruction, harm, chaos and misunderstanding. Such a life as the latter example can make another, different soul ponder its worth. Everything and everyone has a reason, a purpose for doing what they do, in the way that they do it. Given the overview which meditation can bring, or an understanding the many lives which we can have, then there can be a greater clarity as to why a certain individual should behave or experience life in such a manner.

A friend I have, who is a Pagan, has recently dropped her reverence for the male side of life, male energies and indeed males, from her practice, belief and mode of existence. This creates a lack of balance in her life and her resentment and exclusion of these energies is not beneficial. I can understand and sympathise with her reasoning... she sees the male of the species as being the rapists, warmongers, road builders and polluters. With my view of reincarnation, I see it is possible for all of us to incarnate as male or female, that we are a sexless soul which chooses the manifest 'mask' which is suitable for the life we have chosen to incarnate into.

My friend could next incarnate as a man, to experience her soul's pattern through a different way of being. It is not the male energy, the male universal principal, which is at fault, but the way it is being manipulated by the souls involved. Like fire, the energies of maleness can be used for good, or ill. Also, an understanding of reincarnation explains why some souls come into the world with anger, with fear and hurt. Souls are not evil, but can be ignorant of how the harm,or good, that they do, causes ripples to flow out from their actions which affect people directly and indirectly. Experiences earlier in an incarnation, or in another incarnation, can cause people, not just those in male bodies, to rape, steal and cause harm. To give an example which I have experience of, I was raped in medieval France. I felt the grief and hurt of it intensely, my soul carries the memory. Yet I do not wish for retribution or revenge. In this life, I have also suffered sexual harm. It hurts. But I can stand back, away from my body, and imagine floating above the situation. What had affected the soul of the offender so that he too affected another with his hurt? Nothing and nobody is isolated, everything is connected by energies. It is hard to forgive the rapists, the liars, the people who destroy, it is easy to feel we are superior. We all have lessons to learn. Nobody 'deserves' the rape as a lesson, but sometimes we are part of somebody else's lesson. Sometimes, another soul who meant little to us in a past life, wishes to see us again to put things right or to cause harm.

All I can say is that we are all interconnected, interwoven with the web of life and death and life. What goes around will indeed come around. The only tenet to live by is to harm none, to have integrity and honesty, to listen to the voices within and to act with a knowledge that our actions spread out, our energies being far reaching.

When I studied Paganism, I accepted that we all come from The One, the male and the female, joined as a universal energy. One is part of the other, in nature, and in souls, manifestly and spiritually. We reflect this principle with our Earthly Goddess and God concept, a perfect balance, complimentary and in harmony together. To reject one is to reject part of the Self, without understanding the imbalance. I am a Pagan because I value all life, all of it. I understand that the problems which the Earth has today cannot be solved by throwing out the male energy which appears to have ruled for too long, reflecting its worst aspects. There is a balance to be achieved. I do think that fate has decreed, and many souls have chosen, to return at this crisis time for our planet, to try to achieve this balance. We return for our personal purposes and lessons, but as we are all part of the matrix of energies which affect all life, then our purpose is also universal. Of course, I would like everyone to be Pagan and to accept this balance of harmony between the energies of male and female, for the sake of the beautiful planet. All any of us can do is to live by example and learn from everything and everybody as we go.

Anything, be it male energy or be it a knife, can cause good or ill. This can be said for magic. One of the main fears about the tradition of the Wisewoman, Witch etc is that they have the power to hex, curse and ill wish. Magic, or acts of focused will, can be directed for good or for harm. The way I live my life is to harm none, and so my magical acts are directed at healing people, nature and the world. Magic is directed energy, it works. 'Maleness' is an energy, it can be felt in positive, or negative, ways. As Lois Bourne said in "*Witch Amongst Us*", one can frighten an innocent person by sending them a poppet doll, associated with black magic or ill-wishing. It can have been given no directed, focussed ill-wish by the person sending it. It is an object imbued with no magic whatsoever. Yet its connotations are enough to cause the person harm by their own imaginings that it will do so. So it is with the male form. We can be afraid of the soul within, simply if it wears a male guise in this life. Perhaps, in the soul's last incarnation, it was a mother, a nurse, a nun, or some other 'safe' female role!

One of my main lessons of becoming a Wisewoman, and understanding the balance of all nature as reflected by Paganism, is that I do not judge the internal by the external. Nor can a soul be entirely evil, or supremely pure. We are all a balance, we are all learning lessons, and we can act out of ignorance and fear as well as with 'enlightened' intentions. What purpose incarnation, if one cannot learn? To learn by sharing, rather than by teaching.

With Jack's help, I began to understand that part of the quest for my Wisewoman Self, involved an understanding of natural cycles and of the environment. This had once been an integral part of my life, centuries before. I had functioned as part of the rhythms of the natural world, and I had worked my magic and healing arts with a knowledge of nature. One of the first things to do was to get outside more and observe the changing seasons, moon phases and the things which were actually growing during these times. I had decided to re-discover my old skills as a woman who understood the magical properties of herbs and plants, and, as with all my re-discovering of my Self, book learning was not the be-all and end-all.

One of the greatest lessons of choosing to walk on ones own narrow spiritual path, is that there is a large amount of hard work involved. Herbs must be identified in the wild, their properties memorised from many sources and an understanding of how to best use them must be acquired, by practical application and trial and error. For this, I attended evening classes and compiled my own herbal book by my reading as many different types of reference volumes as possible. This was still not enough, I had to go on long walks and look for the herbs and plants myself. Buying them dried in a wholefood shop seemed to be an easy solution, but I discovered, as with all 'magical' practices, that it is the input, personal effort and understanding of the process which makes all the difference. I began to grow herbs to use in simple herbal infusions and syrups, and started to collect seasonal, local plants for drying and storing.

The real magic is the wonderful sensation of working with living things, out of doors, with a sense of continuing a tradition that was in danger of becoming lost in a world full of 'conveniences'. My main personal revelation was that there was a beauty in the simple connection with nature, a poetry for my soul. There was nothing esoteric or complex in these understandings of nature, and I could realise that my previously incarnated Wisewoman Self had also seen the world through these eyes. The only thing which had changed was the lessening, and destruction, of the woodlands, the natural habitats and the hedgerows.

From this point, I began to open out and expand my awareness of environmental issues. My own quest was personal but once again the personal affected my

115

universal relationship, both manifestly and spiritually. I could almost feel my guide and the greater spirits of the land rejoicing as another individual returned to nature with an open heart and a willingness to work with it, not as a separate, superior entity. As John Seymour states in his book *'The Ultimate Heresy'* (Green Books, 1989) "We are part of nature. That is the primary condition of our existence. And only when we recognise this will we awaken from the evil dream that has lead us down the path of self-destruction for the last two or three hundred years. That is, the dream that we, mankind, can 'conquer' nature. For only when we abandon this dream will we realise again that you cannot conquer something of which you are a part." With this wisdom, and my new knowledge that everything that the individual does affects others, (and the manifest levels, and the astral reflection of this) I knew that my 'small' solo efforts were not in vain. My actions in re-discovering natural ways, with new joy and hope, were not isolated, however small and personal they appeared to me. The ripples moved out from my gestures and continued to spread.

I was heartened to read of, and discover, others who were also playing their small part. The sentiments of Sam, an Eco-Warrior with the Donga Tribe, quoted in the book *'Travellers'* by Lowe and Shaw (Fourth Estate, 1993), summed up my own feelings. She stated that her real admiration and her own path lay with "the old witches, the knowledgeable healers, who knew herb lore and food lore. They were like wise mothers and brothers who just knew the garden, the garden of the Earth. " Sam is probably someone who is regarded as, at best, potty and at worst, a menacing threat to established society. Yet her lone voice resonates with me, and our combined wills and energies for the good are powerful, no matter how disempowered and alone we feel. Even though we will probably never meet. This is why I have chosen to write down my feelings and experiences, as our voices travel and we connect via the pages of books which inspire and support.

I will not spend pages on recounting my own formulas and personal interactions with plants and herbs. Many professionals will give a broader view with a medical and scientific slant and their books are a fine starting point. As long as one does not stop at book reading, then the lessons continue outside, with the green energies and ones own individual experience of them. My personal reference would be to the work of Sue Hawkey, who was the lady I studied the basics with at college. She is having her book published by Dorling Kindersley in 1996, which should be available before this work goes to press. As a trained, experienced herbal practitioner, Sue has evidential knowledge, but she also works with the energies of the plants involved. I would also suggest the modern works of Barbara Griggs and David Hoffman, for a continuation of the 'holistic' approach to herbal lore and usage. On the more magical side, *'Herbcraft*

116

Shamanic and Ritual Use of Herbs' by Lavender and Franklin (Capall Bann 1996) provides an in-depth reference to traditional uses of herbs in Britain. I will include the Herb Society's address at the end of this book, for a general reference, as they can put the individual in touch with local groups and garden centres specialising in herbal cultivation. Working with herbs is as magical an act as casting a spell. We imbue our herbal brews, oils and salves with our energies and will, as well as the subtle energies of the plants. This is why it is so vital to go through the process of identifying, growing, finding, harvesting and preparing ourselves. Somehow, after one has been involved with herbs in such a manner, sticking a pre-packaged bag of dried herbs in a cup is not quite the same.

In my first lesson about herbal lore and the value of personal involvement, I learned how to approach my understanding of seasonal cycles, and their traditional, symbolic meanings. No amount of reading other people's interpretations could make me really appreciate what it was that I felt and saw when I had lived alone in the woods in France. What was most important for me, was that I learned all I could, 'remembered' all I could, and experienced all I could. Those three strands of becoming who I was, and could be, were to be interwoven, each having vital significance in the process.

As with herbalism, countless works have been written on the Celtic festivals, Wiccan practice and Druidic celebrations of the cycles. With a broad reading around the subject, one should remain open to the energies of each phase of the moon, each turn of the Wheel of the Year. One should, in my view, open the door and the heart, and step into the cycle. This interaction, as opposed to being a casual, armchair observer and philosopher, is an acknowledgement of ourselves as a part of, rather than apart from, nature. The difference between the way I experience the Way of the Wise, and the way I experienced Christianity is that with the former I can go and feel, experience and be a part of the energies involved in the seasonal cycles. With Christianity the process was static. I had to celebrate things that happened two thousand years ago, I had to accept they happened on faith, and I had to be an observer, rather than an active participant in the 'ritual'. This lack of immediacy and interaction left me 'cold'.

Because of this difference, I do not work well with religion, which appears to me to be inorganic and distant. Later in this chapter, I will discuss my feelings about the organised side of 'The Craft of the Wise' or Wicca (the Saxon interpretation of the name for witches). As with all of the observations in this work, my personal, not universal views and truths, are based on my experience. Many readers may not have had the experiences, and may wish to gain an understanding of such matters which can often be given an air of mystery and elitism by 'insiders'. Readers who are inside, may like to compare their choice with someone who has chosen to remain outside, and alone on their path. Both ways have plus and minus factors. I am just not a religious, or group, sort of person, but I only realise this because I have tried to join in, against my true instincts. I do not wish to paint a 'better' or 'worse' scenario for each way of following ones destiny, but I do wish to dispel some of the fear and ignorance still attached to each way of being. The solitary person may be criticised for being difficult, weird or a loner who is socially inept. The person who practices their form of spirituality in a group may be seen by the solo worker as a sheep without identity, or a yes-person. When one steps aside and actually focuses on the patterns which affect us all; the seasons, the moon, then it is clear that we are all part of larger circles, larger cycles, which make such divisions irrelevant.

Thankfully, Pagan groups and groups from monotheistic religions are now meeting in inter-faith discussions, with a common goal of caring for the Earth and promoting peace and understanding. However, there is still much internal disharmony between Pagan practitioners who have chosen different paths. As with all things, the message is that we may know something in theory (book learning etc) but we must find the will to put it into practice, to actually experience other ways of being, and the unknown, daunting and intimidating. To know one's Self, but to have respect, openness and a non-judgmental attitude, is perhaps the goal to strive for.

But an understanding of our interconnectedness with all things, primarily our own valuable part and connection with the eternal cycles of our manifest home, the Earth, should perhaps come first. When I decided to fully understand the cycles of nature, which have been celebrated, sometimes in secret, for centuries, then I did so alone. I stood in nature, bound to it by my feet on the Earth, inspired by the free birds in the air, driven by the fire in my soul to understand, and heartened by the morning dew of another day, another dance. I was not told what the festivals were about, I did not fully accept anyone else's experience as being my own. My unique perspective of the seasonal cycles appeared to me as follows, using the tradition of symbology to describe the Great Story of the Earth.

Imbolg (February 2nd) is the name given to the first festival, which takes place when the ground is still hard, often clad in snow. To my mind, the celebration is best represented by the Earth yawning and stretching and making ready to rise. Green fingers are reaching out, beneath their blanket of white, ready to throw off the bedsheets and start forth into a new life, a new cycle. For the moment, the Earth waits silently, one eye open, arms outstretched, but still concealed. It is the time of the promise, about to be fulfilled, the promise of life, light,

118

positivity and hope. It is a time of balance and balance shifting. There may not be any outward signs, but if we listen and feel, we can sense the Earth shifting and preparing. It can be likened to the time of the New Moon, a New Moon Goddess, appearing as but a fingernail of silver in the still-dark sky. She is reborn, as is the Earth's new dream, and she is moving slowly towards her own fullness. Her Consort, the Lord of the New Day, can be seen in the pale sky, his sunlight glow a watery promise of what is to come. It is soon to be the time for all to awaken from their slumbers and to bring forth new life. For us all, it is a time of planning, thinking ahead and for dreams which may be made reality in the time of the coming light. It is not yet the time to plant or sow, creatively or of the Earth, but it is the time of preparation. It is the time of the snowdrop and of the snowflake, a time of all things pale and pure, of innocence and hope.

Eostre comes next (around March 20th) and it is traditionally the time of resurrection (a time chosen most prudently for the staging of Christ's own resurrection. The understanding of this time of year goes back far beyond two thousand years. How could it not? It is the eternal cycle of nature, not of humanity's making. In each ancient understanding of the cycles and festivals, we see the equivalent symbology reflected in the Christian calendar. This was originally 'arranged' in order for the Pagan populace to accept the 'New Faith' as another aspect of their understanding of the Wheel of the Year, the Pagan way being established long before.

This was first a faith which was integrated, and then it dominated, so that we are left with a year which reflects Christian celebrations. It matters not which symbology we personally choose to interpret the cycles appropriately, but it is unhelpful for one way of viewing the year to have been swamped entirely by another. This is the folly of creating one way of thinking and one spiritual way as being the superior force. The two traditions should have co-existed as faces of one and the same set of patterns, as they are beginning to do now as neo-Pagans and followers on their 'Old Paths' bring their stories and representations back into use.)

At Eostre, the Spring Equinox, we see the Earth actually rising, casting off the blanket of introspection and bursting forth, refreshed and renewed. The promise is starting to be fulfilled, the first signs are being revealed, the green fingers are breaking through the Earth, moving towards the light of the Young God in his guise as the Sun King. He is also The Lord of the New Day, testing out his shaky limbs, becoming stronger and more confident as he shows himself to the World. He claps his hands together with the sheer joy of being born-again and blessed with his youth and exuberance. It is a time of seeds and of the egg. The prospect of birth, of ideas, dreams and all life, are waiting to hatch, waiting for their time, growing. The Goddess of the Moon is moving towards her half-phase, quickening inside Herself with the prospect of her new life within. She is still the slender dancer, but her maiden's light-footed glide is soon to be replaced by the grace and beauty of her own fertility, her motherhood. She will be mother of All Things. The moving Earth turns between the courtship rites of sun and moon, the youthful Lord and Lady. Upon the Earth there are increasing signs of their coming fruitfulness. The crocus, white butterbur, wood anemone, wild daffodil and flowering coltsfoot all appear, and the sap is rising in the wood.

The consummation of the marriage of the Lady and the Lord takes place at Beltaine (May 1st). The Queen of the May, with a diadem of dew-fresh flowers, takes the hand of the Jack in the Green who is bedecked with the new leaves of the newly greened wood, as they jump over the fire of life together. A transition is made as they leap over the symbolic blaze, a move made towards their changing. All is growth and change at this time, dry twigs to leafy boughs, buds to blossoms. As the Earth is planted with the seeds, so is the Moon Goddess made full by the Sun God, who both become the greater for the coupling.

This is the time of the blessing. The God, growing in his power, the sun reflecting his energy, climbing higher in the sky. He is filled by his own fertility, by his love for his Queen, glowing with the joy of life and Fathering All Life, as a part of the Great Dance. The Goddess, his Lady, is now at three-quarters of her fullness and she is becoming complete in her love, in all she is. In her happiness and beneficence, she bestows her gifts and blessings onto the land. She is at peace with all she is, she is not afraid to leave behind her Maiden-Self to become the mother of All. She is radiant in her new-Self, her sensual curves reflected in the petals of a marsh violet, the ripples in a puddle of spring rain or in the eye of a leaping doe. The Earth reflects the joy of the union, the creation which occurs from the joining of two opposites, in harmony. The people honoured the Lord and Lady, reflecting the cosmic union of Life, as they made love in the woods under the moon, and saw the sun rise anew at dawn. It is a time to create and to take joy in being part of creation.

The summer solstice (around June 21st) is the time when Father and mother Nature proudly display what it is that they have created both manifestly, and spiritually, between them. Their abundance is the abundance of All Life, their offspring is not guarded jealously but is displayed as a bounty to be enjoyed by all. The Sun God is once more triumphant as he beams down his approval onto the Earth, at the height of his power and vitality. He is The Crown of the Day, a beneficent and all-powerful ruler, at his zenith. The Lady, the Moon-mother, is brimming with life-enhancing lunar milk, her full breast offering her plenty. She is divine in her maternal love for the All, her life's blood reflected in the petal of a poppy, the flush of her cheek is the hue of wild basil. Her joy is our appreciation of her gifts. It is time to gather her flowers, for use in healing brews and infusions, and to dry them for later months. The summer Solstice is a time for pure joy, for sustaining the dreams and plans of Imbolg, for rejoicing in the Dance of Life, for being all that it is possible to be. It is a time of fruitful fulfilment of our Selves in our places in the Great Cosmic Oneness. A time to celebrate in song who we are and who we will be. The tune is the thrum of the Lifeforce which links us to all creation.

Lughnassad, or Lammas, (August 1st) follows upon the Year's Wheel as it turns slowly, once more, towards darkness. The peak of light and life has passed again but darkness is not yet apparent. The last of summer's bounty is around us to be taken stock of. We are able to enjoy the gifts of the mother and Father still, although they are standing back, their work done, their presence less active and exuberant. Their plenty is to be harvested, the first fruits to be tasted. The Moon-mother has birthed her only child, and although she watches tenderly over its progress on Earth, her part is played. As a good mother she knows when to allow her child to leave her and to make its own way. Soon, she will have a new role and she gathers her mantle of stars around herself to prepare. She is no longer full, but not quite waning. She waits, she watches, she is pleased. The Earth still stretches, contented, like a cat, under the Sun God's rays. The Lord is no longer the strong, virile hunter that he once was. He was the hunter and the hunted, the wild eyed stag and the wild eyed man. Now he is prepared to relinquish his power and potency for another year. He has Fathered well, and is pleased to have lost a little of his own light and heat in the process of creating abundance. He is a God entering middle age, his mellow light reflected in the colours of golden rod and tansy.

Mabon, or the Autumn Equinox (around September 21st) follows on from Lughnassad. It is the harvest festival, a gathering in of gifts both physical and spiritual. It is a reaping of what has been sown. The Lady is making a patchwork quilt for the Earth's coming slumber. She casts this over the land in the form of ploughed fields, once golden or green, now fallow or full of stubble. The Lord is The Bronze Man, his coat of many leaves is russet, amber and umber, the leaves in his greying beard are nut brown and sienna. He wears a crown of acorns and he walks across the land carrying his staff entwined with ivy. He stirs the four winds with the swirl of his cloak as he passes, and so too the winds of change. The Earth is yawning once more, withdrawing its lifeforce back into the core of its Self, pulling its energy through its pulsing veins to its heart and hearth. The Lady has brambles in her auburn tresses and she opens her arms, laughing, to the small creatures who come unto her to gather their harvests in. Her lips are rose-hips, smiling upon the land, but her eyes are becoming more distant. As she creates her quilt, she reflects inwards, becoming interned, returning inside herself as do the creatures she feeds. Lady-Moon is a waning crescent and the Lord of the Day is now the Lord of the Night.

Samhain (October 31st) is perhaps the most exciting of all festivals. Its old name is pronounced Sowen, but its modern equivalent, Hallowe'en, stirs up much feeling. The misinterpretation is that it is a time of evil, which is no more true of this Sabbat, or celebration, than of any other I have just described. The veils between this world and the Otherworlds are certainly thinner at this time, which may lead to fear by certain people who do not have an personal understanding of death, or of other levels of being. No festival or cycle is evil, nor is it an inversion of Christian belief. The seasonal cycles existed long before any Christian interpretation could be placed upon them, and as Satan is the dark reflection of the Christ principle 'he' has no place in Pagan symbology. Samhain stands on its own, as it always has and always will, open to personal interpretation.

I would suggest that as with anything, an item, a thought or a concept, it can be used or translated for good or ill. Without the will to transform it into a negative thing, a pair of scissors will be a helpful tool and not a weapon to stab with. So the nature cycles/festivals/Sabbats/ celebrations etc will always be there, will always be reflected in all life. It is only humanity's interpretation which differs and which can imply good or ill. It comes back to the point I made earlier, is darkness seen as bad, or the natural opposite and reflection of light, a necessary part of perception and being? There is a saying, "the soul would have no rainbow if the eyes had no tears". Without dark, how would we know the light? Knowing that everything is energies, knowing that everything is connected, that nature and the universe works in cycles, in circles, knowing these things we know that there is no evil, only ignorance and fear of the unknown. We are all a part of Samhain, and likewise, Beltaine, its opposite, its reflection, not of good and evil but of light and darkness. Pagan interpretation has no need of creating an enemy of the darkness, nor does it provide an opportunity for folk to fear the unknown.

At this time, the Lord and Lady chose to reveal secrets to those who ask, visions and trances come unbidden, prophesy is given, divination for the coming year reveals much, and the dead who remain discarnate are closer to our realms. We may speak with the spirits, using the correct precautions and approaches. We place the carved Jack-O-Lantern in the window to ward off unwanted mischevious spirits who may enter our physical and spiritual domain, whilst at the same time welcoming Jack himself in the guise of the Lord of Misrule. He will masquerade in the guise of many, with an air of mischief and merrymaking. The God is also a Cunning man, the Wizard or Merlin, who has his serious side as Guardian of the Veils, Storyteller and Shadowhunter, and who has great wisdom to be accessed. He can guide the seeker into the deeper Realms of Self.

The Lady in her aspect as the Crone, Wisewoman or Hag can share of her eternal, hidden mysteries. She throws open her cloak of midnight blue, studded with strands of starlight, and shows the seeker the truth of their own soul which can be found in her labyrinth. The Moon-Goddess is but a sliver of silver now, past her physical prime but filled entirely with the wisdom of her age. She rejoices still in this phase of her life, for she has loved and she has seen much, more than any younger woman has. She loves to welcome those who are unafraid to see her as she truly is at this time, and she will reveal her immense knowledge about all things if the seeker will face her, unadorned, unashamed to see themselves reflected, revealed in her dark pools. She is the shadow of the black cat crossing a garden path, she is the whispering voice within the cowrie shell, she is the heights and the depths, the firmament and the ocean floor. She is not all positive, she is not all negative. She is herself. She is a circle, a cycle completed.

Samhain was the Celtic time of New Year and the Lady reflects this as she returns to the hidden places within her own Womb-Self, into her Cauldron, into the circle of the cycle of Death and Rebirth. She is first and last, beginning and end, the mystery of All-Connection. The Crone of Samhain is a symbol, an illusionary visionary, and her symbology is of the all-consuming, all-providing, revealing, concealing, life-giving, life-taking Queen of Mysteries. The Lord of Night walks beside her, as always, clad in his animal skins. He walks with the beech nuts and fungi being crushed back into the Earth as he walks in boots of softest leather. She is his destiny and he is hers, and their time is coming.

Lastly, or firstly, Yule (celebrated around the Winter Solstice on December the twenty first). Yule connects as the time before Imbolg, the time when the powers of light and darkness battle over the domain of the Earth. The Lord fights within himself, as Lord of the Night and Lord of the New Day, and the eternal battle gives way, as it must, to the New Day. The Lord of Night gives over his crown to his successor, who is part of him and will return unto him. The old year then dies and gives way to the new, a conception of life, light and hope. The Lord and Lady never totally die, but the moment of their death and conception is of the same instant. They are transformed, brought forth from the Whole, from the Oneness that they make in perfect unison. They return from the Cauldron of Death and Rebirth, which holds everything, and yet nothing. The Lord and Lady then lie asleep, exhausted, under their blanket, embroidered with patterns of frost. They lie asleep under the hard earth, under a dark moon. Even as they rest, and the Earth rests, the Lord and Lady dream of their part in the forthcoming dance. At the Winter Solstice the cycle is done and begun, and the slumber can be filled with dreams looking both forwards and backwards. What went well? What could be worked upon in the new year? On Earth it is a season of withdrawing back to internal concerns and pursuits, of time spent with close relations and friends, and of appreciating the good things we have all made and created from the Fruits of the Year.

I would like to mention here, as a separate issue, that I did not refer to the Earth in the feminine, as is widely regarded as appropriate. I believe personally, that wholeness is only created by the matching of the two opposite, yet corresponding, energies of male and female. These energies can be expressed in any physical relationship, regardless of the bodies involved. It is the energies which are important, not the 'masks' of incarnate being, as I have previously stated. I fail to see how the Earth cannot also be composed of masculine energy, as is the reflective, gloriously diverse, selection of life which dwells there. To give the Earth a solely feminine status is to deny yet again that the male energy can be life-giving, sustaining, nurturing etc. To perpetuate this myth will not, I fear, help us in the balancing of energies we so badly require on our planet.

The above descriptions of the seasonal celebrations may appear naive and simplistic, or old-fashioned to a modern person. The symbology serves as well as any to describe our own parts in the Dance, and who we Be. My preferred way is to use rich imagery in keeping with my love of folklore and art. One may observe that my descriptions do not include a string of complicated God and Goddess titles. This is because I like to keep my interaction with the archetypal energies of male and female simple, and in-keeping with my old way of being. I do doubt if my French Wisewoman needed to invoke a myriad of Deities in order for her magic to work. As an isolated soul, she worked on her own tradition, passed down to her, and her own perceptions of the energies she worked with. Thus, my use of terms like 'Lord of the New Day' evokes powerful imagery which fits the energies of the aspect of maleness which I wish to evoke. Simplicity is my key. In a similar way, I like to keep magical tools and practice as natural and as close to my perceived 'old approach'. I think that all of my magical and spiritual practices would have taken place out of doors, with full contact with the elements and the moon or sun.

As Marian Green suggests in her magical books, why should we worry about the robes we chose to work in when we are indoors, after all, we have chosen to 'wear' a house! To create a sacred space for such workings I would have used the items I had in my vicinity, which adequately represented the energies I wished to work with. Sacred space would be used as a protected place to work in, but also creating such space creates a psychological distance between everyday life and practice and the time spent with the Otherworlds. If one had personal protection (as previously described), then the need for a secondary protection is a formality. The really important role of sacred space is to create that special area where one can cast off the roles and pressures of daily life. The space can be as simple as casting a circle of salt around one's Self whilst moving clockwise (as the sun travels, deosil). This only works if one perceives that one is creating a delineation between the Worlds by the action of casting. Remember, it is the focus of will and visualisation which works, not the action. This salt circle can be cleared afterwards by sweeping with a broom (traditionally used to clear negative energy, but also symbolically appropriate to sweep up one's space). The sweeping should be done anti-clockwise (widdershins, against the suns pattern). This salt casting gives two of the components, protection and a different space. A third way of gaining extra power and assistance in the act of creating your space, is to invoke the four quarters, or elements, and the symbolic guardians thereof.

This is important when one is to undertake a ritual. A ritual is more than a focused meditation or visualisation which may be undertaken in the sacred space. Such a focussed act or visualisation may be doing some absent healing or spirit rescue or clearance (as discussed previously) or it may be sending positive energies for a set outcome to a person who has asked for specific help. Any act of controlled meditation, for the good of others or the All, may be undertaken in the basic circle. A more complex set of gestures or acts of directed will may need a greater protection/injection of outside power. If one considers it, it is obvious the Wisewoman/practitioner of natural magic/Druid/Green Witch etc should relate to nature's elements when requiring help. They are forces in their own right, and ones we all know of and experience daily. To work with them is to have respect. One is not harnessing or controlling them, far from it! They have decided to work with you in the rite.

If one can imagine, the circle you are about to cast represents the Great Cauldron, which, if one is in possession of such an actual item, as the old practitioners probably would have been (a household object) then one can place it in the centre, as a focus. The cauldron can be filled with water, or seasonal fruit and flowers, to represent its birthing of All Life. The other tools which are required (one is working with energies, so one needs tools) must represent the four elements. Therefore, in basic Wisewoman terms, the north quarter (Earth) can be marked with a stone, the east (air) could be a feather, the south (fire) a candle and the west (water) a sea shell. These points are marked out around the central point, or cauldron, which also represents the fifth element, ether. One should always move clockwise around the compass points to invoke the guardians and visualise the sacred circle-space of ritual.

A circle is always used, as nature is cyclic, and so we must work with the flow. The ritual gestures which one employs are always entirely personal, and will work best if they are pleasing to the ear and eye, and so the soul, of the participant. To invoke, summon or request the presence of energies within your sacred space, one will probably find that poetry, rhythmic verse or song is most pleasing.

With the four elements of the four quarters, beginning with north, one must employ the blend of spoken word, visualisation and manifest act which we have already discussed. One must ask for the presence of the Guardians of the Realms of Earth firstly, facing north, holding the manifest representation of the energy. Whilst reciting a simple invocation which could be "O Guardians of the Watchtowers of the North, ye spirits of Earth, I ask that you be present within my circle, to bless and protect my work here" (one should focus upon the element which one wishes to attract, in the case of earth then this could be various aspects including green fields, trees, animals, mountains, stones, hillsides) and once a connection has been made with the element through visualisation, the request should be completed with "so may it be".

Once again, the more respect one gives to the very real powers involved, the more cooperation will be given. Also, of course, the matter of focus and clear visualisation is paramount for successful workings. The mind should not be cluttered with manifest worry or material ponderings, but one should have entered sacred space with a clear head. One is only a time waster if the main concerns are dramatic effect and showmanship. All the smoke and arm waving in the world cannot compensate for focus and directed will.

The calling of the elemental energies is repeated in each quarter until the circle is complete. A time of focus on the fifth element, the central hub of the Wheel of Life, can be achieved as one sits quietly in the centre of the circle. The All, or One, of the cosmic cauldron can be imaged as a very personal thing, and cannot be described by another save as, perhaps, the void or cosmic womb/tomb. Thus is the circle complete.

At the end of any working or ritual within the space, one must remember to thank and ask the leave of any spirit, energy or force one has requested. Thus the quarters are visited again, in turn, and the Guardians thanked and bid farewell. To deny the energies and elementals this courtesy is to not give acknowledgement to their very real presence. I know a couple who forgot to ask

126

leave of the west quarter when they had finished a magical working, and lo and behold, they had terrible floods in their home the next day! Imagine the power of waterfalls, volcanoes, earthquakes and hurricanes, these are the elements you are asking into your circle! A lack of respect is both rude and foolish; it is not wise to forget who you are working with!

As this is not a magical 'how to do' manual, I am not inclined to list a set of rituals and spells to be performed in circle. I will suggest that one thinks about how it is possible to honour the Earth, all life and traditions, by reflecting the seasonal celebrations in appropriate ways within sacred space. Perhaps at Samhain it would be appropriate to sit in circle and meditate on the ancestors and departed wise spirits who may have guidance for others which will come through one as a channel. Perhaps at Beltaine it would be fitting to invite the energies of the Lord and Lady into circle, in their guise of Robin-in-the Hood and the Lady Marian, and to celebrate their union and the coming of summer with a blessing of bread and wine. It is also befitting to dedicate a part of Self to the season, perhaps a commitment to cleaning up the local woods?

If one is adopting the manner of the traditional wise one, then simple tools may be employed as concecrated symbolic tools to direct energy. A magical knife (traditionally black handled, to absorb energy, which is used to cut herbs etc. and which is preferably hand made) may be used to represent the God energy. This use of the knife to direct energy represents the male energies of spring, as the Cosmic Phallus, maleness as non-threatening but powerful, potent and alive. Also, a chalice, fashioned with intention from clay, which was baked and hand-painted, is the Goddess, representing her giving and receiving energy, as we pour our love into her and taste of her gifts. The knife can be placed inside the chalice as a sign of the union, we may drink of the chalice and direct the power of the knife point. This is not passive and active, dominant and dominator, but the harmonious exchange of two vitally important components, eternally switching roles.

I suggest such items should be hand-crafted and painted as again it is the effort and focus which imbue the tools with personal power, the focus of handling and creating which transforms a knife into a symbolic tool. Items may be consecrated by placing them in salt water, or a dish of salt, but this is only necessary if the items are not hand-made. The tools should be dedicated to the purpose one intends, within sacred space. Such a Beltaine act should reflect the season of joy, celebration and union/communion. Blessings can be asked for as personal favours to those in need, and to the Land. Asking for things for one Self is not appropriate, as he or she who walks on the path with truth and a glad heart, despite hardship, is one who is truly blessed and provided for. To ask for favours for others is to intercede for the person, and this is good. The more one does for others, magically and astrally in meditation, the more one gains personally in knowledge and understanding. With this spiritual reward in mind, I believe in never charging financially for spiritual guidance. I accept donations only in fair exchange, and such donations may be of food or of any craft of which the receiver wishes to share.

Interacting with the energies of the One through ritual acts is to be a channel for 'divine' energies. One can 'become' the Lord and Lady through such powerful connection, by focussing entirely on their energies. If one works within the seasonal festivals and moon-phases, all the better. Working with the Crone at Midsummer is untimely, for instance. As is trying to do a creative ritual during a dark moon. To dance the dance of magic is to be aware of the greater Dance. As a Walker between the Worlds, in the created space between the Worlds, everything is possible, with will, morality and an awareness of the Web of Life, the matrix of energies of which we are a part.

As a point of caution here, one should remember that the circle exists as a place which has been created astrally, by visualisation and will, as well as manifestly. One should not step out of it unless a 'door' is cut in the energy which surrounds you. Using the black handled knife, or a magic wand of hazel wood, or a wooden spoon, or even a pointed finger, 'cut' a doorway in the circle's edge, imagining the energy spreading upwards, like a curved wall. The door must be 'closed' behind you as you step out, otherwise the astral floaters and drifters will have full access to your safe place. The circle shines out on the astral, and so it will attract something unwanted if you leave it open and vulnerable. To re-enter, re-open the doorway and close it on the inside of the circle. Try to avoid exiting and re-entering. Nothing should be so urgent as for one to have to do this, toilet requirements should be dealt with before setting up the circle, if possible!

I actually witnessed several cats wandering in and out of a circle which had been cast by the High Priestess of a Coven, once. This gave me no confidence in the safety or sacredness of the circle I was inside, as she obviously had no respect for its boundaries letting cats wander through it. She even broke circle to exit with one of them, and did not appear to let herself out or in! If she had complained of poltergeist activity in her home afterwards, I would not have been at all surprised!

This brings me neatly onto the working of magic, and the practice of spirituality and psychism, in the Coven set-up. There is much mystery surrounding the Coven, and as I have now experienced two separate groups, I would like to share my knowledge of group work. It was Jack who introduced me to the group which worked in Bedfordshire, even though he appeared to have a list of complaints as long as his arm about them. The personalities involved are irrelevant, but the practice involved is a good example for discussion. Also, I enjoy dispelling the mystique which people often court when involved in 'elite', hidden bands of practitioners. I do not subscribe to the vision of a Witch or member of any Coven or group, as being imbued with fantastic powers or chosen knowledge. I enjoy talking to anyone and everyone about my work, beliefs and actions, not to blow my own trumpet, but to dispel confusion, separatism and the inevitable fear and ignorance. The more folk who seek to nurture the 'us and them' myth, the less understanding or tolerance there will be of the traditional practices of the psychics, Druids, Wiccans and followers of the older ways.

I want my practices and ideas to be simple enough to be used by anyone, for the good of All, and the more who attune to the seasonal cycles, and feel a part them, the better for the Earth. Not only that, I want people to be less afraid of the Otherworlds and to re-contact their intuitive Selves, their guides, the spirit realms and all other real, omnipresent energies which affect everything and anyone. I do not feel this is being best achieved by being elitist and sweeping about in a velvet cloak trying to look all-powerful. I do not suggest that it is only group or Coven practitioner who behaves thus. But I would like to give the 'outsider' a peek under the heavy shroud of secrets which can appear to be in operation. I do accept that Pagan practice was not always so tolerated, but now it is not actually illegal, and greater steps are being taken by more and more brave folk to 'come out', it would be nice if we could all do our bit to dispel ignorance.

My experiences of Coven work was of a group, usually of thirteen men and women (the old practice reflected in Christ's disciples?) who gathered to celebrate the Esbats (full moon rites) and seasonal festivals. They also met for group psychic 'practice' (work with tarot, Zennor-cards, aura reading, healing etc). Their group belief and magical almanac was the Book of Shadows which must be faithfully copied out by the beginner before they may become an initiate into full membership. Hence there is an apprenticeship, which is usually undertaken regardless of the individual's previous experiences of psychism and magic.

Thus, a system evolves of master/teacher and student/neophyte. Because of the basic human flaw of needing to compete, this hierarchy can become tense and a subject of dispute. Often the initiate may know more about an area than the High Priest and Priestess. I believe that the only way ahead is to share, and so I could not feel comfortable within this competitive structure of 'levels', although it can work well for one who wishes to pass through various structured grades, on a tried and tested path, which works for others. The reasons that make it a viable system which works for many are as follows.

Group energies; A group can raise far more power than the individual. This great power can be directed into healing, spell casting, or charging an item, like a ring, with positive energy for use as a talisman. Of course, such a belt of energy can go astray if all in the group are not directly focused. Hence the need for the High Priestess and her partner (the reflection of the Lady/Goddess/female principle and her consort)to put the initiate through various tests of their ability and will to work as part of a collective. A group is a circuit, a circle of power and so weak links are not welcomed easily into the chain. Such power can cause havoc if allowed to fly free from the group's concentrated effort, causing much astral, and so manifest, chaos.

I witnessed a huge group ritual which included the raising of energy. The energy was allowed simply to fly free as the group broke up in confusion towards the end of the raising. I saw people staggering off in all directions, with dreadful headaches. Apparently, this enormous group had previously done this and one woman had gotten in to her car immediately afterwards and crashed into a wall. Groups need to work as one, as a whole. Renegades, or the reluctant, should rightly be put through grades, until they can be trusted to be a part of the circuit. The problems of ego can be the very difficulties which break up the circle and jealousy can distract away from the actual purpose. The group energies must be harmonious, and the group must act as one, but this can be easier said than done. Such power can be used for good, or it can cause ill. In the former instance, a group rite, or working, will be a very positive thing indeed.

Reassurance; As I know to my detriment, loneliness and isolation can cause fear of one's Self, and so natural gifts become one's enemy to be fought. With the support of Coven, or group, members, one can share in other's triumphs, mistakes and experiences. One can gain advice and support, and hopefully the confidence to tackle problems. One can also feel intimidated by those who know more and are somehow 'better' than they. But a good Coven should be a life-line and a family to the beginner or the indisciplined, ignorant psychic.

A Coven helps the 'Non-Sensitive'; Of course, there is a degree of sensitivity in everyone, but as with everything there are levels of sensitivity. Remember, we are discussing a natural latent ability, as well as a skill. This can be best likened to art work. Some are natural creative artists, others have a little access to their ability but have learned the necessary skills to get by. A lesser sensitive may have excellent practical skills, or have wonderful counselling skills, or be a

130

superb writer of magical poetry, but they may lack the open channels of a true psychic. Such folk may have the will but not the way to work alone, where they may get stuck or have no luck in communicating with the Otherworlds. However, as a link in the group chain, they are strong and dedicated.

Such a non-sensitive can then work magic and enjoy spiritual communion without feeling as if they are incapable. They form a valued and vital part of the overall collective. The sum of the Coven is greater than the individual parts.

The reason I did not join the Coven was entirely different. I felt that I was not happy with the level of the energies raised at a Samhain rite. Perhaps as I am so sensitive I was used to feeling more on such an important magical occasion? Perhaps it was because I did not feel inspired to visualise the element of water whilst I stared at the sofa and sideboard in the High Priest's front room? (I only practice outside if I can help it and I found the incongruous indoor surroundings in which the Coven cast their circles a little too off-putting. I like to feel the elements and to see them when I am calling upon them for help. I can understand why people work magic indoors, privacy, lack of green space in a city, chilly or wet weather, but I would rather walk a mile in warm clothes with the rain on my face, than I would put on a fancy robe in the glow of a gas fire. To each his own, but that is why I did not feel happy.)

Perhaps I did not join them because, on the eve of the festival which was so important for spirit communion and contact with the Other Realms, the Priestess gave us five minutes of the rite to talk to the dead. I had hardly gone into a state of relaxation by then, let alone reached out to any willing communicant! I simply could not do things double-quick so that the rite would be done in time for the wine and cheese party afterwards! Obviously, social bonding is important to the group/Coven but I felt this was so at the detriment of going about the actual business of being a magical practitioner.

Jack and I agreed on this, we were used to taking all night for our workings if necessary, and someone calling time on us was not appreciated. Jack was, at that time, a Free Bard of Caer Abri and by contrast I attended a rite at Avebury stone circle with him. He could no longer attend the Coven meets, even though he was initiated, as he felt that these Druid rites at Avebury, which were held in the open air, were far more balanced. There is a democratic process at the Avebury (Caer Abri) seasonal rites, and any willing person from any magical tradition can volunteer to offer a poem, song, blessing or representation of the elemental Guardians. I enjoyed the way that there was no leader in the group, as such, only a man who welcomed and facilitated interaction with the site and the season. As I have never been one to approach a site, be it regarded as sacred, or one that I personally connect to, with a set outcome in mind, the open circles appealed to me.

Had I have gone to Barbury Castle, in 1991, with a set, fixed idea of what I would find or see, I would never have been open enough to have picked up the information about my guide. The prospect of visiting a site with hands on hips, demanding a certain response, is alien to me. I do prefer to work with the energies as I find them on that day, at that time of year, and this was how I could respond to the primarily Druid-influenced Caer Abri workings in the landscape. This is not a group to join, nor to be initiated into as such, although one can become a Free Bard within the circle. I now attend the rites when I feel I would like magical company, it is that flexible and approachable.

Jack was a natural solitary worker, as was I, and the experience with the Coven was not one he or I regretted. Our magical practice and spirit contact was more based on free-flowing with nature, in nature. The Coven had been about adhering to strict practice by the book, indoors, with the emphasis on complicated acts of 'high-magic' and the communing with named Deities. I would not state that the Coven was wrong, by any means. Their acts work, within their boundaries and expectations, and they work for the good. I was just very different to them, and indeed, to Jack.

I learned from both he and from them. After working with him, and them, and attending the outdoor, organic celebrations of the Bards of Caer Abri, I found I understood myself far more. I could 'see' clearer in meditation as to what I was, who I had been and who I would become. I knew that Jack couldn't help me with my personal quest, my search for the truth and for Julien. I needed verification of my life in France, and I wondered about travelling alone to the area to see if I could discover any records or clues. I did not have the money, nor the psychic confidence, required to face such a memory in reality. Yet I willed, more than anything, for the truth to be revealed to me in a tangible way. I needed proof of the memory I was basing my whole new life upon. I knew it in my heart, truly. But I really needed verification.

I did not have to wait for a trip to France, for my verification came to me. The fates brought Julien De Saint Pierre back into my life, mere months after my first remembering him.

Chapter Five

"Live your beliefs and you can turn the world around".
Quote from Henry Thoreau taken from *'Begin it Now'* (In-Tune, 1987)

When I first met the man who had been Julien de Saint Pierre again, he was a total stranger to me in this incarnation. Yet something prompted me to forget embarrassment or social etiquette to rush over to him and proclaim "I know you!" I had not thought out what I would say next, yet I knew I must say that, going with my new-found gut-response to all things. I did not recognise the man (who I shall refer to as Martin throughout the text) as Julien, but as another past-life love whose name had been Michael O'Sullivan.

I was not pre-disposed to running up to strange men in public places to regale them with a bad case of New-Age chat up lines but I was utterly convinced that I knew the man. He resembled closely a man I had 'seen' in a life in the 1500s in Southern Ireland. The man I saw before me in the nineteen nineties was extraordinarily like the ex-love of my past incarnation and I felt strongly that it was indeed he. As I was constantly focussed on Julien, I did not expect to find another love, Michael, walking back into my life unprompted. I did not wish to influence Martin's recall of his life with me, had there ever been one, so I did not tell him who I thought he had been. I thought I would wait to see if he had any thoughts or feelings of his own on the matter.

For some years, leading up until the time I met Martin, I had been partner to a man named Wayne. He was an Irish Catholic who disliked my psychism and my questing. We fought regularly and had a stormy relationship which often appeared pointless and unpleasant. Something kept Wayne and I locked together, even though it was a pattern of destruction. Wayne was suspicious and jealous of me, even though I am an inordinately faithful and loyal soul. Our arguments took on epic proportions, with me throwing his clothes into a skip to try and get him out of my life. Somehow he always returned and I let him, as if we were somehow magnetised. When I left him, he would somehow locate my new residence, as if he were fitted with a radar for me. No matter how skillfully I hid from him, he would return, and the fights would continue, I would hit him unceremoniously over the head with milkbottles and he would psychologically torment me. Wayne abhorred my understanding of my Wisewoman Self as he did not approve of my empowerment through Self-knowledge.

I asked to be shown, in meditation, the reasons for our dubious connection and apparent inability to split up successfully. As my confidence grew, my meditations gave me clarity on the matter. I was shown, in the manner of a dream-like, past-life recall, that I had known Wayne before in another life. His name had been Brian, and we had lived unhappily in Ireland together, in the sixteenth century. Brian had been a bear of a man with ruddy cheeks and a drink problem. He had been reasonably wealthy and had, effectively, bought me from my family. I was an attractive girl, wild of spirit, and this was what enchanted Brian with me, yet made him fear me. He would go drinking with his friends, only to return in a drunken fury, convinced I had been with other men in his absence. He would make free with his swinging fists and I would be hurt and deeply resentful. I began to rebel and go out when I was alone. Before, I had not been unfaithful, but had stayed in at home in isolation, and still he had beaten me. I decided to have some fun, and get beaten anyway. With my rebellious streak I enjoyed dancing with the tinker children and gypsy people who passed through. In this way, I fell in love with a travelling man who made music for me. A man with twinkling eyes and a salt-and pepper moustache called Michael.

I had never loved Brian, but I felt sorry for him, deep down. But I was passionate for Michael. We would sneak into the barn together in the afternoons and there we would make love and be happy. We made our plans about running away as we lay in the hay. I was scared of Brian finding out before we were able to leave the area and sadly my fears became real. Brian came home unexpectedly one afternoon after being tipped off by a villager as to my whereabouts, and with whom. Incensed, Brian had brought his 'heavies' with him to put an end to Michael O'Sullivan. They beat him to death in the barn whilst I ran away screaming. I kept on running and running blindly onwards all day and night. I did not stop, driven by grief as I was, until I dropped and I slept where I was. I half expected Brian to come for me in the darkness, but he did not. I was heart -broken and I saw no future for myself. I simply 'gave up' and lost my will to live.

For days I lay where I had fallen, by an outcrop of rocks. I saw nobody, did nothing and waited to die. I eventually passed away from exposure and lack of nourishment, as well as from my pain and loss. I had felt a mixture of hate, pity and sadness as I rose from my body and came back from the recall into the meditation. Wayne had been Brian and that was why we could not get on, but were connected by guilt and anger. Of course, Wayne would not consider such an idea as he was vehemently against psychism. He had witnessed enough strange events in his time, because of me, but they terrified him and he retreated further into his superstitious Catholicism. He did not want me to meddle in the hidden things which frightened him. He did not understand that I had no choice.

I began a correspondence with the man Martin, as it had appeared from our initial meeting that we had much in common. The whole encounter and letter exchange was platonic and was entirely based on a sharing of magical ideas and knowledge, which moved on to discussing our experiences. I dared to mention in one letter that I thought his name was Michael. I said no more than that but I was shocked by his positive response. In his next letter he said that he had always thought of Michael as his true name, and that other psychics had mentioned this to him too. He had also, it transpired, had a strong connection with Ireland and he believed he had an Irish soul-link. He had been watching a film about Irish life, sometime before our initial meeting, and he had heard a woman calling to him on the astral levels. Finally, Martin asked if I had any recollection of a life in Ireland, and did County Clare have any meaning for me? I remember the tears of joy and pain coursing down my cheeks as I read the letter which confirmed that the man Martin had been my once-love, Michael. I also realised that Wayne, Martin and I were somehow destined to replay and change the event which we had been party to centuries earlier. The characters of Brian, Michael and Mary (as I was) had been transposed into their modern equivalents, but the souls involved were the same. Hopefully the scenario would be played out in order to get it right, second time around.

How this incident worked out, with all its complexities, is irrelevant to the point I am making. Nobody died in this lifetime and my relationship with Wayne(Brian) is now finally over. What is important, in this example, is the need for one soul to see another again in a subsequent incarnation. In my case, I had no desire to meet the Wayne/Brian character again, as our soul encounter in Ireland had been violent and unpleasant. However, Wayne/Brian had wished to meet me again, and perhaps wanted, on some higher level, to attempt to make amends. This had failed miserably as we were as incompatible as it was possible for two souls to be. I certainly did not view him as a bad person, but our souls' liaison would always be disharmonious. Obviously Wayne/Brian's connection and desire to see me was far stronger than mine to see him.

There was also the third part involved; Martin/Michael had no desire to meet his adversary again, but he had wished to meet me. I had also desired, in my soul, to meet Martin/Michael. One can observe that the fates brought us together for our individual needs to be met. With the all-important overview of a situation, one can understand that one soul does not operate in isolation in the universe, and that our lives are made by the complex interaction and needs of many souls. Thus it is folly to consider only one's personal soul needs in karmic, rein-carnatory terms, as others have desired to re-connect with us for their own reasons and purposes, however undesirable they are to us. The stronger the emotional link in another life, be it good, like love, or destructive, like guilt, the more likely it is that two souls will meet again. This is why I try not to focus and dwell on those who have done me wrong or hurt me in my lives as I do not wish to see them again under any circumstance, but I must accept that they wish to see me. It is wise to wish to gain insights into a soul like Wayne's, as some root cause must have warped his soul into the suspicious, twisted thing it became. No soul is created with such innate suspicions, but Wayne had obviously had many lives of betrayal or hurt to become who he has in twentieth century England. To his soul, a matter of centuries between our meeting was nothing, a blink of an eye. Time in the Other Realms has no meaning, a thought can be enough to move the soul from one way of being to another. Thus Wayne's soul may have waited and watched until the moment which was fortuitous for his incarnation into his current life, in order for him to meet us both again. Had I not have been a Wisewoman in this life, then I would have had no idea of what was happening between Wayne and I, and so I probably would have suffered a miserable life trapped within our doomed relationship. Life almost kept pushing me back into the situation with Wayne, and he kept pursuing me, and so we would have staggered on and on.

As it is, at least there is no chance of our connection being carried over into yet another life. The whole scenario with Martin was the resolution that we all needed, and I am convinced that Wayne's soul waited around with me until Martin could be brought into our complex web of energies. Thus solved, I do not hang onto my past link to Wayne with regret or unpleasant thoughts. Similarly with others who I know have wished to form a bond by exchanging insults and unhappiness, I have refused to make that astral link. So, as my persecutors in medieval France are lost to me, so will be the incompatible souls who I encounter in this life. Unless it is they who desire a further encounter in future lives. All I can do is not feed that desire by interaction with them.

With the Wayne problem, I could have spoken to his soul on the astral levels in order to understand him more fully. Using the method described previously, I could have asked that his Higher Self be present within the astral circle of light, which I would visualise. If he was willing, on a deeper subconscious level, to do this, I could have found out motivations and had insights into aspects of Wayne's Self which his manifest Being had no idea about. With all credit, Martin also had this ability to access Wayne's Self on the astral, and he could have even attacked it. Wayne continued to wish to be as psychic as a brick and so Martin, or I, could have taken advantage of him by affecting his Self in meditation and with magic (if magic is taken as the direction of one's will). This would have been totally against the tenet of 'harm none' and so the only way to behave ethically was to respect the needs of Wayne's Self and to reason with it and strike a bargain. As Martin had been brutally murdered by Wayne in that past life, it was encouraging to see him want to reason with Wayne, rather than obliterating him in revenge. Astral meddling and attack can be just as devastating as physical harm. As Wayne's Self was indebted to Martin, as it had taken his life before, Wayne's Self was obliged to do Martin's bidding in whatever way was reasonable. However, Martin's integrity forbade him from using this 'power trip' and so the conflict was resolved by Soul-Negotiation.

It was through our association with Ireland that Martin began to reveal other aspects of himself to me. This outpouring included a revelation that he had had much trouble in this incarnation due to one he had had in medieval France. As Martin was eleven years my senior, he had experienced his recall of France before I had even come to terms with my psychism. One of Martin's letters sent shivers down my spine in that it revealed he had been burned at the stake in France in the thirteen hundreds. He wrote of his life near Avignon with such grief and pain that I knew that he was writing from his own souls memory.

At this point in our correspondence, we had met twice, and so our physical connection was no strong enough for the recall to have been a shared delusion. Besides this, he had remembered the life as Julien de Saint Pierre back in nineteen eighty, when I had still been a schoolgirl troubled by poltergeists. He had been a healer, training at a centre in Scotland, and had gone into a meditation there which had lead him to the devastating recall of his horrific death by fire. In response to this recall, he had suffered a physical response in that his whole body, save his back, had broken out in weeping sores and scabs which suppurated. Thus he had had to leave his healing training, as he was in too much pain and his appearance was frightening to the clients. For almost a year he remained with the appearance of having been badly burned all over, and no medical opinion could explain the phenomenon to him. This was a time of introspection and psychic opening for him, and he had then remembered his entire life as Julien, in France.

I had never once mentioned this life to him, but his letter said it all to me. It was astonishing to read something which had been my secret, the subject of my yearning, for so long. In the validation of my own recall, I understood that all I saw, felt and witnessed as a psychic was not somehow my own delusion. The astral and Otherworlds existed and reincarnation existed. I would never expound these discoveries as absolute factual truth, but for me, I had all the validation I needed. Martin was able to fill in all the missing pieces of my life in France. He could tell me where he had been and what he did when he was not in the woods with me and he told me what had happened after I had left the wood. He described the same life as the one I had known, the same meetings under the trees, and so I believed all he said about his experiences in the town. He said how he had been helping a woman he loved to escape into the woods and that he had returned to the town in order to put her persecutors off the trail. However, he was tricked by a woman he had trusted with information, as she turned out to be the lover of a Captain of the Guard. Hence, his own capture and torture, which has applied in order to extract more information about other 'witches', in hiding or no. He recalled yelling "I am not a witch!" just as I had done. He balked against this label as he perceived himself as a healer, Seer and recluse.

He had gone to dwell in the woods, with brief visits to town to heal the sick and disturbed, after his sister had been captured by men and taken away. He had tried to save her, and he had also tried to save the woman in the woods, and both times he thought he had failed. He wrote to me that he had met his sister of that life in this life, and that she too recalled Avignon, the country around it and the events of the past. He had put things right with her, and also been given vital validation of his story with her own recall. Also he had met the woman who had turned him in to the Captain of the Guard, and he had received some verification from her as to authenticity of his far-memory. So, not only did Martin recall the French life, but two other folk remembered it too, entirely independently.

He said to me that he had been an outcast in that life and that the skin condition he had had in this life had also made him undesirable and alone. The burn-like marks had faded with time and with his understanding of their origin. He pointed out how they had been everywhere but on his back where he would have been tied to the stake. He was, like me, not seeking revenge on the people who committed this barbarous act of burning innocents. His torture had extracted no wild confessions or admissions of Satanic worship. He did not see himself as being the Christian version of a witch, in league with devils, as a magician or sorcerer. He was just a simple man who did all he could to help people. For this, he was taken, in the same wooden cart/cell as I too had recalled and he was burned with two other people. One of them had been me. It was then that he asked me if I remembered it too.

I am sharing this verification with you, this personal truth which traversed the centuries, in order to share the satisfaction of knowing that one can trust one's own vision and feelings. My revelations and dreams were not mad but truly gave me insights. I wept with relief as I accepted the actual reality that I had once been a Wisewoman and so I was again. To listen to Self, to that eternal part which knows, is the only way to understand. If one's soul has chosen to bring up images, feelings, memories, then it is trying to teach one and so an openness of heart and mind should be exercised. If this openness exists, then the fates can step in and the wheel of destiny can turn for all involved. Not everyone will remember their lives, as it is not appropriate for all to do so, but everyone can access their Essential Self if they wish, and everyone can listen to their Eternal Wiseperson Being. Books have their place, for support on ones journey, but they cannot sustain a person to the exclusion of all else. Sustenance comes primarily from the Self, in all it was, is and will be.

My postal connection with Martin continued, and strangely, more recall followed. We did not have the capacity to be telepathing so strongly, as our physical link remained weak. I would state that the relevance of my revealing our recall is that it can be observed how the recall acted as a trigger, a confirmation and an inspiration. We both, spontaneously, began to have far memories of a third life in Italy. For me, these images were a clarification of certain fragments I had had, long before I had met Martin. Once, I had actually spontaneously gone into a full trance, and disappeared fully into a 'Roman' life. We decided that we would not share the details of our personal recall until we had met, thus cataloguing the events separately as to avoid tuning in to each others realities.

I was able to relax into working with my Self in recall, meditation and visualisation, using the mini-regression technique I adapted from Richard's 'monk' session. I no longer saw myself as dangerous or slightly mad and I knew I was acting in safety and with clarity. I knew how to access memory and for what reasons I acted. The memories threw up various strange concepts. I had been an Italian woman named Sabine who kept a Mithraic temple with her sister Vada. I had no idea what Mithraism was, and so I was careful to note down as much as I could in order to do some thorough research on the subject, after I had done my recalling. I did not wish fact to affect my vision, twisting what I saw with the knowledge of the historical research I had done.

So I continued to note what I saw. The story was that my sister and I were the well-to-do, happy-go-lucky daughters of a man called Calpurnius. He was a high ranking soldier who was stationed outside of Italy with our brother. We lived with our mother, Lavinia, in a gracious villa on a hill which was surrounded by olive groves and vineyards. Our duties were simple as regards the Mithraeum, we had to keep it clean and stocked with fresh fruit, flowers and water or wine. We performed our devotions there in solitude as we were not part of the actual religious group which met there, but at the same time we were a vital and respected part of the organisation. Vada, my twin, was the Keeper of the Keys, which meant that she was responsible for the access to a secret network of tunnels and caves under the ground, with waterways and boats. Some of the places within the network were used for ritual (for instance, there was a chamber with a hole in the roof which allowed the Solstice sunlight to come through at Midwinter. Also there was a woman's sanctuary which was a

140

place of teaching and ceremony.) The rest of the network lead to the sea, by a complicated set of directions. It was meant for escape purposes.

As Calpurnius was a powerful and respected follower of the Sun God, Mithras, we too shared in a little of his authority and reverence. We had a pleasant existence and we enjoyed our role. Women of our position appeared to have been treated well, and I recalled a safety and security which is absent in my life today. All was well in the life of Sabine. I recalled with special interest a ritual which Vada and I attended which involved a beaten gold plate being held up to the Midsummer sun by the acting Priest. This made the appearance of the Priest holding the sun in his hands as the disc became aflame with the strongest light of the year. Vada and I were allowed to be present at the ritual as we had furnished the arena for the outdoor ceremony, and also I thought it was the most important act of the Mithraic year. Mithras had many associated lesser Deities, but his main Lady appeared to have been Cybele, a moon Goddess whose name I acquired in meditation. Having never been an adherent to complex Deity names or structures, I had no idea if the name was appropriate or not.

In this somewhat idyllic life there came a destroyer. A man, Alexander, a Christian spy, was sent to infiltrate our ranks. He initially tried to court Vada but she was unconvinced of his charm and manner. Her rejection of him annoyed him enormously and so he followed her into the caves one day to see her as The Keeper of the Keys. Vada and I were unused to such persistence and she became afraid of him. I decided that I would be at the gates to the network on the next occasion, and that I would confront him. This shows our absolute certainty that we would be treated respectfully for who we were, as I had no doubt that Alexander would adhere to my wishes. We did not wish to embarrass him by publicly berating him for his actions and so I decided to discretely speak to him in the chambers.

We still did not know that he was not of our order, but a spy. Hence, he did not behave as we were used to the worshippers of Mithras behaving. He did not appreciate being told what to do by a mere woman and so he stole the keys from me and forced me down into the water inside the first cave. He tried to drown me and so I pretended to be dead. I stopped struggling and I believe he ran off, afraid to have murdered someone so publicly noted. He went with the keys to our sacred gate and so his Christian infiltrators were bound to discover what we 'Godless Pagans' got up to in our sacred places. With this same lack of respect, Vada was attacked soon afterwards as she tended the flowers in a small antechamber.

As I had not been killed by Alexander, I remained a living threat to his security in the locale. Our area was one of the remaining Pagan strongholds and so he had to be careful how he went about. Vada and I were bound, back to back, by our braids of hair and we were branded with the mark of the Pagan, which the Christians were using at that time. We were useless to them as we would not speak of what we did, as we were, in fact, only able to participate up to a certain level in the Cult of Mithras. For some reason, the Christian captors seemed reluctant to damage us further, no doubt seeing us weak and expendable women within their own lights, but knowing that this was not so within the area in which we lived. They made a total mess of their approach to us, and having defiled us with their brand they left us be.

For our own Self-respect we knew we had to flee the area. We had lost the sacred Keys to the Christians and we were, personally, too humiliated to continue in our duties. Our sense of pride was enormous and we had let the Cult down. We had to cut our braids off to get free, which was another dreadful thing, to us. We said only a hurried goodbye to our mother Lavinia as we were to leave that night, via the network of tunnels. It was a long and hazardous journey. We would meet with the boat there which would come in at the required signal and bear us out of Italy. It was a terrible thing for us and the caves and caverns seemed terrifying in the dark, some dreadfully narrow and perilous to squeeze through. My final recall was of journeying to a place called Macedonia, where we lived out the rest of our lives, reduced to treading grapes, stripped of our former glories. It was a friendly environment there, but we died in misery that we had lost the life we had loved through another's folly.

When Martin and I met to collate and clarify these vivid memories I was amazed by some of the discoveries. I had actually thought that Macedonia was in Scotland, when in reality it was an area in Greece which had sympathies for the Pagan way. This seemed entirely feasible as a place to escape to, both geographically and spiritually, although I had had no idea of where the place was in my present incarnation! With further research, I chanced upon the name of Calpurnius Agricola who was a soldier of high rank who was indeed stationed out of Italy, in Britain near to Hadrian's Wall. There had been evidence of Mithraea (temples) found in this area and Calpurnius had been the Governor of the region. He was not a well known figure and it was very likely that I would never have chanced across him in a book if I had not been looking out for his name. It was marvellous, not only to have a recall which matched another individual's recall, but also one which could be verified historically through research.

The Cult of Mithras proved harder to research, as it was only featured in out-of-print academic volumes and mentioned in passing by other texts. The general feeling was that the Cult excluded women and that Mithras was a chauvinistic, blood-thirsty bore. My experience, and later discoveries by archaeologists, revealed this may not have been true, as usual we all receive the records of antiquity with the Christian bias. It was stated that Mithras may have indeed had the qualities of Christ, which the Christians usurped and replaced with an image of a ravening evil beast, the enemy to be feared. Christ assumed the role which Mithras had had for centuries; from Sun God to Son God, as it were. I was unable to clarify the aspects of the temples and rituals which I observed, but my research into the subject is continuing, as with all of my research into my 'lives'. I always make notes of details from recalls, however trivial, especially of names, places and events which can be checked. Names such as 'Sol Invictus' which I recall being inscribed upon a ritual blade. This translates to 'invincible Sun' and it was indeed connected with the Mithraic/Sun God Cult, actual proof that I remember this, as it is too obscure for me to have come across it by chance. Also, broader aspects can be confirmed, such as the actual use of underground water systems which were accessed by means of small wooden boats. I genuinely believe that I had a life as Sabine, again with the man who is now Martin, and in a moment I will reveal how I perceive its significance in the overall pattern.

Firstly, what if all of our recalls, our supposed past life memories, turn out to be only elaborate fantasies by which we delude ourselves? Are we giving our Selves greater meaning and relevance rather than accepting the tiny, insignificant sparks of energy which we are? Perhaps we have but one life, and these memories, so called, just help us to feel grander, with more meaning for our Selves? I am ready to accept any concept, any change, with enough proof and the accompanying gut instinct as to its 'rightness'. The reason I have, for now, given reincarnation and reincarnation fantasies, status as a personal truth is that it feels right, it helps me, and on some levels I have confirmation from others as to its validity.

During my memory recall, I become my other Selves,. I feel their pain and their joy, I learn their lessons, I see through their eyes. I have no more respect for the lives that I can 'prove' (by confirming details with Martin and by use of historical reference books) than for those which have no valid proof as to their authenticity. For example, I have a 'feeling' that I may have been a Cathar. I doubt if this is historically true, but my psyche, my Self, has woven me a plausible fantasy as to my involvement with this heretical sect in the early twelve hundreds. I have read Arthur Guirdham's trilogy on the Cathars and reincarnation, after I discovered one of his works contained some reference to the obscure Mithraic Cult. I found no information there, but I did feel drawn to the Cathars.

The difference with my 'recall' about the Cathars and my other recalls is that I had the Cathar 'memories' after I had read the book. Unlike my other memories, which I take as genuine, I had only researched the information after I had suffered long and intense periods of fragmented recollection. However, the feeling associated with the Cathar recall is much the same gut level interaction as I had with my 'authentic' memories. Why did I feel the need to connect myself to a Cathar life, if it is not a personal truth? I believe this is because if one stands above the situation, one can observe the pattern of lives which makes up the Self today. From the Italian life, the French life, the life as a monk and the Irish life alone, we can deduct something about my Self. If these are my key lives, then what do they speak of? A person who likes freedom, reacts badly to groups, has their own simple way of doing things, enjoys the company of a small, select circle of friends, has a penchant for individual spiritual pursuits and who meets with disaster and unhappiness when their inherent integrity, individuality and spirituality is confronted or changed.

In three out of four cases, I was hounded by the establishment in the form of the Church. But it was only a symbol of the energies I found incompatible. The Church was not of my energies, but a representation of the misuse of male energies, power and money. In a simplified form, this is why I came up against Brian, the pillar of the community who was really corrupt and intimidating. The pattern states that my Self, in its many guises (Poppy, Sabine, Mary, Marianne, John) has the same needs and the same root of being despite the centuries and the roles played out. It is the soul of the Wisewoman, simple, spiritual, free and creative. With this Self-knowledge, comes Self-love to be reflected into the world. When we know who we are, we know what we must do to truly 'be'. It is the start of a new journey of honesty.

So why does the Cathar life, myth or fact, fit into this pattern? What if all of the pattern is one great fantasy woven by an intelligent, creative person? My view is that within that matrix of parts that make up the whole, the story of the Essential Self, perhaps the fictitious story of having been a Cathar fits in. It says that even if I was not there in 1244, I could have been, for the way I am would have fitted nicely within the Cathar framework, their basic ethos having been a rejection of material wealth, orthodox spiritual teachings and hierarchies and corruptions. The Cathars were said to be peaceful healers and Seers who lived away from the World but ventured into it to help people. In the greater picture of who I am, I believe that my soul is telling me that I could have chosen to have incarnated during that time, even if I did not, for that is who and what I am.

Fantasy and day-dream are all valid tools for seeing the truth of our feelings, and if my Cathar fantasy is only that, a story made out of my need to have been seen as such a figure, then it still tells me who I see myself as. It still tells me something useful about myself. My soul can relate to the concept of having been burned for my innocent way of Being. The Cathars were eliminated, in the main, after a mass slaughter at Monsegur, of those who willingly went to the stake rather than give up their true way. Do not give up any day-dreams you may have of previous lives, they are almost certainly not meaningless nonsense. Their meaning to the soul is precious enough, be they truth or no.

What of one's changing of sex in different incarnations? To my knowledge, I have also had a life as a black-skinned man who was a healer. In addition, I recall having been a poor boy in Victorian England who lived on the canals with his family. Although I was male I still have the components there of my other female lives, in the former existence I was a man who tried to help people through spiritual and natural means. In my life as the black healer man I had my first experience of losing a woman's baby when I attempted to deliver it, and thus I was cast out of my village community in disgrace. It is strange to think that I had perhaps two lives related to unsuccessful mid-wifery. Indeed, in this life the idea of childbirth has not appealed to me. As a teenager I would run out of a classroom if a film on the birth of a baby or animal was shown. Whether my lives as healers who helped deliver babies are valid or not, my soul obviously wishes me to tackle a fear of child-birth that must have originated somewhere. Certainly there is no traumatic event in this incarnation which would have illicited that response, a gut response of fear, in me.

I do believe that I must tackle this fear, as I believe I once had a skill as a mid-wife. I know that I should challenge the fear within me which is, no doubt, associated with a failure which resulted in great shame and punishment from society. My desire, in this incarnation, is not to have children, but I realise that in my next lives I may have to come face to face with my fears and my reluctance to accept childbirth. My current reasons for not wishing to be a mother include my desire not to add to humanities' chronic over-population of our Earth. However, their are, no doubt, deeper 'soul' reasons for this disassociation with a natural facet of womanhood, which I accept I will need to face. For now, I work with the mother aspect of the female principle in terms of my own creativity and giving to the planet in other positive ways.

As for the canal boy incarnation, I 'saw' this life one day whilst walking the canal path in Avon. I had a spontaneous trance experience as I went through a tunnel, which was quite frightening. I have always loved canal art and boats, but have a terror of water and a fear of drowning that is nearly a phobia. Maybe my spontaneous 'recall' is a way to explain my fear of the canal, or a metaphor for the fear. But the canal boy also had similarities to me in the recall. He was very poor and lived an isolated, simple life with his family in a cold and dreary part of Northern England. He was a sparky yet sensitive lad, somewhat of the runt of the litter, and he died very young after being kicked by a horse on the tow path and being knocked unconscious into the canal, where I /he became trapped. I would say that he was one of those 'unsuccessful' masks I tried to wear in the years after the Wisewoman life. They were terminated early as they were destined to fail. I was a damaged soul, as I still was for the first part of this life. I believe I have gained some healing for my damage, just by understanding. But the understanding is part of the journey and is by no means over yet.

I wished to mention the two male lives which I have recalled clearly, as I wish to reiterate my point about our potential to be male or female, depending on the suitability of each guise for the life we are about to lead. I believe, at present, on the evidence so far of both my own and of Martin's lives, that the soul is sexless, yet both sexes. The soul comes from 'The One', from 'The All', from that great balance of the male and female principle. I also believe that as part of 'The One' we have a soul connection with 'another half'. Together, the Cosmic Egg is made, as with God and Goddess, Lord and Lady, together they create the Whole. I do believe that both souls which make up the Whole have the ability to be either male, or female.

I have no problems about having been male and Martin (my now-husband) has no problems about having been female. I believe that the qualities of the male or female role can be assumed for each incarnate experience, that they are interchangeable within the Cosmic Egg, or Whole. That one half can incarnate without or with the other, that one half can incarnate to learn separate lessons to bring back to and assimilate with the other half, thus adding to the knowledge of the Whole. As the Lord and Lady, Sun and Moon, came from this great Egg, as they are both part of it and together reflect the harmony of opposite principles, so do we. I suppose that we have terms for such 'other halves', soul-mate, soul-partner. The great mystery is, that although we are each complete of ourselves, and that although we have the capacity to be male or female within ourselves... we also are made whole when joined to our other half. We function as a complete unit within ourselves whilst incarnate, but there is no more Cosmic connection or feeling of wholeness-in-entirety than when we meet our soul-mate. With their soul, our own soul has the perfect blend of energies which transcends the chosen male/female way of being. The two souls together create the divine resonance of a union of harmonious energy. Within this union we have personal lessons and we have composite lessons. I do not state that we are incomplete without our soul-partner, as we have the capacity to function as an

146

individual. We remain individual within the 'cell' of our union with the other half, but we have the added completeness of being part of the greatest mystery, the perfect union which reflects the Cosmic All, the union of the interchangeable opposite and its eternal reflection.

I am aware, as I write, having spent much of this incarnation in a state of lonely, isolated fear, that there are readers who will now resent my mention of everyone being part of a Cosmic Wholeness with another soul. It is merely my observation of the patterns, of natural law and personal, spiritual guidance which I share. Yes, I believe that we all have another half, but whether we have chosen to incarnate together this time around, for whatever reason, is not cut and dried. Perhaps your soul partner is at rest, or engaged in another process on another level so as to bring back their new understanding to the cosmic whole as and when you met again. You will meet again. Perhaps in this life, you have other business with other souls who wished to meet you again, separately from your soul's partner. Perhaps you simply have not met them yet. After all, life is not over until it's over (easy to say, but when one is alone desperation can set in).

If you have any recall of anyone you suspect may be your soul-partner, or even if you have not, try to use your wise skills to do some astral accessing. The work will not be immediately easy, or instantly profitable, but the more effort is put in in meditations on the matter, the richer the harvest. If one calls out astrally to the partner for a period of time with a loud enough 'volume', then the person, or soul will hear and respond astrally, no matter how psychic they are in 'life'. The call that one makes will speak to them on a higher level, or frequency, than their daily mode of transmission, assuming, of course that they are incarnate.

Putting out an astral call to the partner is best done in an astral safe place, which one will have to create. This place, which will be individually yours, can be 'built' on the astral realms and it will, with effort, become a 'reality' to the Otherworlds. The safe place can be constructed to one's own personal specifications. If one understands the astral realm as being made of a stretchy, elastic material then one's understanding of the exercise will increase. If the reader has considered the previous statements about the human lower astral being full of our daily thoughts and feelings, made 'real', then one will gather that the astral can take the shape, or form, of any strong will imposed upon it. It can make a 'thought form' or it can accommodate an entity. It is a vast realm which does indeed reflect our realm, whilst having attributes of its own. As above, so below and vice versa.

The astral is not, strictly speaking, 'above us'. It is all around us, but we cannot see it with our normal sight. It can be seen by the third eye or by 'tuning in' psychically to its frequency. It is just on a different wavelength, or level, to ours. There are many levels of being, but the astral is the one closest to our own, connected by our will yet unconnected and a realm unto itself. If this is rather beyond your understanding on a daily basis, then do as I do and think "well, I don't really comprehend how a television or telephone works but I know that they do because I have experience of them". Some people are scientific experts, others mathematical geniuses, who could no doubt equate and explain other levels of existence and communication far more adequately than I. As I am an artist, who is also a psychic, then I could probably sketch you a spiritual impression of the place, but not truly explain it in terms of quantum physics!

I have my own 'safe place' which I created on the Astral, and in a moment I will explain how to go about creating and using yours. I wanted to interject at this point with an anecdote related to the Astral, and to my own influence upon it. As an artist who specialises in detailed drawings and illustrations involving figures, I can spend many hours involved in the creation of one figure on paper. In so doing, I often give the person I am drawing real qualities, like a personality, name, etc. My drawings tend to tell a story anyway, and so I do get highly involved with my characters as I sketch them from my imagination. One such figure, who I called Lian, was featured over and over again in my paintings. She was red-haired and wild looking, not physically similar to me, but a woman who I saw as a 'representative' of my strong nature. She was the red-headed figure that Shirley had described to me back in the days when I still saw her and Richard. Shirley thought that she was either my guide or else a past life image of me. She is neither. Lian also attracted Jack's attention as he admired my artworks. He said "this woman... she is you, I have seen you looking like she does", which I found baffling. I was beginning to think I had been Lian in a past life, perhaps involved with a castle I kept seeing in association with her as I drew her. Then Martin gave me another idea. When he saw my art, he said that he had seen Lian (he even knew her name) during his astral travelling and meditations. She was me on the astral, and he recognised me as her. Basically, I had put so much of myself, and so much energy into creating Lian on paper, that Shirley, Jack and Martin all met her on the astral, whether in dreams or in trance. They thought she was me. I have no doubt that she is still present on those levels, although I have not empowered her for a while by giving her energy through my sketching. She has never approached me astrally, and I am glad. Although she is not my double physically, the effect of meeting a version imbued with so much of the Essential Me, face to face, would be a little like meeting a Doppleganger... unnerving. Yes, she may be a particularly strong part of me from a past life, but I believe, at present, that, for whatever reason, I created her form astrally (without being aware of it manifestly).

148

So, the safe place is like my image of Lian, the more you feed it with visits and visualisation, the more it will glow with a 'life of its own'. To reach a point where you are ready to begin creating your place, first carefully protect oneself, using my method, or another personalised version of it. Better that it be personalised eventually. Then, use the relaxation technique, counted breathing and clenching/releasing the muscles one by one. When you are ready to begin you will possibly find yourself floating pleasantly in a black void. Do not fear. You are in control. You have followed the psychic 'Highway Code', you know how to use your own will as a magical, astral tool.

The void is good, feel yourself floating there, supported, loved. Relax into it. Call upon your guides, known or unknown, to show you the way and also to any God/Goddess principle you may feel close to, or any other archetypal figure you may be drawn to working with. When you are satisfied you have approached a place of deep calm and protection, then begin to paint your picture. You are working on the canvas of the mind, the canvas that you do all your imaginings on. At first you may wish to merely practice seeing your imaginary pictures appear on the canvas. Try making a red teapot appear on this mental screen, or a blue and white stripy mug, as I have previously suggested in relation to strengthening visualisation techniques. Make your pictures familiar but increasingly complex, as a practice. Maybe visualise a jungle scene, or imagine a busy shopping centre. See colours, faces, clothes, shop fronts. Hear the accompanying sounds if you can. Then scrub the canvas clean or turn over a mental sheet of paper until you have a blank screen to work on once more. If you had spent many focussed hours creating the red teapot, then your red teapot would astrally form for you to return to again and again. It would exist on that level to do your bidding. It is the same with the safe place you are about to create.

I think it unwise to describe my very own safe place, but a variant of it will do for an example. You will need to have an idea of an ideal natural setting in your head before you begin. Make a mental list of its parts i. e. "In my safe place I would like a stream, a bridge, a wood of bluebells and a big rock". It won't be until you actually begin 'drawing' the picture on the canvas of the mind that you arrange these in a pleasing manner. Do not be afraid to alter this on the first few occasions of meditating. At first it will still be flexible. Only after repeated efforts on the same thing, the same picture, will your image have a firm astral reality. Even then it can grow or be re-arranged slightly as to how feels right for you at the time.

Let us work with the example list of requirements for the safe place that I have just mentioned. The person with this list is in meditation, relaxed, protected, and has practiced his or her visualisation skills until they are confident to proceed. Firstly they could imagine a bare stretch of grass with a blue sky above it. It is their prerogative, as 'artist' as to what they paint first and to where they put it. This is the composition technique. Will the stream be good running past the rock, or maybe through the trees? Are the trees to my left or to my right? Would a stream coming up from a spring under the rock be nice? Hear the running water, feel the rock. This is your realm, the only place in the universe that is entirely yours. Use it, have it exactly as you wish and do not be hurried. Here, time is your own. This is your perfect place, perfect at this time. It can be changed or moved on from later, if you so wish. For now it is a place from your day-dreams, idyllic, peaceful, safe. You yourself are in the picture of the perfect place. You yourself are lying on the soft grass or sitting atop the mossy rock. There is nobody here but you to walk in the shady wood, admiring the flowers that carpet the floor.

If, and it is only an if, anyone turns up in your space then use a 'checking out procedure' immediately (point a finger, use a mirror or a wand) no matter how familiar they may look. Call on your Guide to assist the intruder out of your place. I have rarely encountered an intruder in my safe place, and then they had no power to remain if I checked them out, found them to be lacking, and then asked them to leave. You are in control. You set the boundaries.

You must return to this place, daily at first if possible, to make it stronger, to make it exist as your space. Believe it does exist! Do slip off into it in quiet moments during the day. I realise that it is hard to revive the imagination if one is not one of the naturally, actively creative and if you are someone who has not picked up a paintbrush since school. I realise that imagination can be stunted by the easy fix of television with its instant images that require no effort. Perhaps certain interactive computer generated programmes will put a spark of creativity back into technology, who knows? For now, many of us have had a part of our creative, imaginative brains switched off. That part has gone to sleep because it was no longer needed. Again, I know that the television has its educational uses and can be stimulating, but again I advocate giving radio and books a try for a while if one wished to 're-awaken' that dozy creative muscle. You are producing magic when you will something to happen, when you actively direct that will using symbolic means. You are creating magic when you direct your imagination into visualising the safe place.

After a while, with practice, one will be able to be in that place, which now 'exists' on another level, immediately after protection and relaxing into trance. I used a technique whereby I had to get to my safe place via steps, and as I descended I became more deeply in meditation and so I became clearer and more focused astrally. By the time I reached the bottom step I was ready to 'see' my safe place. Somehow, reaching this place can be harder some times than others. Do not panic or think you have 'lost it'. It may mean that for some reason the energies are not suitable for trance on that occasion. Do not struggle hopelessly on if the 'reception is bad' and you cannot pick up a transmission or picture. It may mean that you are overly tired, or ill, or worried about a manifest subject. A careful look at one's own energies is needed. Also, do not attempt such activities if you are stuffed full of Sunday dinner (food makes you too Earthed, that is why it is good to consume a small quantity of it afterwards). If you are ill then leave meditation or magical work alone, and concentrate on your manifest self. Trance etc uses up much etheric life-force energy, as does healing another person, or doing divination. The connection with the Other Realms takes effort, remember.

I really do not believe that I should suggest a list of 'safe places 'for the reader to chose from. To each his/her own, and the ideal place should be found within as a response to beautiful things seen in this life, or other lives. I will suggest that a representation of the four elements should be present, and not all of them at full-pelt. A waterfall and a volcano together may be a bit unsettling. Try things like a lake and a mountain, a swing hanging from the bough of a tree (air) and a fiery-red copper beech tree. Or maybe a camp fire, a distant castle with a billowing flag and a river. The combination is endless and good fun to play around with.

I said earlier that I would describe the emotional natures of the elements. I think I can best describe them in terms of a person, the fifth element of Ether being the whole person, psyche, spirit, intellect, body and all. The Ether is the subtle blend of all of the individual's elements of being.

Water could be seen as the blood and tears, the mother's milk, the sexual fluids, menstrual emmisions. Water is connected with our emotions, with flow, with cycles and patterns, with continuity. Water is creative in the form of poetry and art, things of the psyche and imagination.

Fire is present the the spark of our energy, our life force, passion, anger, love making, physical combat, our joie de vivre, our burning desires, the eternal flame of our being.

Air is the breath, the breath of body and soul, a sigh, a laugh. Air is inspiration, ideas, beliefs.Air can be having our head in the clouds or it can be the voice of reason.

Earth is the flesh and bones, it is our root to the World and to our true selves within. It is our will to hold it all together, it is our determination, our solid trustworthiness. We are grounded, supported and sustained by it, from it we grow, from it we are harvested and then planted anew.

I would associate the form of an Elf with the Earth, a nature spirit but solid, almost human. With water there is a nymph or sprite, ethereal but tangible, shimmering in and out of form. Fire has the gnome or goblin figure, solid but by no means human, except perhaps by a long-since forgotten connection of a physical union and air is the will o' the wisp, perhaps a voice in the mists, perhaps a whisper in the ear, the hair lifted by a sudden breeze. All of these ideas are not static, are not final they are ideas, taken from forms I have seen with my 'third eye' all archetypal figures that clad themselves in a recognisable form for us mortals, but can truly be seen as the glowing presences I described earlier.

They too could be present in your safe place, as comforting familiar spirits embued with the quality of the element they represent. You can create such spirits for your safe place, but, at first, it is good to get used to your own company in the place. An art, once again sadly lost in the society we have all created for ourselves. As I have commented before, this society frowns upon the lonely, the loner, the solitary person. Use the safe place as a means of re-contacting your solitary self. Learn to love yourself in this way, to enjoy the space, time alone to listen to any small voices within you and time to know yourself away from all usual relationships and such.

Then, from this safe place one can send out an astral call to another soul, alive or dead, including the soul-partner. If one is feeling confident, one could set up a circle and column of white light and invite your true soul-mate, alive or dis-incarnate, to appear in it. Remember to 'check them out' if they arrive, no matter how nice or familiar they appear. No doubt something very unexpected could occur at this point, perhaps your brother or mother may appear, perhaps you are both of the same sex in this life, or related in a most non-physical way.

Whatever, it is entirely unlikely for you to not like your soul-mate so you needn't worry about a sworn enemy appearing. After all, you are both from the same, harmonious cosmic wholeness to which you will both return. It could be a man, woman or child that you have never seen before, a person of another race or religion to you. The point is, you are speaking to their soul-essence not to their physicality, although they will have to have assumed a form for you to 'see' them astrally. Maybe if they are disincarnate, they would appear for you in the guise of the body they had in the last life you spent incarnate together. All in all,

152

this could be a very moving, life-changing experience. It can be repeated many times, and so a contact of great comfort and love established. It could also prove to cause much manifest change, as on the astral, so below.

Be prepared and know that what you ask, to see and talk to, your true soul-love, may prove upsetting or unsettling in life. Do use your gut-feelings over it, and always check out who appears to you. If you are more faint hearted at first, just ask that you may 'know' more about the partner. This may come to you straight away, as a voice or feeling inside you, or else it could be given to you in a dream or vision later. As with all astral work, the manifest effects are not always immediate, and vice versa. Do not be disheartened if enlightenment is not instant. Keep putting out your astral 'call' and wait. As I can testify, revelations come in the most unexpected manners sometimes. Keep the faith as to the validity of astral work. These things take time sometimes, as we are operating on a completely different time scale.

Do remember that magic works and that directing your will as you are doing is an act of magical intent. Relax, as the psychic and spiritual aspect of ones self can always work better when relaxed. Think carefully about why you want to know your souls love. Are you lonely?Are you plain bored with life as it stands?Then if so, perhaps if you begin to move towards changing things manifestly, by moving house or job, or leaving a pointless relationship, then maybe the astral will shift into gear too. As with all things make an effort, take a step towards the goal you want manifestly. I am a great believer in this, for I have seen the proof that it works.

Finally for this chapter, I will round up with a recap of my rules for all successful, safe trance/meditation/psychic work on the astral. These are my adapted versions of universal lessons. As with the remembering of a story which one wishes to pass on, as long as one does not change the bones of the story, its true meaning, then the muscles and flesh of the story can be altered to fit. The bones of psychic operation are non-negotiable and without them the body of spiritual practice will not stand up for long. It is foolish to adopt either a superior, or a flippant, attitude. It is rather like walking into the supporter's away end at a football match, and proclaiming that your team is best. Someone in the crowd is bound to want to take you up on the matter and the more cock-sure you were, the more they will respond with equal conviction. This can only lead to disaster, a fight at worst, a verbal confrontation at best, but probably not an amicable compromise. It is, similarly, folly to approach the Otherworlds thus, and not to expect a lesson or two in return.

I hope, that if the reader ignores the rules and the guidelines set down here, that the lesson they receive is not too terrible for them. I would encourage free-thinking, questioning of accepted standards and adaptation, but for flagrant flouting of safety regulations I have no sympathy. I would not get into a car with a person who had exceeded the legal limit for alcohol consumption. The rules are there for a reason, in that instance, and so too are they in the case of the astral. The roads of England are an unknown quantity, perhaps the driver would get home unharmed on that occasion or perhaps they would meet with someone driving who was tired or in a rush, or even a pedestrian who was unlucky enough to be crossing the road in front of them.

So too with the astral. Because one 'gets away with' travelling unprotected once, it is no reason to tempt the fates by parading in such a manner again. Who could blame the lion for biting, when it was tempted by a piece of raw meat? It is the nature of the lion to attack. It is also the nature of many astral entities and thought forms to attack. Consider the basic rules as one's psychic sword and shield. And don't forget the chivalry!

1. Have clear intent before one enters meditation. It is far better to have an idea of the purpose than to wander aimlessly about in unknown country. Even if the idea is as simple as visiting the safe place, understand where you are going and for why.

2. Protect and astrally survive, using the blue light protection in any suitable form that religiously covers all of the participant. A blue egg, suit of armour, space suit, the choice is yours. Use silver reflective symbols at the portal points, be they crosses, roses, stars or any personal talisman. Visualise the full suit plus protective symbols as clearly as possible for maximum effect. Go through each stage of the putting on of the protective garment slowly and thoroughly.

3. Spend quality time on astral work, not just when a few minutes at the end of the day crop up. Give the work priority and have patience. Patience is a virtue, virtue is a grace. Grace is a little Witch with astral egg on her face if she doesn't give her work time, energy and focus. Do not give up unless something feels wrong. If it feels right, then persevere. The effort will reward you. *"Failure is often the line of least persistence"* said Zig Ziglar in *'Steps to the Top'*(Pelican, 1985).

"Never give in, Never give in, Never give in, " said Sir Winston Churchill.

4. Relax! Learn how to relax. Use herbs, music and candles in small healing rituals of daily life. Give personal growth and understanding time and listen to what the body and soul are saying to you. Create relaxing mantras, or chants, to sing to one's self. Captain J. A Hadfield said in his book '*The Psychology of Power*' (Macmillan, 1919), "This art of resting the mind and the power of dismissing from it all care and worry is probably one of the secrets of energy in our great men. "

Without relaxation, there will be no meditation, and without meditation there will be no Self-knowledge gained greater than the fleeting glimpse we gain of our Selves as we run hither and yon in daily life.

5. Relate to the guide, like belly-buttons we all have one in this life. Relate with love, truth, wisdom and understanding and be prepared to accept the same. The guide relationship is a partnership. If one cannot 'see' them them at least relate to them with thanks for their constant protection. Ask them to be with you during all spiritual acts, and know that they are there, even if they are invisible to you at that time.

6. Visit the safe place, make it stronger by visualisation on a regular basis. Spend time working there, but also recharging one's Self.

7. Do not attempt to influence anyone adversely on the astral realms. Do not even attempt a beneficent working in which you believe what you are doing is right. Do nothing against another's will, even if you believe it is for the best, as one has not the overview, and such acts could cause ripples of harm and confusion. Only ever do magical, astral work with the consent of the person you seek to represent. Be approachable enough in your daily life for others to come to you to ask for help for themselves. Remember the law of three fold return. Any bad, foolish or manipulative act performed on another will reflect back on its sender eventually,three times as powerfully as when it was sent out. Know the consequences of performing such acts. Do not be fooled by the effect not bouncing back immediately. It will, in time.

8. Say please and thank you, to those who are visible to you or not. If you have asked for their presence, they will be present. They do not exist for your use and pleasure alone. Beings, all beings, exist in their own right and deserve respect and courtesy.

9. No matter how small the astral working was, always eat and drink a little on returning to the manifest so as to connect and ground one's Self

to the Earth. Similarly, always make notes in the Book of Shadows and Light. It is surprising that even the most trivial journey or astral guidance can seem relevant in future weeks, and one always wishes that the information had been logged somewhere for future reference. A little effort, as usual, goes a long way.

Chapter Six

"So that.... " She considered for a moment, eyes thoughtful, *"so that you can put it into perspective. So that you can see all your life as a part of what you are, but not all of what you are. You were a priest. And so you still are, I think. That is a good thing, it has opened your sight to the spirit, to the unseen, to the holy. It has played a part in shaping the soul, in making you what you are. Now you feel empty and hollow. Perhaps that is a good thing too, because it is shaping you once again. "*

"Shaping me? To become what?"

Quote from Gael Baudino from *'Strands of Starlight'*

We are all shaped by our experiences whilst retaining the Essence of our own Essential Self. The growth and learning that comes from experience, be it seen as negative or as positive experience, takes place around our central core, the root that is the Eternal Soul. Our learning on the manifest level, when we have chosen to be incarnate in the physical, is a blend of knowledge gained and the influences of people and places we have experienced. The growth comes from the assimilation of this learning into the Essential Self. It does not change the Self, although a subtle change of the shape of that Self may occur gradually, but it makes that Self better, more understanding, more loving, honest and wise. Our aim is not to incarnate for life after life to attain some standardised state of absolute perfection. Does this state reflect the natural World? Is the fox, the eagle, or the salmon trying to strive for something better than it is? This takes me to the tale of the dissatisfied oak tree who longed to evolve into something he deemed as better, more perfect. I will give a brief account of this tale, which I created to help children understand the value of Self in a world which tries to regulate us to the perfect model.

There is an oak tree in a wood who is not growing as he should. His branches are short and weak, his fruit is stunted and his leaves are a sickly yellow colour. The oak tree spends his time looking at the apple tree. The apple tree is in perfect health. The apple tree radiates happiness and contentment for who and what he is. He has marvellous fruits which people love to come and collect to enjoy. He gets much praise. His blossoms are appreciated and admired. He is a

157

158

fine tree who knows he is a fine tree and so he flourishes. The apple tree acknowledges the oak tree and all the other trees in the wood, but he is contented enough to stand alone. He concentrates on his own growth, his own development, and as long as he harms nothing he is happy to do so. He knows who he is.

The oak tree envies the apple tree. He wanted to produce fruit which the humans can eat and enjoy. He wishes to produce pink blossoms. But no matter how hard he tries, all he can produce is acorns. His acorns are not worthy, he feels, and so his fruit become small and shrivelled. He loses all his confidence and feels inadequate in the presence of the apple tree. One day the unhappy oak spots a lone squirrel sitting sadly in the pile of dead oak leaves at the base of his trunk. The squirrel is crying because the oak tree used to provide all of the squirrel's winter store of acorns. Now the old, tired squirrel must trek miles to the next oak tree. The oak tree is shocked that any other creature could have been relying on him.

For the first time in a long time the oak looks about himself. He notices that the apple tree is now bare of fruit and standing quietly. Nobody is making a fuss of him now, yet the apple tree is still happy. The oak sees the horse chestnut tree with the children collecting his conkers. He sees the beech tree shedding his nuts. He sees the ash tree who is growing no fruits but who is just growing happily, being himself. He sees the beautiful shades of red and gold in all of the trees' leaves. He realises at last that he too has worth and a role in the wood. As he understands his own unique role and his part in the Dance of Life in the wood, he gets a new surge of life. His sagging bows, wilted leaves and poor fruits all begin to grow anew. He can feel safe and happy with the knowledge that everything in the wood is valued as a part of natures great plan. Everything and everyone has their own special season. A season for growing, giving and simply being. The real role of the oak is to simply 'be', just as a fox simply 'is' a fox. The eagle wants to be the best eagle it can be, the fastest, the best fed, but it still wishes to be an eagle. It is the same with the Self. The story of the oak is simplified here but the message is still clear.

The aim is to know thyself and then to simply 'be' that Self in the best way that we can. How many of us would stand by to watch a friend spend hour after hour in frustrated combat with a violin, trying to master the instrument only to produce a few tortured squeaks from it? We know the friend cannot hold a tune when they sing, and would not recognise middle C if it came and tapped them on the shoulder. It is a waste of time for us to hopelessly grind away at being a musician because we so desperately admire a particular violinist.

If someone you knew and liked was involved in such folly then you would be best to remind them of what it is that they do best. You would perhaps praise their carpentry skills and point out that the violinist could not produce such a beautifully carved table. If the friend refused to acknowledge the worth of their craft as a woodworker, thinking it a lesser craft than that of the musician, then we could do one of two things. Either we could do as the squirrel did to the oak tree, and create a situation whereby the friend realises that their skill is needed and appreciated in the World. Or else we could deduce that the friend has worries on another level about their Self and is perhaps not satisfied with their own current *modus operandi*, or way of life. It would be your role as that of caring friend, to spend time talking to that person to find out why they felt their current situation was unsatisfactory. One cannot change them, but one can encourage the change of the circumstances that surround them so as to be more beneficial to that Self.

That is the lesson, as I see it. We will only ever be a better, wiser, kinder, more compassionate version of who we Essentially are. The man that we see as a drunken, lazy, sexist football-mad thug will not evolve in a hundred incarnation's time into a Buddhist of great spiritual enlightenment. However, he may have had several incarnations as women in the meantime and come back as a man who has learned how to balance himself and to channel his natural exuberance and love of group activity into a positive role. He will still be the same soul who once liked a bit of a riot, but now his energy will have been directed into a more beneficial role, due to his balancing experiences as persons on the other side of violence, or abuse, in other lives.

As I have stated before, it is abhorrent to me that we should all evolve to exactly the same perfect ideal before ascending permanently to a state of nirvana in some distant, un-Earthly dimension. If we have evolved to the best of our abilities as ourselves on the Earth, then we should either incarnate to help others, or take on the role of Guide in the Other Realms to a similar human soul. I do not, for one moment assume that I am so evolved as to have returned to Earth in a helping role, but that is what I am aiming to do and there is no time like the present to start helping as best we can, right now.

Everything is made of energy, therefore everything is energies, therefore we are all inter-connected, all of our actions having repercussions in the World, whether we can see them or not. The soldier in the trench in World War One did not see his commander or general, far away in a safe office somewhere, yet the generals decision affected their life, and the life of the man that they are destined to kill when they are ordered by the general to go over the to. and so the family of the man who they kill gets affected and so it goes on.

As we choose the incarnations we have in order to learn the things we need to learn and to meet the souls we need to meet, then we have already seen that this choice is not isolated from the choices of other souls who wish to see us again, for whatever reason. Thus their will comes into our destiny. Like it or not, we are all connected, the ebbs and flows of energy between us may sometimes be tangible (instant attraction, loathing someone on sight) or may be imperceptible to all but the trained psychic. But they are there. So too is our connection to the Earth, to all life. If a table or a cup is made of energy and has an energy field around it, however slight, then how much more of an energy field, or aura, does the living thing have? Each tree, blade of grass, butterfly or bird, each rabbit, pet dog, horse or tiger, all have a life force, a consciousness, a purpose and a way of being which is essentially Theirs. Each decision is far reaching, each choice affects more than just ourselves. This does not mean that the only way to be is hyper-sensitive, avoiding treading on the grass, refusing to eat anything that has been grown of the Earth. The key is to be aware, to be respectful and to learn to work with the energies, not against them.

This is the role of the Wisewoman, as I perceive it today. If I asked myself the question 'who do I wish to become, in becoming a Wisewoman?' then I would include those three things in my list of attributes I would like to have. The Wisewoman is aware of all life. She strives for the overview, not only so that she can know her own Essential Self but so that she can work with the most understanding with the needs of other selves. She does not act out of fear or ignorance but tries to gain a fuller picture. She forgets her own human feelings of passion or anger when faced with a problem and lays out the information she has in the most balanced way possible.

She communes with her Guides and with the spirits and principles within the Other Worlds to have more insight into the needs and problems of another human soul. She does not act without first communing with these spirits, as she is aware that she needs the greater picture and that the dis-incarnate ones have less connection to Earthly emotional feelings on the matter then she herself might. She knows that they are there to help because of their own wisdom and to them she is respectful. She values her Guides as friends who require attention and input from herself if the relationship is to last. She accepts their protection and superior wisdom, but she is not humble before them. She knows her own limitations in this life and knows that she is doing the best that she can, as her own Self. She is true to that Self and loyal to her protective guiding spirits.

The Wisewoman knows that to gain an overview psychically that she must practice her own magical arts in order to become more accomplished in the ability to 'See'. She combines her learning with that of the Other World. She spends time on meditation, trance work and in going deeper within her own nature so as to gain a greater understanding about the sacred nature of all life. She knows that her psychism is a gift, a talent given, but she must work hard to become better at it, for the benefit of all. She knows that the artist would be a fool to never paint a beautiful picture for the World to enjoy although they have a natural skill. So the skill will become neglected and unappreciated and those without natural talent may achieve more than the neglectful gifted artist, just by hard work. The Wisewoman wants to use her skill of divination in the World, as she wishes to heal others with a blend of her herbal and plant lore combined with her ability as a spiritual healer, by which she channels the power of the Other Worlds and of the Cosmos, into the body of the sick or disturbed. She realises that she is no more, no less important than any one that she meets or works for. She realises that she too is a tool, a channel by which the Other World energies of insight, healing and peace may be brought to this World. She is not proud, but she is pleased with who and what she is, with her part in the pattern of all life.

So, with her knowledge, with her overview, comes new wisdom, new understanding, new compassion. She is never static, always open. She knows how to protect herself and how to protect others. She sees the complex matrixes that lead a person to act certain ways in this life that may seem grossly unacceptable or bewildering to others. She tries to step into other people's shoes. She can tune into a soul astrally, or through manifest contact using laying on of hands or through psychometrising a personal object. She can see their past, present and future and all the possibilities and probabilities thereof. She can see the pain, hurt and damage of another soul that may cause terrible actions in this life. She knows when to intervene and when not to. She never acts against the will of another. She seldom acts unless she is asked to intervene. She knows when to be silent and when to listen, and she knows when to speak and to act. She knows, most of all, when to withdraw within, to go back inside herself, to be alone. She takes stock, she makes new promises to herself and to the Earth. She is not afraid to be alone, knows no fear from man nor spirit. She knows who she is and her part in the process. She has no fear to face who she is. She is at peace.

The Wisewoman, she who I wish to become, has no need for religion. She has experienced the persecution of the Christian or Catholic Church and yet she is not bitter, not a person who seeks to avenge that injustice in this life. She sees the fear and ignorance of that establishment and there is pity within her, not hate. She understands their fear for they are part of a hierarchical system, part of the State. Their fear is for loss of position within the structure, loss of money, power and security. Their fear is that they will have no afterlife, for all their talk of God and Devils. Their fear is that when they die there is nothing, nothing at all, and so in this life they try to cling on to that structure which gives them shape and form, which gives them a reality, for the Church, the State, is only made of people, frightened souls hiding, hoping that no other will discover their lack of real faith, their lack of spiritual belief. They cover themselves in wealth and status, the riches of the Church, that church which would be an abomination to the Jesus of historical fact. How he would have despised the trappings of the men's fear and greed. A greed to have more as to make themselves more real, more valuable in the World, but it is easier for a camel to pass through the eye of a needle than it is for a rich man to enter the house of God, or so it says in their very own Bible.

Those who tortured and killed the Wise Ones and the weak of the burning times did so as to protect themselves. If there was somebody else burning then it was not them, but it could have been and they knew it.

The Wisewoman feels sorrow for those who seek absolution in material things, in man-made structures. The Bible is man-made, and seeks to disempower the woman, to discredit the power of the Wise. It values things that the Wisewoman rejects, it creates vast structures that could house fifty homeless people and then it locks the doors to these houses of God at night. All is fear. There are some who are making links, lighting candles and trying to understand the Old Ways within the church structure. The Wisewoman would reach out her hand to them. They can no longer hurt her. They could never hurt her. For she knew that her body was transitory and that her soul was Eternal, and that one day she would understand the damage that their fear caused to her and so be healed.

The day of her own healing has come, but the woman I wish to become still rejects the structures of religion and of society. She sees no need to deify her Guides, the guardian spirits and the universal principles within the universe. Although she is of the Old Ways, of Pagan beliefs, she does not worship. She respects. She has no need for structure or to put other humans between herself and her contact with spirit. He also respects those that do, and she wishes them well upon their path. Upon her own path their is no structure, no hierarchy, nothing but pure connection, sometimes spontaneous, sometimes pre-planned.

She knows her God and Goddess to be the male and female principle in their Essence. She loves and respects their difference, their balance. She does not reject the male principle because she has been born into a female incarnation. She relates to her Lord and lady in trance as valued, respected friends. She knows the Lord as both the spirit of night and of day, of darkness and of light, of death and of birth. She does not see him purely as the negative aspect of man.

She relates to him as Herne, protective in the best male sense, strong in the best male sense, and honest, wise and true, values that are equally of man and of woman. He is her male principle so as to represent her True Self. She is a Wisewoman involved with nature, nature magic, natural lore and Earth energies.

Herne is the Spirit of the Greenwood, Father of all life. He is the young man and the Father too, and he does not require that the Wise woman kneels before him or treats him as a distant and lofty King. He is but another being in the universe, a bigger, older, wiser, kinder more understanding being whom the Wise can tune into, can invoke as protector and Guide, oracle and benefactor. He is a spirit that embodies the qualities of both the hunt and of the hunted. He sees both sides, he has an overview of all life. He can also appear as one of the hunted, a stag, the fox, or as the hunter, an owl man, a man in skins with antlers atop his head. Herne is also the Wiseman, the male principle of the waning year. His symbol is that of the Sun. He can be met astrally as the Avatar of the Male Principle. He has many guises. The Wisewoman I seek to be, relates to his guise as Herne. He requires no supplication, no wealth, no offerings. He needs respect and love, not worship. You will find him outdoors, not in a temple or at an indoor altar. He is alive, and is kept alive by contact with the energies of those, like the Wisewoman, who practice the Old Ways, the Craft of the Wise.

The Wisewoman, she who I am becoming, realises that she is a manifest representative of the female Goddess principle. The Wisewoman does not worship herself, she knows and respects who and what she is. So it is with the female principle, the Lady, who she represents on Earth. She contacts the Lady in the other Worlds for for inspiration, for her greater wisdom, perfect understanding. She seeks to be the Lady. The Lady is reflected through her daily life, through the Wisewoman's acts in the world.

She recognises that her own incarnation reflects the cycles of nature and of the female moon principle. She understands that her life can also be apportioned as is appropriate to the three aspects of the triple Goddess of Death and Rebirth. She sees that each phase of the Goddess cycle is as important as the last. The Wisewoman does not wish to become a Goddess herself, in the traditional sense of having followers and devotees. She does not wish others to surrender their will to her, rather she wishes others to step up to her as equals on the path of life. She will work for others, with others, not against them. She seeks to empower herself and others, not to provide all the answers for them. The Wisewoman who I seek to become sees her own Lady, the representative of the Great Female Principle as reflecting all life, being all life, and she too requires acknowledgement and respect, not blind adoration. Her way of being is available for all to attune to. It can be emulated and appreciated by any soul

164

with the desire to do so, and the effort to do so. She seeks to empower us, in all her aspects.

I would like to be the Wisewoman who accepts and cherishes the stage of her female cycle of life that she is in. When middle aged she does not long to be a youth. She recognises her own youth as a phase that is now past in this life. she remembers it well, recalls where she has come from, and what she has learned from it. Youth is about physical growth and vitality and psychic openness. We all of us are more receptive to the Other Worlds in our childhood and adolescence, to varying degrees. An active or subconscious decision can be made at that time to shut the door on the psyche. But it is always there, for a return to it in later years, after some reflection on the matter. It may need care and attention but it is still with us, that intuitive, responsive, ancient side of being.

It saddens me that in many years to come, that part of us may have become so under used as the generations go by, as to become dysfunctional, like an appendix or tail bone. It is vital for the psyche to be kept alive, to be stimulated and inspired. And for this we must dispel the fear and ignorance of our young. Look at the popularity that Halloween has, in England and the United States. The young are ever drawn to the unknown, the unseen, for they are closer to their own memories of the Other World and spirit. The questioning, the searching for truths, the interest in all things hidden is a trait of the young.

In our schools with their over-crowded classrooms and regimented curriculums, lack of personal contact and lack of funds do not facilitate the continuation of such a questing attitude. The individual is often overlooked and is bombarded with rapid-fire facts, many of which are based on a history or perspective of the World that should have been re-assessed long ago. They are often presented with a male-dominated, Euro-centric perspective and instilled with a competitive streak, to the detriment of understanding and tolerating others of a different nature or ability. The problem of bullying is still rife within school structures. The child often feels hopeless, useless and swallowed up by a system that he or she feels they are powerless to change. As a former teacher I do not blame the teacher, for they have their own personal motivations for perpetuating myths in the classroom. They need the job. They are so exhausted by the demands of the situation that they themselves have stopped thinking, or caring. The motivation becomes money alone. As a Wisewoman I could not continue as a teacher in a state school, my own sense of personal morality would be in question if I continued to support a system which, by its own structure, loses the ability to encourage personal growth and questing. It is contrary to my Self.

The true Wisewoman sees her own youth as a time of questing, like the young deer allowed to roam the forest alone for the first time she spends time experiencing what works for her, and what does not. She learns some hard lessons, but enjoys the process, knowing that she is adding daily to all she is, because she can. And who is she? She sees visions, hears voices, has dreams. She looks within herself and without, having the vital energy to explore her World, her part of the forest. She remembers who she may have been, and is working out who she may be. She finds out who she likes, what she dislikes. Her own values are being shaped, something coming to her instinctively like a memory, others being found out by looking around with eager, hungry eyes. Youth is a time when truth, honour, justice and freedom matter a great deal. The young woman will reject, rebel against, test out and accept what feels right within her and what makes sense in her logical mind. She wants to change the World and to improve herself. She is the Maiden, the Young Lady, the Maid Marian, the Slender Moon Dancer. She is not feeble, although delicate as a flower. To her at this time all things are possible. She has the fleet foot of the filly, she will not be bound by convention. She will do as she chooses, or she will run.

Then, she starts to bleed and so is connected to all those others who bleed and have bled. Her blood link is to the Earth, a reflection of its life force, a promise of its new fertility. She can be as terrible as the sea, dashing the body of a mere man against the rocks, such is the power of her flow. She recognises this power, latent, untapped, within her and she smiles. She looks forward in hope, creative, instinctive, wondering about what it is she shall conceive in the World, with whom she shall conceive it. She searches, her feet barely touching the ground, her hands reaching out, now touching the velvet fuzz of a peach, now reaching out to pluck a jewel from the firmament. She may be feted with rose petals and words. Still she bleeds. Greedy fingers may pluck at her but they cannot stay her jig of life. She can hear a calling and she may fight it. 'Over here... ' the voice calls, destiny, fate. She finds her place.

The wheel turns and the woman within her is growing, born of the connection between blood and the Earth, intuition and the stars. She is entering into the time of summer rains and fires in her belly. She may try to deny who she is or she may reach out to her calling, those inner voices. Her feet may be still now, but her soul is still searching. She catches a glimpse of her face in a pool of still water, caught between two rocks on a deserted beach. Fine lines have appeared around her eyes. She knows they are there, and has no fear. Each one of them tells a story of laughter or of tears, of her learning to let go, to love, and to know when to move on. She loves those lines.

She loves her freedom also, and she wanted to set others free. She builds a nest but knows how to fly from it, tethered only to the Earth by the finest silver cords. She has found her place, but still looks with interest at other places, as she glides over the face of this world, of other Worlds... her bright eyes missing nothing, seeing All. Her voice is rich and full, she is brimming. Her hair is made from plaited corn. She is red, gold and green, of blood, of sunlight, of the land. In her hands she may hold a baby blackbird, or a bunch of fragrant orchids. Perhaps she has given birth to her own baby, maybe to a child, maybe to a dream. Perhaps she has found her soul's -love?

She gazes out to sea, becoming the sea and so she is the highest wave, the gentlest eddy, giving birth again to all the varied life in her depths. She is the zenith, singing with life, filled with milky full-moonbeams and rocking her Earth to sleep. She is woman, mother, her mother, our mother. She gives, she sees, she knows. She has no name but the bees hum their thanks to her. She feels and sees everything, drinking it all in, spilling it all out, like the tide, like a baby. She brings others to her place of calm, warm and soothing, and she comforts. She looks back only to remember and to learn from memory and feeling. She is now middle aged, with her hair still bound in plaits held together with ragged robin and fronds of weeping willow. She does not close her eyes to her own reflection, seen in the eyes of All, all she loves. She moves. The Earth turns.

The Wisewoman who I wish to become knows that there is a Season of Sorcery, as there is a season for all things. She sees her old age as a gift of greater wisdom and greater sight. She is not afraid of the dark, she is the darkness, of the bats and the mice and the empty womb, filled now with only secrets, hidden. Her smile is bright still, though her eyes may be dimming, as her sight comes from within as well as without. She is the Grand Lady, so often denied her dignity and her ease within society. She looks at the youth without envy, knowing that on the turning of the Cosmic Wheel that she too shall return in youth, perhaps a little wiser, a little richer than ever before. But in what body, in what guise? She hugs her knowledge to herself, the Old Crone, happy in dark places but still dispensing light. She reflects upon the fruits of her waxing life, the harvest of her waning one. Her skills in the Arts of the Craft come to the fore. She is sometimes feared, her proximity to Death and her consort, her soul-partner the Lord of the Death. Yet she is still of the same Essence that she ever was, still a part of the Female Principle. She knows this and she turns her gaze upon those who approach her in awe and trepidation. She laughs, twigs snapping, brittle bones breaking, turning to dust. She holds out her withered hand, extending her knowledge to be carried on and carried on.

She is the full of the Earth's ancient wisdoms, for she has travelled much into the Other Worlds and has witnessed many things. She is full of truths. Her truths are personal. And if one can see beyond her withered, wrinkled skin, the dry and papery rustling of that skin as she beckons, then we will hear her words. Words like the aromatic smoke of resinous woods which burn in the crisp November air, her breath with a hint of cider-apples and cinnamon, words which are yours to pass on. Hers is the voice of the dying, of the Dead. You are near to her and she throws back the hood of her cloak to reveal a smile like a tear in the very fabric of being. If you have the will to look into the eyes of that grinning skull, those empty sockets, the connection into the Void, and so into the womb of conception she will tell you.

The Wisewoman that I wish to become, that I am becoming, would tell you this. That you are seeing her truth, her way of looking at things. And that you must find your own. Her truth is valid, is to be respected and learned from, but it is individual as her Essential Self, and it is hers. She may point you in the right direction, but when you turn back to her for confirmation as to your path, she will be gone. Gone back into the Earth, to feed it, to nourish, to give back to it. But her spark of life remains, alive at the instant of death. Waiting, watching. Watching you. Your choices. She learns from you, too. This is your journey.

Finally, the Wisewoman that I am becoming wishes you well upon your journey, unto the Self, unto the Lady.

168

Pathworkings

A pathworking is nothing more, nor less, than a meditation or piece of trance work undertaken with a specific purpose in mind. The difference between it and a 'standard' meditation is that you will have used a planned route to get to your pre-determined destination. You will need to sit down before entering into trance and consider what it is you wish to know, or who it is you wish to meet, and to decide what means of visualisation would be most fitting for this. What I mean by most fitting will become clear as I share with you my first idea for a pathworking, I will explain why I chose certain settings and 'props' within the visualised scene.

The problem that I found originally as a beginner following the suggestions of other practiced Witches and Occultists as regards pathworkings was that I couldn't remember the instructions that I had read in their books after I had gone into meditation. As I am a very visual person, I found the only way to remember their instruction was by reducing their directions into a series of images for example a hill, a door, steps, a candle, a tree. I could not for the life of me memorise a list of directions per se, although I suppose that as with all familiar routes one needs to study (don't forget, it's all hard work in this game!) the 'map' that one is given, and decide which are the key points. As I used the image to recall where to go next, so could a list of words be used. But when one is in trance one cannot suddenly snap back into the manifest in order to check with the book that one has remembered it correctly. There can be a nervousness as a beginner that if one forgets the instructions then one will get hopelessly lost and never return to reality again. Not so. It is possible to return at any time from a meditation. You are in control and by your own will you can change things. As long as one bids the Guide or anyone else accompanying you on the journey a hail and farewell, with thanks, then one can abandon a meditation at a point at which it seems you have forgotten your way.

The two things that are wrong with the pathworking directions of another person are that a) you can forget their instructions, particularly if the thing is very elaborate and wordy and b) because you are following another person's rules, one can feel boxed in and a little restricted. It may feel as if there will be no spontanaiety on such a journey. Well, unexpected things will, and do, happen on any astral/Other World journey, so do allow for any diversion that comes your way on a previously well 'organised ' route. It would be a little silly to think "well this wasn't in the plan, I think I should ignore it and keep ploughing forwards as I had decided to". Chances are you may miss some great guidance or revelation that had cropped up spontaneously.

Be flexible within the other person's structure. What is good for the beginner about using the structure is that it is tried and tested. It works. It will get a pre-ordained result. However, I have to say that as is the case with any aspect of the Craft of the Wise, like the brewing of herbal remedies for example, if it doesn't taste/feel right for you then don't go ahead with the course of treatment. Do not feel a failure because somebody else's cure does not work for you. Perhaps the reason for failure is one of those described previously for example fatigue, illness, being over-full in the stomach) or maybe it simply doesn't suit you. You are unique, and have a special blend of energies. Never feel you are not good enough because someone else's way does not automatically work for you. The benefit of trying someone else's way is so that you get experience and build your confidence up so that you can create your own way.

Before ever attempting any pathworking, one should have used an astral method of meeting the Guide. The Guide should then be somebody who you ask to accompany you on all astral workings. He or she will be glad to assist, but do remember to get to know them and to learn who they are, and their own individual way of being, before dragging them off with you into new situations that may be somewhat overwhelming at first.

The Guide is a being in his or her own right, not a deity, not someone who requires adoration. Think of them as your valued friend, and treat them accordingly. They are not there to do your bidding, to be dismissed or discounted at your pleasure. If you treat your Earthly friends that way then maybe it is time for a serious re-think of attitude. If you are a natural psychic, then chances are that you tuned in to your Guide long ago. If so, perhaps it is time for you to meet them again, as if for the first time, and to have a honest talk to them about your relationship. All relationships need input and maintenance. With the Guide you can be sure that they will be willing to discuss anything and everything with you, as long as it is the right time for you to do so. It is not your place to 'know everything' immediately. Allow your relationship to grow steadily, be patient, and do always remember that your Guide has specifically picked you to work with.

Do not be surprised if the Guide changes at a point in your life. You have not been 'given up on' by the last Guide as a hopeless case. As we have seen, our lives have transitional phases and changes that are akin to the seasons in the Wheel of the Year. Perhaps a new Guide will be more appropriate for a new phase, or maybe for a particular lesson that is coming in this incarnation for your Essential Self. I myself have been through a transitional phase, and so I have been introduced to my two new Guides, both representing female energies. One was my mother, in my Italian incarnation and the other appears as a Native

American grandmother figure, the Hag or Crone archetype. I have welcomed them both into my life, accepting that they must have new lessons to share with me. In spirit, I thank my last Guide and hope that he will return at a later date to renew our treasured friendship.

The Guide can be of any soul, be they past or present or future who one has known incarnate. They can be a soul with a similar 'vibration' to your own, or with attuned energies to your own. Someone you will never meet in life, or someone you were very close to only years ago before they passed over. The Guide can be less of a person, more of a representative of a Principle. In my case, my 'Red Indian ' Guide was a representative of the Great Spirit of his Earthly culture and way of being. Similarly, one's Guide could be an Elf, a representative of the Spirit of the Green Wood or a Faery Queen, a representative of the Spirit of Earthly Mysteries and Enchantment. Whoever you meet, be they a shown to you as a child, as a man dressed in a soldier's uniform from the Eighteen Hundreds or as somebody clad in the manner of an old Shaman they are a being in their own right, appearing in a manner that is recognisable to you, or which will appeal to a strong part of your Self.

Learn how to 'check them out' by use of a pointed wand or mirror, learn to recognise their way and to see through any spirit who may seek to fool you by masquerading as your Guide. Your Guide may even test you out thus, by sending a false representation of themselves to you so as to see if you have learned the lesson of astral protection. It is for your own good, there is precious little point in proceeding into the Other Realms if you cannot even be bothered to test that you have invited the 'genuine article' to travel with you. Visualise yourself carrying a mirror, magical tool or special stick with you at all times in meditation and on astral journeys. This, once pointed at the supposed Guide, with the directed will that they reveal their true Self, is the simplest means to test any spirit form.

As a note here, the Guide may also be accompanied by a totem animal or creature. I have never, so far, heard of anyone who has a speaking animal as their Guide. The animal is not a human, has not a human soul or way of being. The animal is not lower in the astral ranks than a human and I do not believe that my pet cat has the potential to 'evolve' into a human. Cats are cats, have cat souls and evolve to be the best cat that they can be, big or small. No matter how I try to talk to my cat as a person, or to dress her up in a coat and hat and try to make her eat her greens, she will remain oblivious to my will and remain a cat. I can talk to my cat by transmitting images telepathically and my cat can relate to my energies.

So is it with the 'totem' or Guide animal on the astral. I do not believe that they will speak, but they will certainly use their qualities to communicate telepathically, and through feelings, to you. The animal may be with you because of a manifest link (the faithful hound, the favourite horse) or they may be relating to you because they are drawn to an aspect of your Self. Maybe you can relate to the fox, admiring its way of being, its beauty, and find that in life you see foxes at particularly important times, perhaps when you are having a crisis, or feel in need of a boost of energy. The fox is your protective symbol, and will lend its own qualities as the hunter and the hunted, the swift, the intelligent, the brave, to your work on the astral.

You can ask to meet your animal Guide as you can ask to meet your 'human' one. Think if you have any particular animal that you closely link to in life, maybe you would even like to be that animal. Or maybe an animal that you miss the company of in life. Or maybe even a mythical beast which you have always wished was 'of the Earth'. I have no doubt that there are dragon Guides and unicorn Guides, as the amount of human thought that goes into creating and sustaining these beings (who may, or may not, have once manifestly existed) is considerable. In the same that way that we of the 'Old Ways' keep the archetypal Gods and Goddesses alive who represent various aspects of the Great Male and Female Principle, then we can also add to the life force of such creatures. It matters not if the Goddess principle of Rhiannon once walked the Earth, nor if there actually were dragons living in caves in England. It is what they represent that matters, and the energy that they give form to.

To meet with the Guide, or to re-establish a relationship with them, then one must travel to the 'safe place' as previously described. I will no longer remind the reader of the 'highway code' believing that it would be a foolish person indeed who would not have noticed, and heeded, my warnings thus far. Once in the safe place, one must create a portal. As the body has portals then so has the Earth, places where the connection is weakest, the veils thinnest, best shown in the reflection of all things in the great cycle of nature.

Think of any Earth portal, or bodily portal, as being like Samhain, or Hallowe'en. Then the mists which separate the Other Realms from our mortal World are such that, with the will, we can peer through them and gain insights. Think of anywhere on this Earth where you have visited, which has given you a feeling of connection, or 'Other Worldliness'. This may have been enhanced by a time of day, a state of the weather. It may have been an accepted 'sacred site' on a leyline or 'vein' of energy, or it may have been at the bottom of your garden as a child, hidden under the ivy or sitting on a wooden bench looking at a sunset. Use these memories to set your scene in the safe place. You have been to your

172

safe place so many times now, in journeys to the astral, that you are happy enough to add to it or to make changes. Alter the weather to a state which makes you think of mysteries revealed, of magical revelations. Alter the time of year thus, and the time of day. Let us assume then, as an example, that one has an oak tree in the safe place. It is now Autumn and the leaves are russet. There are acorns in proliferation. There is a slight breeze. The water in your flowing brook is cold and reflects the colours of the sky at early dusk. It is late afternoon. There are no flowers in bloom. There is a faint smell of wood smoke. You look around and see no one, hear perhaps only the noise of the water over the mossy stones, maybe the cry of a rook to its mate.

You are going to create a portal for your Guide to come through. For this, you are going to find a piece of flat ground, previously empty in your safe place. You may choose to construct a portal here that you will be happy to leave in the place, so consider the spot you chose well. This is your place, as always. Think about the concept of a portal as being a doorway, a gateway. Think literally of pleasing shapes for doors and gates. Think also of things that we way pass through. We may go under a bridge, through an archway, through a hollow tree, may pass between standing stones, can go through a tunnel or a cave, between two trees or across a style. Chose an image that fits with your environment.

To have an actual door, one need not build a wall, or building about it. All we need is a door, free standing. By all means, do build the wall or structure, but as the door is symbolic it has no need of Earthly trappings. You are going to make the door a reality by using your will, by visualising it in the finest detail, by making it a reality in that place which now exists astrally. If you choose, perhaps, a strong wooden door of the medieval type, bound with metal strips and studded with iron nails for strength, then see it in all its details. How does it open? Feel the locks, the hinges, the wood itself, with your hands. If it is a doorway made between two standing stones then see the lichen upon them, the marks of time. Smell the stone, feel its chill surface. Walk around the doorway, front and back. It is your will that only the person who you ask for directly will be able to come through it, and only then when you have drawn a circle of blue protective light around it. You can hold the person who comes through the portal in the circle of light until you are certain that you have checked out who they are. This is your place, with your rules. Make the rules fair and you will have no problems.

When one has touched the created door, to feel its astral presence, and when you have walked around it, creating a circle of protective light (some people prefer pale yellow as a protective colour, I prefer blue and silver) then you may retire to a place outside of the circle and ask that your Guide come to you through the portal. This requires patience, concentration and an openness of heart and mind. Expect the unexpected, so to speak. Wait. Be peaceful as you are waiting. They will come. When they do, no matter if they appear as your Great Aunt Gladys or as a dashing Arabian Prince you must check them out before allowing them out of the circle. Never cut corners or be slap dash. Show your intent to be a careful astral practitioner. Any false presence will be bound by you to disappear back to whence they came if they show themselves to be something other than what they have claimed to be. Only when they show up to be a true shape and form of the energies that they claim to represent, then can they be invited out to join you. At this point you can go for a wander about your safe place, and show them around. Or else you could sit down together. Have an idea of things you may ask, three questions are enough to begin with. Any more and you will never remember all the information to bring it back to the manifest. Maybe you could establish who your Guide was in life, or else what it is that they represent as a being. Why are they with you? What is the connection? And a question that should always be asked is "is there anything I particularly need to know at this specific time?".

As with my Guide, they may speak to you through images and thoughts rather than normal conversation in your Earthly tongue. They may show you things, or take you on a journey on the astral to reveal something to you. In the future they may show you the future, or your past lives, or the possible outcome of a present problem. At first, do not overload them with questions and needs. Think about what you can give back to them. They do not expect material rewards or homages, but it is good if they can see you acting on advice they have given you, or trying to solve a mystery they have set for you. Most of all, they require sincerity, gratitude and respect. Start as you mean to go on. Thank them for their time, clarify any points they have made with you before they depart, and ask for their continued presence with you, both in daily life and in meditation. If they are your genuine Guide then of course they will be happy to comply. See that they leave via the portal, and remove your circle of protection. The door is now closed, and can only be opened on your say so, through the drawing of a further circle.

As the time goes on you will not require the portal on the astral. You will get used to asking the Guide to be with you, and so they will be. This is the same for in life. If you are a little sceptical at first, ask that the guide tells you of a 'sign' in meditation, that one can find in daily life on the manifest levels, in order to 'prove' their existence and presence. This could be anything, the guide will choose. I was once given an extraordinary piece of guidance by a deceased relative who realised I was slightly disbelieving. "When you find the sixpence, you will know it is all true" she told me. Sure enough, weeks later when I had dismissed her words as the fancy of my imaginative Self, I found the sixpence. I was sitting on the floor reading when the coin literally appeared, as what I would call an 'apport' (a material item manifesting by spiritual means) on the floor next to me.

The guide will do this for you too, if you ask. They do expect us to be healthily sceptical and not to believe any old tosh, just because it is psychically transmitted to you. Also there is a lesson here, give it time. It is customary that when one stops worrying about a thing and relaxes about it, then is it possible for it to happen. Our energies need to be flowing, not uptight and hostile, for us to receive clear guidance, as can be seen with the scrambled, rather manic messages I received as a frightened youth.

The guide is always present, then, at all times. Not like a Genie for you to uncork the bottle of the astral for, to get them to 'perform your will' for you. Nor can they grant wishes. They can be asked politely to be closer to the manifest in order to advise or protect you. A good guide will never tell you what to do, although they might, by way of teaching you a lesson in manners, if you begin to order them around. The Guide, is, by the nature of its being, closer to our Realm. There are many dimensions, or levels, not for 'ascended beings' but for those less dense and more of spirit. Perhaps of those who have never been incarnate. Those are the ones we cannot easily see or contact, even psychically. The guide is far closer to our world, but is still a spirit walker between the Realms, not of our dense manifest existence, although they may have once been. They can relate better to our lives here, whereas some beings would not be able to give insights as they are too far removed form our physical existence.

I repeat, I do not believe that these beings are supremely all-knowing, perfect creations. I would be highly suspicious of any spirit guide who declared that they knew everything and had the only relevant information for the salvation of mankind, yet this is precisely the sort of things that people get told by their 'guides'. Personally, I prefer a little localised guidance about relations, friends and colleagues, rather than cataclysmic global declarations. Perhaps some mischevious entities enjoy passing on such 'almighty, all-powerful revelations, or perhaps we all receive what we astrally 'put out' for. In terms of astral fishing, I am contented with one fish for tea, which I can share locally, rather than a net full of larger, more impressive catches which I cannot use.

Now that we have contact with our guide we can take he or she on our pathworkings with us. He or she can be protective and helpful as we step out of the safe place, making a deliberate astral journey into the unknown. Here are two ideas for journeys to meet the male and female principles in their guises as

Herne, Lord of the Trees (in his phase as the Wiseman) and of the Wisewoman, Crone or Waning Moon Goddess.

Pathworking to meet the Wise Man

Before I begin the description of this suggested journey, let me say that Herne is nothing to do with the Christian concept of the Devil. He is purely a Pagan figure, a Horned God with the antlers of a stag, representing the chase, the hunter and the hunted, the grace and strength of his aspect as the young, virile, God of the Green Wood, The Robin in the Hood, the Jack-in-the-Green. He was used by the Christians as a tool of fear and guilt, a representation of evil, because they wanted to eliminate the older Ways by making them as corrupt, as depraved and sinister as their own minds. I should not have to state this fact, as it seems to be one that many are coming to understand and accept this, but as we have already seen, the 'medieval' is still alive, and been actively kept alive in some circles.

Herne was a symbol of the people's hope, he reflected their simple lives, he would give to the poor after stealing from the rich. He was, in fact, very similar to the sort of man that they say that Jesus was. Yet, Jesus's representatives sought to eliminate the symbol of empowerment for the individual, the reflection of all natural life, by making it seem unnatural, by discrediting it as evil. Herne is not a symbol of fear, but of protection, of truth, wisdom and justice, of the cycles of nature, the male principle. To meet him is to be part of his Dance of Life and Death, then around again. In his guise as Wise One, Lord of the Waning year, Father Shaman, he is a man of prophesy, of revelation, of journeys into the darkness to find the light once more. He is the way of the Wiseman, perfect balance to the Wisewoman. In accepting his principle we accept that Great Union, the harmony of united opposites.

He is within us all, in the next life we could walk his way, we may too be clad in the male body. To reject him, for the sake of rejecting all the negative things that those souls clad in the male form have wrought upon the Earth, is to reject part of ourselves, is to shut out so much joy and understanding in life. To deny his principle is to deny part of the Whole, and so to create an imbalance within and without. I suggest that one undertakes this journey with an open mind and heart. Many times I have met his principle, been held inside the folds of a leafy cloak, been stroked on my cheek by his Fatherly green fingers. Do not be afraid. If you are a man in this life, his is your own way, your own role, your own path to Wisdom. If not now, then one day.

176

For this journey, one must follow the usual rules, protect, relax, invoke the Guide. Then open the third eye and begin to visualise. Imagine yourself to be walking along a quiet lane, in daylight. To your left and right there are trees in the process of shedding their leaves, bushes bearing the last of their fruit, some last blackberries and rosehips remain, a few elderberries and sloes here and there. You marvel at the colours in the leaves, the colours of rich spices, chilli pepper and saffron, floating down around you, dancing on the path before you in the light wind. Leaves all about you, twirling, spinning, falling. The branches of the trees appear almost black against a sky the hue of blanched almonds. A single ray of weak sunlight filters through the cloud.

To your left you notice a raised bank of earth beneath the trees, with a single track running faintly, but discernably on it. You approach, and see that the track goes over the mound and away into the trees. There is nobody about to follow you, and you decide to see where it leads. The track is barely visible, and as you walk it you notice the wind picking up and the trees closing in around you. The steady beat of your feet and the noise of the leaves being pulled from the swaying branches is all you can hear. The track leads you up and down, over more earth banks and down slopes, around the trees. You pause occasionally to staff from the flat, grey rock next to him and beckons you over. He is not an intimidating figure, but rather like the figure of some gnarled old tree, very ancient, very wise, and still strong. As he stands you notice that his white hair and beard be-lie his stature and size. Although he is a man past the prime of life, he is still straight and tall, with a broadness of shoulder that suggests a past physical prowess. Yet he is slender and his eyes dart quickly over you and then away, seeming to notice every fresh leaf that falls in the wood around him. His garb is held together by twine and frayed hemp rope, rough hewn sacking forms the folds of his cloak. Yet his boots are made of the softest leather, and he has a fine bag made of the same, hung around his body. He finally greets you with a voice that betrays no sign of age.

" The place is here and the time is now, so it is and so it shall be."

You look at him, expecting more, but he is gesturing for you to follow him, out of the clearing and deeper into the trees. You notice as you walk behind him that his staff is made of live wood, of ash. You see a deer peering from out of the safety of the trees at your presence and it does not flinch away as you pass by. A hawk alights on the shoulder of the man in front of you, staring down at you disconcertingly as you struggle to keep up with the silent man who leads the way. To where?

The man who is leading you suddenly disappears, ducks under a low branch and is gone. It takes you a moment to realise that he has gone inside a small dwelling which is almost entirely disguised by the trees. In the dim light you see the cross beam above the doorway which has no door, and step inside the man's dwelling.

His Amulets, feathers, woven bags and dried plants hang from the low ceiling. There is a fire burning there already, the smoke leaving by means of a small gap in the interlacing of branches that create the roof, packed closely between with earth. The fire smells of pine resin, and you realise that you are tired from the journey. The man only has one chair, a wooden seat upholstered in a worn green velvet cloth. He offers it to you and you sink down in gratitude. The chair is more comfortable than you would have guessed. The man turns and produces a wooden bowl for you to drink from. As you accept it and drink, the liquid tasting like mulled wine made from the last of summer's gifts, infused with the pale glow of the sunlight of the waning year, bitter and yet sweet, you feel more relaxed, more at ease with the strange, silent man. He turns again and produces a heavy leather-bound book for you to look at.

"The lives of all are within. Ask what you will", Herne says. He passes you the volume and the pages fall open upon your lap. "Ask, ask", he repeats. You cannot see the pages in the dull light. As if hearing your thoughts, the man lights a candle for you. As he does so, the pages come alive as you ask your questions. You may hear the man's voice, or see images on the paper. He may tell you all you need to know, at that time, or it may be revealed in the book. You may ask him who he is. You may ask about his arts of divination, or his ways of journeying. You may ask to return to him in the future, to be taken upon a journey. You thank him for his knowledge and care.

When finally you have seen and heard all there is to know at present, the man suggests that as you are tired from your travelling that he return you to the place in the universe which is your safe place. He will ask you to close your eyes and to imagine that place. To hold it in your inner vision. To be there within yourself. You do not feel as if you have moved from the chair, yet when you open your eyes you are in your safe place, with the presence of your Guide. You may then return to the manifest, after thanking the Guide for their presence, unseen but felt, throughout the proceedings. On your return to the manifest, eat, drink and write of your first meeting with the Wiseman principle.

The next journey described is to meet the Great Sorceress within us all, the Cosmic Grandmother, the Grand Lady. This journey is a vital part of becoming a Wisewoman, or indeed, a Wise One. For whether we be in male or female form at present, we all have the capacity to be either. If we do not acknowledge both the male and the female principle within us and as a universal principle, then there will be dis-harmony both of our souls and of the universe. We cannot put the balance right by ignoring and rejecting the male principle, just as the female principle has been ignored and rejected for hundreds of years. The female aspect of us all, of the All, has always been there, as will the male aspect be there even if we do not acknowledge it. All the lack of the acknowledgement does is cause damage, imbalance and dis-harmony, both personally and globally.

It is like ignoring or disregarding ones own true nature, including one's skills as a psychic. They will still be there, and rejecting them will cause a build up of damaging energy which will be expressed manifestly as well as spiritually. I appreciate that this may take time for some of us to accept as damage done can go on to inspire the creation of damage, as we have seen. All I am doing here is saying that be you male or female in this life, work with both principles of The One. To become a Wisewoman, one must meet the Wiseman, her polarity, and vice versa. If I labour this point, it is because I see it as vital for the way forward.

A Pathworking to Meet the Wise Woman Principle

One has protected oneself and is relaxed. The personal Guide has been asked to be present, to protect and accompany you on this journey. Then visualise yourself to be walking along a cliff top path. It is a day with a sky the colour of cold steel, and the wind is beginning to whip your hair into your face, making it difficult to see the path. It is somehow exhilarating, yet a little frightening. The rocks lie below you, jagged, slate coloured, against which the sea is crashing relentlessly, white foam covering the savage peaks and troughs of the rocks, then revealing them afresh. There is a curious music to the crashing of the waves, almost comforting, almost compelling, it makes the blood in your veins course a little stronger. You feel connected to that powerful tide, simultaneously drawn towards it and then repelled by it as you continue to walk.

The path begins to curve downwards and as you get lower you can see an outcrop of rocks on which the cormorants huddle together, one occasionally stretching its wings against the cold spray of the sea. Everything seems to be drawn out with a hard pencil, sketched in shades of cobalt and lead. There is nobody to share this scene with you, for everyone else has been driven indoors by the damp, clinging air and the biting wind. The surging, choppy waters are barren of human life, no boats bob in the distance, no surfers stand at its edge. It is a feeling of heady excitement that leads you on further down the winding path that appears to end up on a small patch of deserted beach, the sand also seeming to be a shade of grey in the stormy halflight, a light tinged with sickly yellowish green. You feel that if you slipped and fell, your scream would be snatched from your mouth, torn from your soul and smashed against the rocks to be lost forever into the sucking tide. You feel small, helpless and vulnerable, but you also feel part of it all, the sea, the sky, even the solid rocks below.

The old track seems to somehow spiral around as it descends. You are concentrating so hard upon the path, and not losing your footing, that you do not immediately notice that you have reached the cove below. You notice at once that a blazing fire has been started by a cave mouth. You are freezing cold and damp with the air and spray, and decide to hurry over to the blaze to warm up. As you do so a movement catches your eye. A hooded figure is moving with its back to you by the water's edge. It is a figure unbothered by the waves which wash the figure's bare feet, then ebb away again. The figure is collecting pebbles, driftwood and broken shells. They have pockets full of such treasures, and still more in their hands. They have turned towards you now and are moving in your direction. You stand your ground at their fire, trying not to show your blatant curiosity about the strange dark figure who is hopping towards you like a manic, cackling bird. The person is simultaneously clutching their wet cloak around themselves and holding onto their collection of goodies from the water's edge. The legs below the cloak's lining are pale and thin, also the legs of some strange bird, the feet like that of an old crow. The figure dances in front of you, dropping its bounty at your feet for inspection. You do not wish to appear rude, although you are certain that the collection will be dull and useless.

As you stoop down to look, the figure thrusts a silver chalice under your nose. You are amazed at the beauty of the goblet from such a poor figure. You look up to thank them, but they are now standing in the shadowy cave mouth, huddled back into their cloak. You drink the hot brew gratefully, tasting mugwort and meadowsweet, the whites of an egg, milk and moonlight, and perhaps a hint of the sea. It tastes wonderful, and you look down at the stones and shells with renewed interest. Suddenly you can see colours again, a real shock to the senses after the monochrome of the day. Stones of brick red and mint green, pebbles streaked pink and turquoise, the water on each bringing out subtle shades, dusty madder rose, duck egg blue.

You are amazed by each one of them, each more beautiful, more special than the last, more fabulous than any jewel. There are fossils of forgotten creatures pressed into pitted limestone, driftwood shaped into gnarls and swirls like ancestral faces filled with their individual ancient wisdoms. You pick up a large

180

conch shell, creamy smooth and patterned with peach and tangerine. You trace the spiral of its curves, you look inside, into its labyrinth. You hear the voice of the Goddess.

You find that you are standing inside the shell, inside the cave itself. You cannot see the figure, but you know that they are there with you. You take their hand and they lead you off into the caves, deeper into the darkness, with the tangy scent of all life in your nostrils. The cave walls feel damp and slippery to your trailing fingers. The figure is hurrying on, pulling you with them and their urgency to reach some unseen destination becomes your own. You wish to see them, to see their chosen journey's end. As you are thinking this the figure with you lights a candle. Before you in the rock there is a door made of a heavy, green-brown wet wood, studded with limpets, hung with seaweed. The figure hands you a key, a huge, old, rusted key. Your hands are so cold you doubt you can turn it in the lock, but you do. With a creak and a groan the door opens and the figure gently pushes you inside. Inside is a round room, cut into the rock, with a fireplace off to one side in which a roaring fire is already burning. In the centre of the room is a wooden table, with a bench on either side of it, and with two goblets set out, as if the figure had been expecting your company. There are torches alight on the walls of the room and the light is now bright enough for you to see who you are with. There is no need to peer under their hood, for they have removed their cloak, at last, and sit down at the table, opposite to you, so that you can see them completely.

Your host, the woman, is old, terribly old. Her face is a mass of lines and furrows, the skin like parchment. The eyes are almost as pale as the hair, but the hair is like a sheep's fleece, shot through with spun silver, and the eyes are like the shadows on the moon. She smiles, like ice cracking in the thaw, and she throws back her head. The laughter bubbles out, like the laughter of a young girl and she grasps your hand, the hand that lead you, moments before, through the impenetrable darkness is ropey with blue veins and delicate as that of a small child. But the grasp is firm, warm. Her other hand is under the table, hidden. You look at the simple shift of some black cloth that she wears, the blue mark like a crescent moon on her temple. She is unadorned and her flesh has forsaken her, almost transparent, luminous, yet sagging, falling from her bones. Yet she has the presence of one who is clad in the most precious jewels, the richest, most sumptuous fabrics. She sits straight, straighter than a woman of half her years. She has nobility and an aura of great strength and wisdom that is almost as intoxicating as the brew which she has prepared for you. You breath in the scent of the drink, of herself and her room. She smells of the fur of a vixen, curled up within her Earth, of the roots of Elecampagne, of the inside of the conch shell.

From underneath the solid table she produces three bright cloths, three squares of silk in red, green and yellow. She speaks; "Take each square and in it wrap up a question, a problem you wish to solve, a truth which you wish to be revealed". So, you take the green square and visualise one thing to do with your material life which you wish to know at that time. Imaging it placed inside the square, wrap it up within the fabric. Hold it there within your vision, wrapped up and held.

Do the same for the red, with a question about your spiritual, psychic self. And finally for the yellow, for a question that you have about the Greater Scheme, of life itself, of the World and the Other World. Give these back to the old woman before you.

She then stands and moves to the fire. She clutches the first bag of fabric to her withered breast and closes her eyes, breathing deeply. Then she casts the bag into the flame. From the flames, pictures arise in answer to your question. The woman speaks to you also, accompanying the images in the flames with her voice. She does the same for the red square of folded cloth and for the yellow. She has shown you three things, given you three answers from the flames. You sit for a while longer, thinking on what you have seen and heard. She may speak to you again, or she may sit, waiting.

As you eventually look up again, a second door has appeared in the cave wall, opposite to the first. It was not there on your arrival, or was it? Things do not appear as they originally seemed in the small room, the woman watching you has hair that sometimes seems the gold colour of ripe corn, or perhaps that is only a trick played by the fire light. She gestures to the door, and you stand to take your leave. You pause to thank the woman and ask if you may return to her again. Expecting her to take your hand you are surprised then when she clasps you to her in a hug of farewell. The small, bird-like body is frail, yes, but it is strong and taut as a wire, and hums with energy. She opens the door for you and you see that you are back in your safe place. You step out onto familiar ground and turn to wave a final time. But the door is gone, and so is she. But is she? You feel your hand clenched around something small, and you open your palm to reveal a stone washed smooth by water, water which has made a hole straight through the middle of it with its relentless ebbing and flowing, its power. You leave the stone in your safe place. It is to be your astral talisman, thrice blessed. You can use it on other journeys to protect you and to bring about magical acts of will. It can be used as an astral focus of your energy, your own power. You say goodbye, with thanks to the presence of your Guide and slowly return to the manifest, to eat, drink and make notes.

Some Words About Magic

We have already established what magic is, the direction of will, the focus of energy for a specific purpose. We have already seen that it works the more if the focus is strong and the will truly directed with strength of purpose. We have looked at the consequences of using the direction of one's will to affect another's, and the fact that such magic will rebound upon you sooner or later. We have even seen that in the Craft we can use tools to symbolise certain aspects, the chalice as the Lady for instance, and as the focus of our will, as we can focus on a candle to channel our energy in the required direction. Tools are only that, they are not necessary for magical acts. But they can help. The finger can be used to direct protective energy, or to 'check out ' a being astrally, but it is nice to have a knife or Athame that we have made ourselves and imbued with its purpose, with our own energy and the properties that it symbolises, that is; protective, male aspect, sun energies. I acknowledge that a lovely shop-purchased metal Athame can be consecrated for personal use, but I do not see it as part of my Craft as a Wisewoman. I like to keep my tools to a minimum, because I like to work all magic outside. I do not wish to acquire valuable one-off items that I could lose outside and which I could ill afford. My attitude is that I will use now what I could use in 1300. A wooden spoon to direct energies, or a stripped hazel twig.

Although there are probably many Occultists who would balk at this idea, I believe that the Wisewoman that was, would have been happy to have used the same kitchen knife for cutting her herbs as she used for stripping her hazel. It was an all purpose tool, and only as important in magic as the importance that she placed on it. It is only an extension of her will, after all, not a sacred item. We are not entering the ranks of the Church here, by giving mere material items any over-blown value. A magical tool is only as indispensable as we allow it to be. It should be remembered that it is a conductor of our energy, and that is all it is.

In the case of the knife, it is traditionally associated with the element of fire, and masculine (phallic) qualities. The wand is an air element implement, also male. The wooden spoon serves the same purpose, and no doubt the Wisewoman used the same tool to stir her brews and to cast a circle. As long as the item has been held up as an implement of importance and magical relevance, then it need not be consecrated by any special means. A tool buried in salt, or in the Earth, or kept out for the three nights of the full moon, will be blessed and cleansed enough for use and a simple 'prayer' of dedication to the appropriate forces should be said.

The Wisewoman knew that the Chalice would be her ordinary drinking cup, hers alone. The point is, that the Wisewoman lead a life of magical integration, that all acts of eating were as sacred as a specific act of directed magic. The Wisewoman saw herself as an representative of the Goddess principle incarnate, so all of her acts would be appropriate to having such a role. This does not mean, as we have already seen, that it is appropriate to have an elevated sense of worth about being a Wise One. It is saying that we are all part of the divine principle of The One, and that in this incarnation we may be representative of either its male or female side.

When choosing a tool for an act of magic, perhaps we should keep this in mind. Keep it basic, and preferably homemade. One can imbue a wand with a lot of power whilst stripping the bark and oiling the wood. It is the same principle as when employing a candle in magic, in order to focus an act of will onto it. If one spends time before lighting it, rubbing the shaft of the candle with a chosen oil (a vegetable or wheat based oil, infused with herbs and flowers one has picked one's self) and carving words or symbols into the wax, then the candle becomes filled with your energies, with the energies of that particular focus which you have in mind. Otherwise, it is just a candle.

I would recommend that the Wisewoman would use a knife (black handled), a wand or spoon, a wooden bowl for holding salt or earth, and a chalice or drinking vessel, to represent the female principle, and to hold the element of water. Other simple accoutrements would be a cord or coloured thread for use in both banishing (cutting) spells and in binding acts. Both must be done with the person's permission, and only if the full implications of the act will harm none. We may banish ill health, or bind two willing lovers together. The morality of binding or banishing someone who is causing another harm, who has asked you for help, should be checked out with the Guide, as should all magical acts. They have a greater overview than we have, and maybe can advise you on an implication of what you are about to do that will not be beneficial in the long run. We must attempt to see the probabilities and possibilities of what we do magically as best we can, but do ask the Guide before acting. A selection of candles, oils and scraps of cloth are also useful as tools. Any household, or found item which seems appropriate, if one incorporates some individual power into it by say embroidering on cloth, painting on glass or carving into wax, wood or metal can be given the status of magical tool.

As has been stated, I believe in working magic outside. Here is a further reason as to why tools should be kept to a minimum. As with the relaxation tape mentioned in an earlier chapter, tools should not be so vital to us that we cannot be spontaneous and create a magical act on the spot. Most magic takes place on the astral, through our visualisation and connections there anyway, and our magical acts on the manifest only reinforce our astral workings. When we work outside, we make that astral connection stronger. We have stepped out of the energies of physical existence, towards the energies of the Earth, of nature.

We can perform any magic outside, for the majority of it goes on in the mind. Think how much better one can perform a spell of banishing ill health if we use the method of calling up the astral body of the sick person into the circle of fire, or column of light. We can even ask them to come through our portal in the safe place. Then we can assess the energies of the astral body, with the Guide's help, or with the help of the principles of male and female, like Herne and the Lady. We can give astral healing and then send the person back to their rightful place in the universe, without them being disturbed at all physically. We can accompany the astral act with a physical act, to strengthen it.

The same with the act of binding two lovers. We can call them up astrally, in the safe place, and can effectively join their souls with love and understanding, truth and wisdom. We can echo this manifestly to seal the spell. What I am saying is, magic need not be full of clutter and of great moanings and chantings in strange tongues. It takes place, for the most part, in spirit or astrally, in the Other World. As we are of the physical, as well as having access to the spiritual, we can reflect our will here on Earth too.

Do not huff and puff to a distant hill or green place, laden with unnecessary baggage. On the path of the Wisewoman, we need only have our will, the knowledge of how to direct that will accurately astrally, and the understanding of the best method of how to reflect this manifestly. That is magic, with our feet on the Earth and our heads full of stars. This will always work best outside, where the connection is strongest. The Guide and the universal principles that we seek to work with astrally will always appreciate a step towards their realm as they make a step towards yours. Try to get out when casting a spell by an act of will, try breathing fresh air whilst you relax instead of centrally heated air, try lying on the Earth, with your gaze to the sky to feel your connection to all life, the energy of the Earth will hum through you and your mind will be opened to the vastness of the cosmos (so much more so than if one is lying on the bed staring at a lampshade!)

Do not worry about having to go outside in a fancy robe and so freezing yourself half to death. Wrap up warm. The spirits and the Guide are not looking at your physical self, they are dealing with the soul. We are not of the same mind as the Catholic cardinals et al, surely, so as to believe that The One will only look favourably at those of us clad in ceremonial garb, the likes of which probably cost the month's wages of a poorer soul? I accept the practicalities which I have listed before, but I am sharing my joy in communion with the elements, with the knowledge that it is worth the effort.

When working with the elements outside, it is appropriate to consider several practical points; a) your particular act of magical will needs to be worked in close proximity to a particular blend or individual manifestation of an elemental natural force and b) if your magical act of will would benefit from the invocation of a particular representative of an elemental principle. By a) I mean that if the spell was particularly concerned with the emotions, dreams and creativity then performing it by some form of running water would be appropriate. However, as this may not be geographically viable for you, perhaps b) should be considered and the an elemental of water should be invoked for protection and help. If one is outside then it is far easier to tune into the elements astrally. Do have a manifest representation of the element you require the help of, as a physical focus point, e. g. a chalice of liquid. Visualise water strongly in all its natural forms. Tune into the spirit of water, how would it feel, how do you perceive it to appear. As ever, use the third eye.

Unfortunately, I once attended a group meditation in which the leader insisted in running her hands back and forth in a washing up bowl of water. All it evoked in me was the sound of a woman with her hands in a washing up bowl full of water! The elements are rather more impressive than that, and strike chords within our very souls.

Also, as discussed, to reflect the cycles of the natural world we are best advised to work within a circle. When outside, or anywhere that is not your home environment, it is not necessary to cast a full circle with quarters/representations of all of the elements; the simpler version is adequate if done with care. An understanding of the principles involved is required as one visualises a protective blue circle of fire around the participant, which could be directed by the knife, spoon, wand or finger. Do know where the compass points are, and ask for the element of that points' blessing and protection (if you do so, remember to thank them also at the end).

You do not need great billows of incense and flickering candles to alert all and sundry to your presence. This is a private, solitary act of magic, not a public performance. Do use the circle of protection, always. Do protect yourself, and do not allow any one, physical or spiritual, into your area without checking them out. Just because they are outside, does not instantly mean that they are benign nature spirits. To let a human into the circle, cut a doorway, then close it after them. Take the same safety measures as are always prudent, and do not get carried away that all in the cosmos is wonderful and beautiful just because you are out in nature. Sadly, the astral is inhabited by the same entities, human debris etc as when we are inside, be they clothed in the guise of a nice little leprechaun or no... check them out. If they are the real article, they will not mind, and if they are not, then good riddance.

If you are working indoors do have your altar reflect what is happening out of doors, for example a full moon, or springtime. An altar can be a table covered in attractive cloth and which is home to one's magical tools. It is nice to have a space in the home which is special, an area to meditate in and which puts one in the mood for working with energies. I would recommend, then, that this altar area should reflect whatever is happening in nature, for instance the use of pine cones for decoration. This altar space encourages the participant to set aside time for magical and spiritual practice, and it should be pleasing to the eye as a reminder of the natural world outside. One does not need to worship at the altar and it is not supposed to be either redundant but showy, or expensively clad but incomprehensible to the owner. Again, this is not the Church! The word altar can be changed for another, more appropriate one, by the user if needs be.

With this reflection of nature in mind, do spend time and effort when considering the most appropriate course of spiritual action to take, considering the moon phase and the time of year. Before performing any magical act, draw up a version of the Wheel of the Year which means something and which resonates with you, the active participant. Understand your interpretations of the old understandings that new moons are for conceptive wishes, full moons for culminative ones and dark moons for banishings or tidying up lose threads. These are rough guidelines. Follow your intuition, there should always be room for change and growth within common acceptance of symbology.

Do not be impatient. Do not attempt to go out at Samhain with a desperate need to get a new idea off the ground for a friend. You will be working against the natural tide of the season. At Samhain, one should be outside looking for guidance, connecting with the Old Ones and the spirits of the departed. Forcing your will through regardless of the festival or season will be counter productive and frustrating. Work with the flow and you will not be disappointed. Know what the festivals mean to you personally, and to others individually. Celebrate them accordingly by tuning into the energies of the Earth at that time, and to the cycle of Being that the festival represents, for instance, birthing, or growth and vitality. Direct the energies present into your magic for the benefit of others.

To recap, one should only ever work magic for others. Guidance can be for you, personally, but your gift is not for self-indulgence. As a rule, we receive all that we need personally when we choose to dedicate this incarnation to the service of others and of the planet. I am afraid that great material wealth was never one of the things mentioned on the 'job specification' of the Wisewoman or Cunning Man! There is a quote at the beginning of this book as regards material well-being. As long as we have all we need then what more can we ask? Wealth is no bad thing, but as a Wise One, the worth of wealth in terms of the Other World should be negligible. Each day I get by fed, clothed and sheltered is a blessing for me. I live in a time when I will not be tortured or persecuted to my death for my natural way of being. I enjoy the gift of my new life, and I share my natural gifts as best I can. I want for nothing. When one is in tune with the Essential Self and way of being, and so in tune with the One, the Whole, then things tend to slide into place naturally.

In a similar vein, do give back to those who give to you. We take guidance from the Guide, we take energy from the Earth and we take the attributes and individual powers of the elements. We work with the principles of Moon and Sun, Goddess and God. Do we get to give back? Yes, if we respect, thank and try to inspire others to do the same. Try going to a local wood or green area with a bin bag and pair of rubber gloves to clear away bottles and human rubbish. Alert your local paper to the mess you have found there. Write to your local M P about the new road that is being proposed in your area. Know what is going on and get involved physically, not financially. Plant seeds in wild places to grow more trees. Go out and enjoy the environment. Put back your energy of love and joy into it.

You need not make elaborate offerings to the spirits or to nature. Give thanks by word and deed. Know your local area, introduce people to it. Go to areas that may have been abused by negative human input and do an energy clearing by use of visualisation of cleansing, protective energies. Work with the Guardians of certain sites. Perhaps invoke Guardians appropriate to others. Love nature, the elements, the spirits. Love is an energy. That is a gift if the energy is directed back to the source from which you benefited. The Wisewoman practices green magic, natural magic. It harms none, gives back all it can.

Do go with the flow. My most used words, no doubt, are spontaneity and intuition. Do use them. Enjoy magic, it is one of the most marvellous things about the Craft and being of the Wise. There is magic to be found in the acts of magic! If meditation is the fertile, well-worked, tended field then magic is the fine crop to be harvested from it. Use your own personal creativity to make magic. I was once told a story by the Green Man, or Herne, which began "once upon a time, there was a land of the woods where the greening reached to the edge of the sea. And in this land there were green people who by dance and

188

song, story and picture and most of all by love, and making love, kept the land green, and cared for." Do use art as a focus for magical will, however primitive your art is, it comes from within.

Perhaps learn a skill to dedicate to the Old Ones, a musical instrument that you can use to raise power with, a drum or bhodran, a penny whistle, guitar or mandolin. Traditional instruments of the country in which you live, made of traditional, local materials. Think primary school and make your own hand-decorated shakers or bell-sticks. Become acquainted with folk tales, especially local ones. Understand what it is they say, although they may be veiled in the secrecy of the hidden Pagan faith. Learn to interpret their code of symbology in your own way. Ask the Guide or the beings of the Other World to tell you stories. Make up your own symbolic tales that reflect seasonal tides, male and female principles. Use song, poetry and story to raise energies so connected. If you cannot sing, chant or speak a poem with feeling. Make it as simple as:

'see the Maiden, she returns,
greening the land as she walks,
bearing the light of this new season,
for the Earth and all its children'.

It is the rhythm which we build up which builds power, and this can be chanted over and over with the ad-libs and variations which come forth with it. Use one's creativity as a charm, a spell, a raising of power and a focus of energy. Use it to connect, to dream and to record. Use it, it is of the lifeforce, and is your unique manifest way of interpreting it on Earth.

As a couple of final pieces of advice, don't be afraid to fail occasionally. The first person who comes back to you immediately with the complaint "your spell didn't work" will not be the last! Timing can be a funny thing, and when one is a worker with the Otherworlds then their sense of 'now' can be far removed from ours. Be specific when asking for something, or else your idea of 'soon ' could be their idea of in the next few years! Asking for 'by the next full moon may it be so' will stand you in better stead.

As you check with the Guide before and after creating magic, make sure there is no blockage to your request manifesting in the world. As long as one has followed the highway code of psychism, and followed the stages of raising power, visualising, representing the connection manifestly using tools etc, and directing or sending the imagery and power then there should be no major disasters. The only real disaster is to see a mistake as failure. It is another lesson, and nothing more. As Julia Soul says (quoted in '*Bag of Jewels*', In-Tune

Books, 1988) "if you are never scared, or embarrassed or hurt, it means you never take chances. "Taking chances without adequate safety precautions is foolish both in astral and manifest terms, but one who never chances, never grows. Embracing one's past and ones future is a matter of being happy with the Self. I hope that this book has adequately shared my joy in discovering that Self, and I hope that with knowledge and understanding, the reader may be inspired to do the same.

Blessed Be!

On Becoming a Wisewoman

I accept my material poverty,
For I value my own creativity,
I accept that I know, yet I do not know,
That I learn from All, and so do grow.
I see myself, past, present, future,
I see myself in all nature,
Reflected in cycles of the Earth
My part in the Dance of Death and Rebirth.
I learn from my Craft by work and toil,
For the love of Self and for the All,
May my words have simple eloquence,
To dispel fear and ignorance.
May I with respect, and with compassion,
Free all from the energies of oppression,
May my magic come from intuition,
And all my acts be done in wisdom.
May I stand with understanding, in the light,
May I not deny my second sight,
On with the journey, and if it harm none,
In love and truth my will be done.
May all who read this be at peace,
From bonds of confusion be released,
And in starlight, find themselves,
A Spirit Walker between the Realms.

Addendum

Since completing this book I am moved to write this piece in addition. Having journeyed on from the point of completion, both spiritually and materially, I must reinforce the importance of the truth 'to know is to accept that I do not know'. I wish to reinforce it by use of a further personal example which reflects just how valid this truth is.

If anyone, but anyone, had inferred that I would not be with the man who I have described as being my soul-partner two years after our coming together I would have dismissed them as a fool. Yet here I am, twenty seven months after our reunion, with a new man, on a new path. Why? Does this mean all I have written is nonsense and invalid? Does it mean that I was deluded and wrong to share my views? By no means. I have had to accept that just because I did understand, that I did know, it does not mean that I will continue to do so. The lesson for me, a universal lesson, is to be flexible, to practice what I preach and to be open to growth through change.The man I called Julien de Saint Pierre was undoubtedly my soul-mate.This is a truth. People have soul-mates, this is also true. But there are lessons that sometimes we must share with other souls, things we must learn as individuals to bring back to the unit of the soul-partnership.

There were things I could never learn or experience in this life with that man, due to circumstances beyond my control. As much as it bewildered and hurt me at the time,I know now that there are things that my soul must feel and witness apart from his, and vice versa.The coming together in this life was a relatively brief one, yet it was a touching of home base, to feel reassured and then set off on life's journey again.The pattern of the soul is far richer and more complex than I could ever have imagined when I began writing this book. It is well to be open and to know truly that one really never knows. The soul has its own agenda, and in this there is strength, not sadness. For there are undoubtedly always returns, as I have discussed here in this work, using my own incarnations with my soul-mate as examples.

A question my Guide has recently posed to me, however, is do I believe one can change soul-mate at a certain point in the soul's evolution? My Guide has left this one with me to work upon as part of my personal quest. Is the soul as constant and as rooted as one would think, an unchanging core which wears many guises over the centuries, or does it too evolve, albeit slowly, barely perceptibly over millions of years? What is such a time scale to the eternal soul? If this is possible, then am I to consider the fact that my time with my old soul-mate is passed and I must bond with a new one, letting the old one go free? To be open to such questions, such challenges to the essence of one's belief is to my mind to be truly spiritual. This means not acting on whim or fancy for convenience sake, but truly considering that we are still in spiritual infancy, and so we must respond to all possibilities with wonder and awe. This includes accepting that we do not know, this is the real knowledge. We must be as open and as explorative as we were when born anew into the world in this incarnation. I learn this and pass it on.

For myself, I am happier than I have ever been, personally. Yet again I am on a journey with a man I have known before, in medieval England. This time our memories seem to be of great joy and happiness, which makes a refreshing change for me! I still maintain that knowing who you 'be' (including where you have been in other lives) is central to development. This does not mean dwelling on the past but learning from it, assimilating it into our current existence and stepping with good faith into the future. The universe is unfolding as it should, do not resist even when you do not understand. I for one have found much peace in this.

Poppy Palin, Bath 1997

Useful Addresses and Contacts

East Midlands UFO Research Association, 8 Roosa Close, Hempshill Vale, Bulwell, Notts. NG6 7BL
(Their magazine is available at six pounds for a yearly subscription. Their hotline for sightings of strange ariel phenomena is on 01159 275 623, or, 01159 847 894)

Truth Seekers Research, 25 Upper Canning St. Ton-Petre, Mid-Glamorgan, CF41 7HG (magazines, lectures etc)

British UFO Research Association, Suite one, The Leys, 2c Leyton Rd, Harpenden, Herts, AL5 2TL.

Psychic Questing Conference information, PO Box 189, Leigh on Sea, Essex.

Free Gorsedd of the Bards of Caer Abri, c/o The British Druid Order, PO Box29, St Leonards on Sea, Sussex, TN37 7YP.

Postal and local courses on Wicca (basic), Vivienne and Chris Crowley, BM Deosil, London WC1N 3XX.

Courses in natural, magic (solo path), Marian Green, PO Box 42, Bath, BA1 1ZN.

Pagans seeking Partners should write to Ann Balard, 14 Wimbledon Place, Milton Keynes MK13 9DR.

Greenleaf (eco-activism and neo-Paganism), George Firsoff, 96 Church Rd, Redfield, Bristol 5.

The Cauldron Magazine, Mike Howard, Caermorgan Cottage, Caermorgan, Dyfed, Wales, SA43 1QU. (Please do not mention The Cauldron on the envelope).

Dragon (eco-activism), Adrian Harris, 39 Amersham Road, New Cross, London, SE14 6QQ, tel 0181 244 6001.

The Herb Society, 134, Buckingham Palace Road, London, SW1W 9SA.

The Pagan Federation, BM Box 7097, London, WC1N 3XX.

The author welcomes correspondence and queries, with a stamped addressed envelope or IRC, plus a first class stamp or IRC for forwarding by the publishers, please.

FREE DETAILED CATALOGUE

A detailed illustrated catalogue is available on request, SAE or International Postal Coupon appreciated. Titles are available direct from Capall Bann, post free in the UK (cheque or PO with order) or from good bookshops and specialist outlets. Titles currently available include:

Arthur - The Legend Unveiled by C Johnson & E Lung
Auguries and Omens - The Magical Lore of Birds by Yvonne Aburrow
Book of the Veil The by Peter Paddon
Caer Sidhe - Celtic Astrology and Astronomy by Michael Bayley
Call of the Horned Piper by Nigel Jackson
Cats' Company by Ann Walker
Celtic Lore & Druidic Ritual by Rhiannon Ryall
Compleat Vampyre - The Vampyre Shaman: Werewolves & Witchery by Nigel Jackson
Crystal Clear - A Guide to Quartz Crystal by Jennifer Dent
Earth Dance - A Year of Pagan Rituals by Jan Brodie
Earth Harmony - Places of Power, Holiness and Healing by Nigel Pennick
Earth Magic by Margaret McArthur
Enchanted Forest - The Magical Lore of Trees by Yvonne Aburrow
Familiars - Animal Powers of Britain by Anna Franklin
Healing Homes by Jennifer Dent
Herbcraft - Shamanic & Ritual Use of Herbs by Susan Lavender & Anna Franklin
In Search of Herne the Hunter by Eric Fitch
Inner Space Workbook - Developing Counselling & Magical Skills Through the Tarot
Living Tarot by Ann Walker
Magical Incenses and Perfumes by Jan Brodie
Magical Lore of Cats by Marion Davies
Magical Lore of Herbs by Marion Davies
Masks of Misrule - The Horned God & His Cult in Europe by Nigel Jackson
Mysteries of the Runes by Michael Howard
Patchwork of Magic by Julia Day
Pathworking - A Practical Book of Guided Meditations by Pete Jennings
Pickingill Papers - The Origins of Gardnerian Wicca by Michael Howard
Psychic Animals by Dennis Bardens
Psychic Self Defence - Real Solutions by Jan Brodie
Runic Astrology by Nigel Pennick
Sacred Animals by Gordon MacLellan
Sacred Grove - The Mysteries of the Forest by Yvonne Aburrow
Sacred Geometry by Nigel Pennick
Sacred Lore of Horses The by Marion Davies
Sacred Ring - Pagan Origins British Folk Festivals & Customs by Michael Howard
Seasonal Magic - Diary of a Village Witch by Paddy Slade
Secret Places of the Goddess by Philip Heselton
Talking to the Earth by Gordon Maclellan
Taming the Wolf - Full Moon Meditations by Steve Hounsome
The Goddess Year by Nigel Pennick & Helen Field
West Country Wicca by Rhiannon Ryall
Witches of Oz The by Matthew & Julia Phillips

Capall Bann is owned and run by people actively involved in many of the areas in which we publish. Our list is expanding rapidly so do contact us for details on the latest releases.

Capall Bann Publishing, Freshfields, Chieveley, Berks, RG20 8TF